The Future Shape
of Christian Proclamation

The Future Shape of Christian Proclamation

What the Global South Can Teach Us about Preaching

Edited by
CLEOPHUS J. LaRUE
and
LUIZ C. NASCIMENTO

CASCADE *Books* · Eugene, Oregon

THE FUTURE SHAPE OF CHRISTIAN PROCLAMATION
What the Global South Can Teach Us about Preaching

Copyright © 2020 Wipf and Stock Publishers. All rights reserved. Except for brief quotations in critical publications or reviews, no part of this book may be reproduced in any manner without prior written permission from the publisher. Write: Permissions, Wipf and Stock Publishers, 199 W. 8th Ave., Suite 3, Eugene, OR 97401.

Cascade Books
An Imprint of Wipf and Stock Publishers
199 W. 8th Ave., Suite 3
Eugene, OR 97401

www.wipfandstock.com

PAPERBACK ISBN: 978-1-7252-5248-6
HARDCOVER ISBN: 978-1-7252-5249-3
EBOOK ISBN: 978-1-7252-5250-9

Cataloguing-in-Publication data:

Names: LaRue, Cleophus J., editor. | Nascimento, Luiz C., editor

Title: The future shape of Christian proclamation : what the global south can teach us about preaching / edited by Cleophus J. LaRue and Luiz C. Nascimento.

Description: Eugene, OR: Cascade Books, 2020 | Includes bibliographical references.

Identifiers: ISBN 978-1-7252-5248-6 (paperback) | ISBN 978-1-7252-5249-3 (hardcover) | ISBN 978-1-7252-5250-9 (ebook)

Subjects: LCSH: Christianity—Southern Hemisphere. | Preaching.

Classification: BR161.3 F88 2020 (paperback) | BR161.3 (ebook)

Manufactured in the U.S.A.   07/31/20

Contents

Contributors | vii

Introduction | 1
—CLEOPHUS J. LARUE AND LUIZ C. NASCIMENTO

Voltear la tortilla: Preaching and Theological Method | 12
—ELISEO PÉREZ-ÁLVAREZ

The Passion of the Christ? or The Passion of Mel Gibson? | 40
—ELISEO PÉREZ-ÁLVAREZ

Preaching in Brazil and the Formation of Brazility:
Experience and Vulnerability as Homiletical Locus | 47
—ABDRUSCHIN ROCHA

How Are They to Hear without a Preacher? Homiletics
from a Cuban Protestant Perspective | 70
—CARLOS EMILIO HAM

The Hermeneutics of African Caribbean Homiletics | 92
—CAROL TOMLIN

Trinidad & Tobago Preaching: The Gospel According to Calypso | 116
—CATHERINE E. WILLIAMS

Singapore: Preaching in the Power of the Pnuema | 136
—JOHNSON LIM

Preaching to the Javanese People of Indonesia | 158
—SARI SAPTORINI

Embracing an Ocean Homiletic: Fiji's 'New Exodus' and the Sermons
of Tuikilakila Waqairatu and Tevita Nawadra Banivanua | 169
—JERUSHA MATSEN NEAL

India: Homiletics from the Underside | 189
 —Alfred Stephen

Existential Realities and the Preaching Dynamics
of Some Nigerian Pentecostal Preachers | 214
 —Babatunde Adedibu

"To Each Its Own Meaning": Interpreting the Bible
in Nigerian Context | 232
 —Deborah Doyinsola Adegbite

Contributors

Cleophus J. LaRue—Cleophus J. LaRue is the Francis Landey Patton Professor of Homiletics at Princeton Theological Seminary. He specializes in the theory and method of African American preaching.

Luiz C. Nascimento—Luiz C. Nascimento is Professor of Religion and Society at Seminario Teologico Batista de Nordeste, Feira de Santana, Bahia, Brazil.

Eliseo Pérez-Álvarez—Eliseo Pérez-Álvarez is Professor of Systematic Theology and Philosophy at the United Theological College of the University of the West Indies in Jamaica. He has published two books on sermons and also essays on theological method.

Abdruschin Schaeffer Rocha—Abdruschin Schaeffer Rocha is a professor in the undergraduate and graduate programs at Faculdades Unidas in Vitória (a school of theology of the United Presbyterian Church in Brazil), and Director for the Distance Learning Program at CEFORTE (Center for Theological Formation) of the Wesleyan Methodist Church—Brazil.

Carlos E. Ham is Pastor of the Presbyterian-Reformed Church in Cuba as well as President and Professor of Mission/Diakonia and Homiletics at the Evangelical Theological Seminary in Matanzas, Cuba.

Carol Tomlin—Carol Tomlin, an award-winning educator, is a Visiting Fellow at the University of Leeds. Tomlin is the leading expert on African Caribbean preaching in the UK and senior leader of Restoration Fellowship Ministries.

Catherine E. Williams—Catherine E. Williams is Assistant Professor of Preaching and Worship at Lancaster Theological Seminary in Lancaster, Pennsylvania. Williams's work focuses on dismantling white privilege in the teaching of Christian preaching.

Johnson T. K. Lim—Johnson T. K. Lim (PhD, University of Queensland) is the Director of Baptist Institute for Contemporary Christianity in Singapore. He has been facilitating academic doctoral seminars in Asia in the areas of Hebrew, Hermeneutics, and Homiletics.

Sari Saptorini—Sari Saptorini is a lecturer of Discipleship at Indonesia Baptist Theological Seminary in Semarang, Central Java, Indonesia. She has spent considerable time in the inland areas of Indonesia preaching and mobilizing the churches in mission.

Jerusha Matsen Neal—Jerusha Matsen Neal is an Assistant Professor of Homiletics at Duke Divinity School in Durham, North Carolina. She previously served as the Dean of Studies at Davuilevu Theological College in Nausori, Fiji. She taught preaching in the Fiji Islands for three years.

Alfred Stephen—Alfred Stephen is Professor of Homiletics in Tamilnadu Theological Seminary, Madurai, India. Stephen focuses on Contextual Homiletics and Eco Homiletics in his Homiletic reflections.

Babatunde Adedibu—Babatunde Adedibu holds a PhD in Missiology from North West University, South Africa. Babatunde is the Provost of the Redeemed Christian Bible College, Mowe, Ogun State, Nigeria and an Associate Professor at the Department of Christian Religious Studies, Redeemer's University, Ede, Osun State, Nigeria.

Deborah Adegbite—Deborah Doyinsola Adegbite is the Senior Lecturer in Biblical Studies and Theology at Bethel Institute of Theology & Biblical Research and Redeemers' University. Adegbite's area of specialization is New Testament History and Theology.

Introduction

CLEOPHUS J. LARUE AND LUIZ C. NASCIMENTO

The Movement and Shape of Christian Preaching

CHRISTIANITY IS TURNING BROWN and moving south. Philip Jenkins notes in his book, *The Next Christendom: The Coming of Global Christianity*, that by the year 2050, Christianity will be a religion of people of color living primarily in the southern hemisphere.[1] The Christian church, according to Mark Noll, has experienced a larger geographical redistribution in the last fifty years than in any comparable period in its history. The redistribution has been so massive that the typical late twentieth-century Christian is no longer a European man but a Latin American or African woman.[2] That movement is currently underway and shows no signs of abating anytime soon. Aberdeen Missiologist Andrew Walls observes that at the beginning of the twentieth century the heartlands of Christianity lay in Europe and North America. More than eighty percent of professing Christians lived there. Christianity, says Walls, was both a Western religion and the religion of the West.[3] Today, Europe is no longer a Christian heartland. The Christianity the West has known is in recession and has almost dwindled out of recognition in Europe. Christianity is in decline in America, especially in the mainline churches. Owing to exponential growth in recent years, well over half the world's Christians now live in Africa, Asia, Latin America,

---

1. Jenkins, *Next Christendom*, 3.
2. Noll, *New Shape of World Christianity*, 21–22.
3. Walls, "Christian Scholarship," 171.

and the Pacific.[4] While Walls warns against declaring where Christianity will thrive in the future, he does point to its movement, diversity, and demographic transformation in the Global South as one of its great strengths.

Samuel Escobar notes in *The New Global Mission* that migration patterns and refugee movements have helped bring a multiplicity of cultures—as well as the different forms that the Christian church has taken among them—to Europe, the United States, and Canada. At the heart of European and North American cities, Third World cultures, as well as varied expressions of the global church, have taken root. From the missionary perspective, indigenous churches from faraway places have become sister churches down the street.[5] This has consequences for Christians in Western nations because the form of Christianity that has developed in the Southern Hemisphere and has reached the great Western cities is a "popular" form of both Catholicism and Protestantism that we might call "grass-roots Christianity." It is marked by a culture of poverty, an oral liturgy, narrative preaching, uninhibited emotionalism, maximum participation in prayer and worship, dreams and visions, faith healing, and an intense search for community and belonging. Evangelical leaders who have long emphasized the clear and correct intellectual expression of biblical truth and the rationality of the Christian faith especially need to be sensitive to this new expression of Christianity.[6]

The massive southward shift of the center of gravity of the Christian world described by Walls in his essay has been hailed by Swiss missiologist Walbert Buhlman as "the coming of the Third Church."[7] He points to the fact that the first thousand years of church history were under the aegis of the Eastern Church, also known as the Orthodox Church, in the Eastern half of the Roman Empire. Then, during the second millennium, the leading church was the Western Church in the other half of what used to be the Roman Empire. Those familiar with the history of theology also perceive how theological themes, language, and categories have reflected this historical situation. Buhlman goes on to say that the Third Millennium will evidently stand under the leadership of the Third Church—the Southern Church.[8]

Drive and inspiration to move forward and take the gospel of Jesus Christ to the ends of the earth, crossing all kinds of geographical and cultural barriers, is the work of the Holy Spirit. There is an element of mystery when

---

4. Walls, "Christian Scholarship," 173.
5. Escobar, *New Global Mission*, 14
6. Escobar, *New Global Mission*, 15.
7. Escobar, *New Global Mission*, 15.
8. Escobar, *New Global Mission*, 15–16.

the dynamism of mission neither comes from people in positions of power or privilege nor from the expansive dynamism of a superior civilization but rather from below—from the little ones, those who have few material, financial, or technical resources but are open to the prompting of the Spirit. Many Western missionary organizations started in the nineteenth and twentieth centuries as humble and insignificant efforts of visionary people before they grew to become large, well-financed organizations. It is not merely coincidence that the form of Christianity that has blossomed in recent decades, especially among the poor urban masses, is that which emphasizes the presence and power of the Holy Spirit: the Pentecostal movement that started among poor, marginalized people. In the words of one of its historians, Pentecotalism is the "vision of the disinherited."[9] Another aspect of this new scenario is that while many non-Western cultures are highly receptive to the gospel of Jesus Christ, paradoxically, it is within the Western world that we find less receptivity to it. Lesslie Newbigin, a missionary in India for thirty years who then returned to minister among working-class people in Britain, notes that "the most widespread, powerful, and persuasive among contemporary cultures, modern Western culture more than almost any other is proving resistant to the Gospel." Patterns of church growth prove the validity of this observation in the case of North America and Europe today. Several of the old mainline denominations show decline and fatigue with significant numerical losses. Are we here confronted not only with the resistance of Western culture but also with the impotence of the Western churches, crippled by a loss of confidence in the validity of the gospel or by a loss of creativity to change the forms of church life as cultural changes require? Escobar says that in cities where the gospel is preached in a relevant way, where people form a welcoming community and where structures such as house churches are created to respond to the urban challenge, the church is still flourishing. In many cases churches of ethnic minorities within declining denominations are also growing vigorously. This constitutes a tough new challenge to partnership in mission.[10]

Perhaps the single most striking feature of Christianity today is the fact that the church now looks more like that great multitude whom none can number, drawn from all tribes and kindreds, people and tongues, than ever before in its history. Its diversity and history lead to a great variety of starting points for its theology and reflects varied bodies of experience. According to Walls, the study of Christian history and theology will increasingly need to operate from the position where most Christians are, and that

9. Escobar, *New Global Mission*, 19.
10. Escobar, *New Global Mission*, 20.

will increasingly be the land and islands of Africa, Asia, Latin America, and the Pacific. Shared reading of the Scriptures and shared theological reflection will be to the benefit of all, but the oxygen-starved Christianity of the West will have most to gain.[11] Jenkins, agreeing with Walls, notes that while the numerical changes in Christianity will be striking enough, there will also be countless implications for theology and religious practice.[12] Preaching will be one such practice affected by the movement of Christianity to the Global South.

This work is an effort to advance the discussion of what Christian preaching will entail in those different areas of the globe where Christianity is growing. It is not an effort to outline a theology of preaching for all to follow, or a one-size-fits-all homiletic as a gift from the Global South to the Christian West; rather, it is a tentative effort to identify and describe certain practices, emphases, and methods of preaching in different parts of the world where Christianity continues to grow—i.e., the Global South. This collection of essays is by no means exhaustive nor is it necessarily representative of all the cultures and areas of Christian growth in the world. It is a snapshot of preaching in various places that allows us to look in on homiletical practices among different cultures. In any number of places, the influence of contemporary Western homiletics will be apparent. In any number of essays the works of Western homileticians and especially American homileticians will be analyzed and incorporated into the theories and methods of the contributors to this volume. This volume is not an effort to deny those influences, rather it is intended to look at the ways in which Western homiletics is reshaped and refashioned to explain, illuminate, and/or clarify the practices of homileticians in the Global South.

Preaching at its best is always contextual. It is always directed to a particular people, in a particular place, in a particular time. It always takes into account the situations in life (*sitz im leben*) into which it is proclaimed. For much of the twentieth century, white, Western homiletical theory was deemed as normative for Christian preaching. What worked for the majority culture in America was supposed to work in every setting, regardless of the particularities of the contextual experiences of the listening congregation and world. Today we know better. While we certainly can draw upon and learn from the centuries of homiletical wisdom acquired by the Western world, it will no longer be the primary conversation partner at the homiletical table and most assuredly not the only voice at the table. We have much to learn from those areas of the world where Christianity is growing.

---

11. Walls, *Cross-Cultural Process*, 47.
12. Jenkins, *Next Christendom*, 6.

Some years ago, Old Testament scholar John Bright declared that the church lives in her preaching. Always has and always will. No church, says Bright, can be any stronger than the Gospel it proclaims. Christian preaching is playing and will play a major role in the shape of the Christian witness in the twenty-first and twenty-second centuries. Andrew Walls describes the people living in Asia, Africa, Latin America, and the Pacific as the New Representative Christians: those who represent the Christian norm, the Christian mainstream of the twenty-first and twenty-second centuries. He rightly assesses that what those Christians think will come to matter more and more and what the people in the Northern hemisphere think will matter less and less. He even speaks of a possible northern theology to describe the future of theological reflection in the world:

> The most significant Christian developments in theology, for instance, or ethical thinking, or the Christian impact on society, will be those that take place in the southern continents, not those that take place in the West. The development of theological and ethical thinking and action in Africa and Asia and Latin America will determine the mainstream Christianity.[13]

There is a determination on the part of homileticians and preachers in parts of the Global South to stress the importance of one's context, culture, and history in the preaching event. They also express a determination to say "yes" to the particulars of their socio-cultural environment even when the majority culture in America and the white Western homileticians in different parts of the world express apprehension in the name of normativity and so-called "best practices."

Our writers are most definitely aware of white, Western homiletical theory, but they are not bound by it in the development of their own particular homiletic. They have little regard for anyone claiming their method to be "normative" or "universal." They own up to the contextual nature of their preaching and expose the faulty normative claims of the Western world. They have neither tried to reinvent the wheel with respect to homiletical theory nor accepted completely the theories of white homileticians about the most effective means of communicating the Gospel in the twenty-first century.

Andrew Walls said you could never talk about the rise of Christianity, for it is inclined to grow in one area and die out in another. Thus, what we are describing here is the movement of Christianity with respect to preaching in the opening decades of the twenty-first century. We are not claiming to identify any noticeable trends or systematic movement in Christian

13. Walls, "Christian Scholarship," 173.

preaching in the Global South. What we offer here are glimpses of how Christian preaching is being taught, practiced, and advanced in those countries where Christianity is growing; in those places where statistics show it is most vibrant and alive.

In chapter 1, Eliseo Pérez-Álvarez bases his essay on the metaphor of "voltear la tortilla," which literally means the flipping over of the corn tortilla. Since most of the world thinks of North America as the top and South America as the bottom of the world, the bottom of culture, and the bottom of significance, flipping is necessary in order to affirm the cultural and geographical being of *Abya Yala*, which is the original name of the Caribbean and American continent. To further clarify his metaphor of "flipping," Pérez references the 1943 painting of Uruguayan Joaquin Torres Garcia, "Inverted America," which flips the map and places South America at the top. Pérez describes this as the first map with openly political overtones. In the *voltear la tortilla* metaphor, Pérez applies his liberating homiletic to six different areas of thought and action. In terms of preaching, flipping the tortilla means to permanently approach preaching from the place of oppression. The people of South America and the Caribbean must ask this probing question each time they preach: is the being of non-White people present in Sunday preaching? If not, then whose traditions, whose logos, and whose experiences are we preaching? He further states that *voltear la tortilla* targets post-colonial homiletics by "honoring our own authorities while learning to pray 'lead us not into imitation.'" A sermon entitled, "*The Passion of the Christ*? Or The Passion of Mel Gibson?" is included to show us what preaching looks and sounds like when the tortilla is flipped and imperial homiletics are set aside.

Brazilian homiletician Abdruschin Rocha argues in chapter 2 that preaching presupposes subjects whose language is deeply determined by historical-social conditions. Thus, the processes and conditions from which the production of language takes place must take into account human beings in their history. Owing to this epistemological reality, he believes the postcolonial discourse that continues to impact Brazil is inadequate and proposes a type of decolonial preaching in which experience and vulnerability become a homiletical *locus*—by which he means the context from which the sustaining discourse develops. Rocha out and out rejects the highly colonial discourse that currently sustains a way of being church in Brazil and is distilled in the preaching that is practiced in the pulpits of Brazilian churches. He believes decoloniality supposes a deeper project which is set in motion beyond the mere historical overcoming of colonialism and neocolonialism. "Decoloniality," according to Rocha, "has a spectacular and sufficient set of experiences capable of constituting it as a category from which to construct a new discourse capable of sustaining a preaching more liberating, more dialogical and more connected with the demands of our own place."

In chapter 3, Carlos Emilio Ham makes a case for the importance of biblical hermeneutics in the interpretive process for preaching. Hermeneutics for Cubans, Ham argues, is far from mere academic discussions with their philosophical and idealistic presuppositions; rather, it is the technique of reading out of their concrete situations in the light of scripture. The very survival of the Cuban people depends on such readings. The abrupt collapse of the European Communist bloc, a deeper imposition of the trade sanctions by the American government, and internal mistakes by the Cuban leadership thrust Cuba into a deep economic crisis at the beginning of the nineties, undoing the higher standard of living Cuba had enjoyed since the Revolution, with free health care, education, and so forth. Biblical paradigms help the Cuban clergy to be faithful to the Gospel in the midst of the crisis and offer hope for the future of not only the church but also the country.

Ham acknowledges the homiletical challenge is his claim that Scripture itself is not the Word of God, especially since the preacher is called to reveal Scripture as the Word of God through the sermon. However, he claims that Scripture's message becomes the Word of God when it is interpreted and applied to the life of the congregation and lived by the community. So, he says, revelation comes not only to those who wrote the Bible but also is completed by the preacher who is bridging the message and applying it to the life of the community in its own context.

Carol Tomlin in chapter 4, an essay on the "Hermeneutics of African Caribbean Homiletics," describes the movement of Pentecostalism from the United States, to the Caribbean, and finally to Britain. While acknowledging the African American founding of Pentecostalism in the States, she traces the movement of Pentecostalism from Jamaica to Britain to the mass migration of the Caribbean population to the United Kingdom during the postwar period. The early migrants, commonly referred to as the Windrush generation, were instrumental in developing African Caribbean Pentecostal churches in Britain.

Tomlin argues that the preaching event is the most prominent feature of African Caribbean Pentecostal ecclesiology. While African Caribbean preaching mirrors aspects of global Pentecostalism, there are distinct characteristics to the expression of Pentecostalism in Britain. She outlines ten broad areas particular to Caribbean Pentecostal preaching. Stressing the importance of preaching in context, Tomlin argues that preaching does not operate in a social, cultural, or theological vacuity but rather is appropriated in particular contexts. For example, Black Pentecostals approach the Scripture with various pre-understandings and suppositions that are inextricably linked with prior experience, which might impact their interpretation of the biblical text. She also makes note of the recent shift in British-Caribbean Pentecostal preaching away from an over-emphasis on end-time messages to preaching that addresses the socio-economic and political challenges facing African Caribbean communities in the United Kingdom.

In chapter 5, Catherine Williams, a native of Trinidad and Tobago who now teaches homiletics at Lancaster Seminary in Lancaster, Pennsylvania, argues for the recovery of an authentically "Trinbagonian pulpit idiom." Invited to lecture at a regional Bible college in Trinidad and Tobago, the title of her lecture was "The Gospel According to Calypso." The students were initially cool to her lecture, having been taught that the world of calypso was not a place where Trinidadian and Tobagonian Christians did any sort of exploration. In times, says Williams, the students came to see that much that may truly be called preaching is integral to this local art form called calypso. Students and active ministers had been socialized to dismiss this musical speech as homiletically worthless. Williams notes that such non-acceptance of the calypso art form and its cultural jewels predisposes the students of Trinidad and Tobago to the continued wholesale esteem for and use of imported, ill-fitting homiletical patterns and styles of preaching. "I believe," says Williams, "that somewhere in the pile of post-missionary, post-colonial, Trinbagonian rubble there *is* a homiletical gem that is the gospel according to calypso." In an effort to make Trinbagonian preaching unapologetically contextual, Williams outlines five specific characteristics that stand in contrast to preaching that has greater ties to a colonial homiletical legacy. These traits are: (1) pragmatic content, (2) a hermeneutic of experience, (3) the sermon as communal, (4) the use of vernacular, and (5) robust affect and embodiment.

Johnson Lim of Singapore in chapter 6 argues that in spite of all the preaching aids and tools available to us today, preaching still lacks power because the Holy Spirit is MIA—missing in action. Lim argues that preaching that has a lingering effect or that inspires, impacts, and influences the listeners, is pneumatic or Spirit-filled preaching. In our preaching today, with its focus on the preparation of the sermon and its failure to incorporate the work of the Spirit, Lim claims that we are putting the homiletical cart before the homiletical horse. He says there is no unction (pneuma) in the pulpit, there is no action in the pews. His essay offers a corrective balance to this neglect by asking three vital questions: (1) Why is the work of the Holy Spirit important in preaching?; (2) What is unction in preaching?; and (3) How does one obtain unction in preaching? Lim pursues his scholarship on preaching with intellect in one hand and a desire for the anointing of the Holy Spirit in the other. He makes no excuses for his pursuit of the transcendent while at the same time maintaining intellectual rigor in his quest for a deeper knowledge of the work of the Spirit in preaching. He, along with other writers in this volume, is quite conversant with Western scholarship and integrates the thinking of Western homileticians and theologians into his work. More and more North American homileticians, especially those in the mainline tradition, seem reticent to speak of the Holy Spirit in preparation for preaching or to identify and describe its movement in the preaching event. Among any number, it seems to be a tacit assumption that the preacher is relying on some aspect of the Spirit in their preparation and proclamation. Lim brings the Spirit to the forefront and argues for its importance from beginning to end in preaching.

In chapter 7, Sari Saptorini of Indonesia describes the importance of tradition in the preaching of the Javanese people of Indonesia. Indonesia is made up of 17,000 Islands and hundreds of ethnic groups, but the Javanese are the largest group of all with approximately 85 million people. Saptorini argues that anyone who would preach with authority to Javanese Christians must have a firm grasp on the important role that tradition plays in their lives. So embedded is tradition in their culture that she argues that the Christian preacher must be able to convince their audience that the Bible is the ultimate authority in the life of the believers. Consequently, the Scriptures must take a primary place in the preaching of Javanese Christians.

Jerusha Matsen Neal in chapter 8, writing about the experience of the Methodist Church in Fiji, describes the way in which church leaders employed the metaphor of exodus in new ways to affect societal change at a very troubling period in the island's history. Methodist clergy under the prophetic leadership of Tuikilakila Waqairatu sought to employ this metaphor as a way of steering the church away from its past abuses of power while asserting the importance of the church's role and voice in an increasingly secular landscape. Through preaching, the clergy sought to frame their new exodus through the imagery of the ocean as opposed to the imagery of the land. The Fijian ministers' awareness of context and their skill in employing the exodus metaphor in new ways—an ocean homiletic with a fluidity of boundaries—led to new understandings of exodus and hope for the Fijian people. According to Neal, "To shift the conversation away from the role of the land in Fijian ecclesiology and toward the role of the ocean is a risky, cruciform decision in this context. It requires the letting go of static certainties and stepping into an unknown future."

In chapter 9, Alfred Stephen centers his homiletic on the sufferings of the poor in India—primarily the Dalit, often termed as the backward castes.

Dalits have historically been excluded from the four-fold varna system and were seen as forming a fifth varna. The contextual preaching to which Stephen is calling us is born out of the sufferings of the Dalit people. Long known for their suffering and injustice at the hands of those who consider themselves to be a higher caste, Stephen claims that a hermeneutic that addresses their reality is absolutely essential to preaching from the underside. He proposes that preaching from the underside will have a hermeneutics of resurgence, convergence, and relevance as its foundation, which he believes will allow for the creation of a new community among the Dalits; one in which love, acceptance, and equality will be the norms of life.

Babatunde Adedibu in chapter 10 argues that the redrawing of the political map of World Christianity has led to the emergence of a distinctive indigenous appropriation of the Christian faith across the Global South which is a variation from the Western dominated influences. The obvious implications of this seismic shift in the center of gravity of the Christian faith has led to variegated expressions of the historic faith in terms of liturgy, preaching dynamics, creativity and innovations, ritualization, and religious idiosyncrasies and diversities amongst churches—particularly of the Pentecostal stream. Thus, she argues that the twenty-first century might be labeled the "Global South Christian Century" due to the radically changing ecclesial landscape within this context. Even though Nigerian Pentecostal churches lean toward the prosperity gospel, Adedibu observes that many provide vital services to a number of dispossessed Nigerians.

A critical aspect of preaching that will most definitely be affected by the shift to the Global South is biblical interpretation. Adedibu highlights "Interculturation hermeneutics," as championed by some African scholars. Interculturation hermeneutics takes its cue from life outside the academy. She notes that the general experience of African Christians was that African social and cultural concerns were not reflected in missionary and Western academic forms of biblical interpretation. Inculturation hermeneutics arose as a response, paying attention to the African sociocultural context and the questions that arise from it.

In chapter 11, Deborah Doyinsola Adegbite addresses some of the sociological issues behind popular religion in Nigeria. She focuses primarily on the development of deliverance and prosperity preachers in the Nigerian context. She attempts to explain why ministers who are basically uneducated have such broad appeal among the masses. The influence of the worldwide Pentecostal movement continues to influence Christianity in many parts of Nigeria. While she is critical of deliverance and prosperity preachers in general, she does concede that some of them manage to provide much needed educational, medical, and social services to the people. The preachers, who are largely untrained, reflect the popularity of the various strains of Pentecostalism. Many are pre-critical in their preaching and continue to believe in the longstanding fears of demons and evil spirits active in the lives of the parishioners.

    Cleophus J. LaRue and Luiz C. Nascimento

Bibliography

Escobar, Samuel. *The New Global Mission: The Gospel From Everywhere to Everyone.* Downers Grove, IL: IVP Academic, 2003.

Jenkins, Philip. *The Next Christendom: The Coming of Global Christianity.* New York: Oxford University Press, 2002.

Noll, Mark A. *The New Shape of World Christianity: How American Experience Reflects Global Faith.* Downers Grove, IL: InterVarsity, 2009.

Walls, Andrew. "Christian Scholarship and the Demographic Transformation of the Church." In *Theological Literacy for the Twenty-First Century*, edited by Rodney L. Petersen and Nancy M. Rourke, 173. Grand Rapids: Eerdmans, 2002.

———. *Cross-Cultural Process in Christian History.* Maryknoll, NY: Orbis, 2002.

Voltear la tortilla
Preaching and Theological Method

Eliseo Pérez-Álvarez

The last will be first, and the first will be last.
[Read:] She who laughs last laughs best.

Matthew 16:26

An enticing appetizer at the beginning of a meal along with a palette cleansing, coffee-flavored dessert at the end can be a great help in digesting a not-so-tasty dinner. In like manner, covering up for our less-than-stellar sermons with enticing introductions and sugary endings may well be all we are doing in our present-day preaching.

"What you tied in the Eucharistic table, you loosen in the pulpit," is a saying in the Latin America that shows us the sorry state of homiletics in many parts of the world. The jibe is intended to suggest that the clarity of the historic Christian witness, frequently observed by the faithful at the Eucharist, is often muddled by our insincere and superficial preaching. Far too often, our sermons are plagued with bad jokes that fall flat in the pulpit or filled with Greek words and theological jargon unfamiliar to the listening congregation. Still other homilies come off as mere entertainment so weighed down with platitudes and generalizations that they offer less substance than a chat over coffee. Though much of our preaching theory has come from the White Western world, it could well be that an inverted world where the Global South is at the top could have more to teach us than the mere displacement of geography.

Alexandrian Claudius Ptolemy (second century CE) has the credit of drawing the first atlas placing the North-up. In the Middle Ages cartographers "oriented" maps towards Jerusalem, the city where Jesus was crucified and resurrected. In the tenth century Ibn Hawqal, the Arab cartographer, chose to place the South up. In 1943 Uruguayan Joaquín Torres García painted "Inverted America," i.e., the first map with openly political overtones: South America at the top.

This is precisely the meaning of "voltear la tortilla," namely, the "flipping over" of the corn tortilla in order to affirm the cultural and geographical being of *Abya Yala*—that is, the original name of the Caribbean and the American continent.

Abya Yala means the fertile land or the "land full of life," according to the Kuna culture of the formerly Greater Colombia. However, for more than 525 years the North Atlantic empires keep re-baptizing "the fertile land" as Latin-America, Anglo-America, Ibero-America, Euro-America, and so forth. The hidden agenda is to acculturate us, to impose their hegemonic culture and steal *Abya Yala*'s logos from our ancient civilizations.

Voltear la tortilla continues to discourage respect for the "doctrine of discovery." On the other hand, it continues to encourage placing the South as a co-equal interlocutor within the *oikos*, or our common planetary home. It seeks to place our Southern experiences as the point of departure—in this case, a liberating homiletic—to provide the "last rites" to the Southern country folks who still suffer "nortemanía"[1] (North-mania) or having a crick-in-the-neck always pointing towards the North Atlantic world.

Voltear la tortilla is a permanent reminder of Uruguayan Mario Benedetti's dictum, "The South also exists." In flipping over the tortilla, I will dig into the theological method in my task of stirring the homiletical pot while venturing some answers to a myriad of provocative questions, such as: What are the hidden presuppositions behind each homily? Methodologically speaking, is the being of the non-White people present in our Sunday preaching? Is our exposition of the Bible liberating, or romantic and alienating? Do our sermons probe deeply into the plight of the folks who belong to the oppressed classes?

The theological method or structure has to do with the wider hermeneutical framework, which will be addressed in six sections. The first section will deal with methodological conversion, namely, the indissolubility between thinking and doing, between listening to the good news and actualizing it right away, between theory and action, or, better yet, with discipleship as the epistemological place to know Jesus.

---

1. Phrase borrowed from Fray Servando Teresa de Mier.

The next subtheme will elaborate on the hermeneutical *locus* in preaching, namely, the poor and their many faces: for instance, the Native *Abya Yalans*, the African *Abya Yalans*, and the Immigrants. The third segment will deal with the theological *locus* or its particular historical location, namely, oppression. I will problematize and qualify the Methodist quadrilateral and I will spice it with the Church Base Communities Method. In this respect, the womanist metaphor of intersectionality will serve to unpack the multiple oppressions of classism, heterosexism, racism, ableism, ageism, and marital status-ism, among others, in the single goal of transforming the sinful structures that perpetuate them.

The fourth part will revolve around preaching and social location. Let me hasten to state that, from a Southern perspective, the social place is social, not individualistic. The community or collective self has primacy. We-ness or *nosótrico*, the *amáutico* and the "I 'n I" are core interpretative keys in the articulation of the sermon.

The antepenultimate taste that should inform homiletics is the suspicion of ideology. Instead of canonizing the Apostle Paul, the Jews from Berea "examined the Scriptures every day to see if what Paul said was true" (Acts 17:11). Critical thinking will swallow catechetical and apologetical preaching that follows the lectionary in a rigid and frigid mode. Social sins and decolonization will spice the cooking of a sermon. By being suspicious, we are actualizing and re-contextualizing homiletics while following Jesus' example: "You have heard that it was said...but I tell you..." (Matt 5:43–44). The last portion of this essay will grill the universal versus the particular debate. There we will uncover how incarnational homiletics, well rooted in its concrete context, converts local preaching into a universal value.

1. Methodological Conversion: Theory and Practice

It is the fact that the one and only thing that can maintain the liberating character of any theology is not its content but its methodology. It is the latter that guarantees the continuing bite of theology.

JUAN LUIS SEGUNDO[2]

Voltear la tortilla has to do with Abya Yala theological methodology, which thinks and feels theory and practice in the perichoretic dancing of praxis: "What matters is faith working through love" (Gal 5:6).

---

2. Segundo, *Liberation of Theology*, 39–40.

Our way of theologizing and preaching, then, is a lively relationship between thinking and acting. It is the dynamic correspondence between knowing and doing. Bluntly speaking, Jesus is the *hodos* or the way because his praxis is his preaching and vice versa.

Take for example the rite of baptism. It was a convenience to adopt either the Trinitarian formula (Matt 28:19) or the "in the name of Jesus" (Acts 2:38, et al.) formula instead of the much earlier liturgy taken by Paul from the oral tradition: "[In your baptism] there is no longer Jew or Gentile, slave or free, male or female. For you are all one in Christ Jesus" (Gal 3:26–28). The Christian baptism then is the end of religious wars—Jewish or Greek or Voodoo, Santería, Mesoamerican, Andean, Macumba, Rastafarianism—and the emergence of a classless society and an ethos of equal gender opportunity.

To divorce theory from practice is the hidden card Western empires still use in order to avoid the ways in which our understandings of social justice are directly related to and grow out of our baptismal vows. Even those we deem imperfect or even inferior are equalized in baptism and brought into a classless society. When baptism ceased to declare us as one and equal in the eyes of God, as stated in Galatians 3:26–28, it lost much of its original understanding. Thus, in time, children born outside of marriage were baptized on weekdays instead of the day of the Lord, i.e., Sunday, for they were clearly inferior. Since unmarried men were excommunicated, and thus no longer entitled to the promise inherent in baptism, some mothers were forced to present their brothers as fathers in order to participate in the baptismal rite. (Ironically, to address God as Father in the Caribbean is the norm, in spite of the fact that in several countries three out of four children are born out of wedlock, just like Jesus!)

Prior to raping our women, Whites proceeded to baptize them, since the Bible states very clearly "Do not yoke together with the infidels" (2 Cor. 6:14). Western Christians first dehumanized us so that through the baptism we—indigenous, Blacks, Mulattos, and Zambos. . ., could be "whitened" and granted an imposed identity. Blacks throughout history opposed the imposition of this whitewashed identity along with its Christian imprimatur. Malcolm Little, the son of a Grenadian mother, rebelled against this understanding of baptism and changed his last name to "X" in order to pay homage to his millennial civilization and denounce his stolen identity. Beginning with St. Augustine, baptism was used, not to equalize and unify, but rather as a weapon to proselytize the "pagans" and to terrorize unbaptized children. (Luke 14:23). For slaves, baptism meant the end of passions but not the end of slavery, as was apparent in the message sent by naming Lubeck's human flesh trade ship "Jesus." Zinzendorf subscribed to that conviction in his 1739 preaching to the slaves in St. Thomas, the US Virgin Islands, when he said, "God punished the first Negroes by making them slaves, and your conversion will make you free, not from the control of your masters, but simply from your wicked habits and thoughts, and all that makes you dissatisfied with your lot."

Though baptism is no longer used to justify our enslavement, it has not returned to its original status as the great equalizer. In our day, baptism, under the influence of imperial Christianity, Christendom or "churchianity" has come to mean little more than a social event or an investment in the afterlife. From voltear la tortilla we come once again to see baptism as the great equalizer as was evident in the first baptismal ceremony.

Voltear la tortilla homiletics means a rupture with Western theology that despises preaching for its supposedly unscientific character. This is evident through the way North-Atlantic scholars in general polarize practical from speculative theology, Christian education from theology, Doctor in Ministry from Doctor of Philosophy, professional CV from academic resumes, religiosity from religion, crafts from arts . . . God's talking from God's walking.

Western theological method considers praxis, in the best-case scenario, as *poiesis* of production or, in the worst, as United States pragmatism. Praxis, however, is not mere activism empty of an enlightened theory but rather has to do with the mutually informing relationship of knowing and doing: "They have the understanding to know me, that I am the Lord, who exercises kindness, justice, and righteousness on earth, for in this I delight" (Jer. 9:24).

Voltear la tortilla fries thinking and doing in the same skillet. This homiletic relinks, from religion or *religare*, our system of beliefs with the everydayness of our entire life.

2. Hermeneutical Locus: The Poor and Their Many Faces

Liberating homiletics emerges from the *Abya Yala* theologies, which deplore the unnecessary suffering caused by sinful political structures. "For I was hungry. . .thirsty. . . a stranger. . . naked. . . sick. . . and in prison and you came to me." (Matt 25:31–46).

Flipping over the tortilla articulates an ecclesiology that prioritizes the option for the poor, "For yours [said Jesus] is the Reign of God" (Luke 6:20). Being exhaustive in dealing with the many faces of the poor goes beyond the scope of this essay; therefore, let us sample only a couple of them:

2.1 The Native *Abya Yalans*

The first ever global revolution against economic neoliberalism took place within the Mayan community from Chiapas on January 1, 1994, as the *Sub-Comandante* Marcos recorded: "To the Mexico of the basement one arrives bare foot, or with sandals or rubber boots. . . . The Mexico of the basement is indigenous . . . but the rest of the country doesn't count, doesn't produce, doesn't sell, doesn't buy, [and] namely, doesn't exist."[3] According to Uruguayan Eduardo Galeano, "the masked man unmasked," the racist system that keeps our ancient population oppressed for more than five centuries.

This racism comes from the North white supremacy and hate speech—"The only good Indian is a dead Indian" (Sheridan)—but has also been internalized in our Southern countries: "The Indian is not to blame, but the one who trusts them" (Mexican saying). In spite of that, there are stubborn voices that keep flipping over the tortilla to keep their humanity afloat, "The Mexico of the basement is the one that doesn't have anything to lose, the one that has everything to win. The Mexico of the basement doesn't give up, doesn't sell itself, it resists."[4]

In order to articulate their cosmologies, the ancient philosophers and theologians from *Abya Yala* roast together their wisdom, experiences, liturgies, myths or sacred narratives, faith, hermeneutics, different epistemologies, and sermons. Eleazar López is right when he points out that indigenous theology, contrary to imperial dogmas, neither attempts to demonstrate the rationality of faith nor tries to clarify the teachings of revelation in an organic and systematic way vis-à-vis reason. For the Mexican theologian, the goal of the "indigenous theologies" is to rescue God's "saber y sabor" or knowledge and savor; It is to demonstrate how God is "Present among the poor, to show with which dishes and spoons our people eat the divine things, and with which gourds (*jícaras*) we drink the things of the Spirit."[5]

If, on the one hand, North-Atlantic empires built Christian churches on top of sacred indigenous shrines, on the other hand, our native *Abya Yalans* treasured their Goddesses, Gods, and Wakas under the Christian altars and also in the very chest of the Virgin Mary and other Bible saints. "S/he who laughs last laughs best!"

From *voltear la tortilla* follows the myriad legacies of our mother cultures that are actualized during preaching—their indirectness while speaking to avoid impositions, their use of the diminutive as an endearment style,

---

3. Subcomandante Marcos, "La larga travesía," 3.
4. Subcomandante Marcos, "La larga travesía," 4.
5. Hernándes, "Una misión descolonizadora."

their reverential rhetoric, their giving up in an argument for the sake of maintaining sorority and fraternity, their parsimony and soft tone of the voice, their story telling, their poems, their testimonies, and so forth.

For ages, it was considered a blasphemy to preach in a non-European language. Within the Roman Catholic Church, it was not until February 15, 2016, that Pope Francis authorized *Náhuatl*, one of 68 Mexican languages, as a legitimate liturgical tongue. In addition, it was not until 2019 that the United Nations declared an International Year of Indigenous Languages. *Náhuatl* language is spoken by more than 1.5 million and read by thousands. The fear of immigrants is a traumatic experience for some Euro-North Americans that comes from centuries ago. Many of them also still feel threatened by the Afro-Amerindians and by the Apaches who were never conquered.[6]

Voltear la tortilla refers to the tenacity in facing the so far 69 empires of history that have insisted on monolingualism. To preach in the 7,000 world languages is to continue overcoming Babel's "Babylonian Language Only": "And yet we hear them speaking in our own native languages!" (Acts 2:8).

2.2 The African-*Abya Yalans*

The African presence and legacy in the Caribbean, Latin America, and the USA is paved with myths such as the divine curse to Ham (Gen 9:18–28) by darkening his skin, ignoring the fact that the more melanin we have, the more resistant our skin is. The Gibeon event (Josh 9) has been preached to sanctify slavery and apartheid of Africans.

The myth persists that Africans arrived in *Abya Yala* as *tabula rasa* or as blank slates, namely, cultureless. If that was the case, let us ask Greece, Rome, and Christianity if they are not in cultural debt to the African continent. Europeans in *Abya Yala* needed African menial workers alongside their physicians, agronomists, artists, philosophers, sailors, griots, mineralogists, and you name it. The slave trade was a brain drain as well.

The myth persists that Africans ended up embracing resignation when the opposite happened. We now know that the Cimarron, or indomitable horse, and their *cumbes, palenques, quilombos,* or oasis emerged all over. Africans never capitulated. In fact, one of their main legacies is the idea of freedom, as it is preached, sung, danced, written, enacted, worshiped, and tasted through comfort food!

The myth is that hard labor decimated and almost extinguished them, when the truth is that the (currently) more than 150 million African-*Abya Yalans* have outnumbered the Indigenous population of the whole continent.

6. García de León, *Misericordia*.

Africans brought their ways of talking, walking, and clapping with them. They also brought along their ecological culture, their sayings, and their legends. Their oratory or oral tradition also crossed the Atlantic. Like the *corridos* or story telling in a form of song, which does the work of a local newspaper or a chronicle, by artistically improvising with "code words," Africans used their tapping (*zapateo*) and improvising of songs to communicate with one another since drumming was banned. Africans taught Indigenous people other fishing, ranching, and agricultural techniques. Europe and *Abya Yala* were enriched by African philosophy, theology, science, esthetics, literature, music, wisdom, poetry, architecture, sports, and of course, l'haute cuisine!

José Vasconcelos came out with his idea of the "cosmic race" or the mestizaje by getting rid of the indigenous and African presence of Mexicaness. This educator really denigrated us, by literally taking the nigger out of us, understanding nigger, of course, as a person from Nigeria.[7]

Voltear la tortilla reminds us of the fact that the medieval paintings portrayed Africans as dignified human beings. It was not until the transatlantic slave trade took place that they were robbed of their humanness. An example of the brutal physical and mental dehumanization is the filthy *Journals of Thomas Thistlewood: Sugar and Slavery in Eighteenth-Century Jamaica*. The Industrial Revolution did not mark the end of human trafficking; it was more of the same economic oppression under the guise of freedom. The police substituted for slave drivers, or, as Jamaicans say, the Babylon.

It was in 1503 that the first batch of Africans landed in current Haiti. Some sources claim that 14 million Africans were transplanted to the *Abya Yala* continent from the sixteenth to the eighteenth centuries, without taking into account the slave contraband. Following a more conservative historian, we stick to the following figures: 12.5 million Africans were shipped to this continent and 1.5 million died in the ocean; 11 million survived, 10.5 million were traded in the Caribbean and Latin America, and only 450,000 were sold in the USA.[8]

Not all Africans were slaves. Some came as the master's crew, others as soldiers, and therefore they were able to get *encomiendas* or *Abya Yala's* land, their inhabitants included! Furthermore, one third of the slave ships transported females, who, in Adriana Nevada's opinion, ended up

---

7. Fernández "Afrodescendientes." In Mexico Afro-Mexicans are counted as Mixtecos or Amuzgos. In the USA prior to 1924 Latin Americans were counted as white. In 1930, Mexican-Americans were counted as "non-White." One decade later, they were considered white. In 1950, Puerto Ricans were classified as White, unless they appeared as some other race. In 1980, Hispanic was transformed into an ethnicity.

8. Gates Jr., *Black in Latin America*, 2.

as housekeepers, wet nurses, nannies, and cooks. Maria Elisa Velázquez has already proved in her seminal study that female Afro-Mexicans such as Donna Susanne di Nobrena and Nzinga Mban de Ngola enjoyed great privileges due to their African rank, nobility, and economic power.[9] The population that got their freedom worked as teachers, merchants, midwives, in public dining rooms, making pottery, tailoring, and shoe making.

If Mexico in the sixteenth century got the majority of the African population in our continent, Brazil would soon emerge as the second largest country of the world with Africans, after Nigeria, with its 60 million Afro-Brazilians.

Verna, the root of the word vernacular, was the name of the female domestic slaves, also called "the help." *Voltear la tortilla* in the English-speaking Caribbean is the empowerment of the people's vernacular ways of knowing, preaching, and worshiping with Patwa-Patois, Creole, and their sister Pidgin. It is celebrating polyglotism, since, after all, "standard language is a dialect with an army and a navy," according to the 6,000 to 7,000 world vernacular languages and the political refugee John of Patmos: "After this I looked, and there before me was a great multitude that no one could count, from every nation, tribe, people, and language" (Rev 7:9).

Western racists have preached the carrying of the cross by Simon of Cyrene (Mark 15:21) for centuries in order to justify African descendants' slavery. They missed the point that Simon was only following the Empire law, which made it compulsory for a non-Roman citizen to carry any burden for one mile. There is nothing in God's will nor anything intrinsic to being African that mandates slavery.

In the Letter to Philemon, one sees another classic example of White supremacy style preaching that had great appeal among uninformed traffickers in human flesh who saw Onesimus as a prime example of the ideal, quiescent slave. Onesimus, however, did not willingly submit to his enslavement. Rather, he is a fighter whose humanness is not negotiable and Paul and Philemon know that. Historically, in Suriname, the transcending rulers and the collectors pretended to stop *Bush Negro* uprisings through fear and severe punishments. However, the slaves kept rebelling from their 400 plantations. *Bush Negroes* probably share the record with Haiti of the highest run-away community of the world. Suriname women were fearless too; they stored wheat, corn, beans, and squash seeds in their beautiful curly hair. Once they reached a safe place, they shook their heads and fertilized their new free land in the middle of the wonderful jungle. Jamaica owns the record of the most insurrections per square meter in the world, with

---

9. Velázquez, *Mujeres de origen africano*, 33..

more than 400. Taking their cue from the scriptures, the Suriname people intuitively understood that Onesimus was definitely a Maroon (fugitive slave) and not a "yes sir," person as many pulpits portray him.

Haitian Vodun keeps afloat centuries-old, uprooted African cultures: "It's better to rely on two magics rather than one!" Shango Religion in Trinidad keeps alive self-worth, self-confidence homiletics. Jamaican Rastafarianism keeps preaching, mindful of the beauty and prophetic values of the Reign of Jah. Having said that, let us consider another face of the generic poor, the immigrant.

2.3 The Immigrants in Irregular Situations

Martin Luther stated that the theologian of the cross names things for what they actually are.[10] That is a very relevant reminder today as we live under the tyranny of euphemisms and the dictatorship of the semantics of migration, namely, the constant changing of the meaning of words, backed by the powers that be. Such constant change of meanings confuses the issue and distracts us from root solutions.

Therefore, in dealing with immigrants who do not own a "passport," we need a "password" to unpack the dehumanizing narratives with which the powerful have veiled this reality; we need to unveil reality from the many layers of lies in which it has been covered. Then, we need to unveil "reality," as the "royalty" defines it, or we have to question metaphysical reality totally divorced from physical reality, as it has been defined by the neoliberalist system.

Such unveiling reveals, for instance, that immigration should be understood first as the only possible solution available to millions of children and adults around the planet facing situations of extreme poverty and violence. That is in contradistinction to considering migration as "a problem" or "a crisis" by those who "don't want to upset their peaceful digestion," as president Reagan said after the bombing of Grenada.[11]

In the ecumenical creeds, we confess that God emigrated from heaven. From the book of Genesis, we learn that Adam and Eve were asked to leave the Garden of Eden (Gen 3:23–24), thus becoming the first immigrants in the history of humanity. According to anthropologists, our human ancestors mimicked animals in departing to other lands in search of food and water.[12]

---

10. Luther, "Heidelberg Disputation" no. 21.

11. Ronald Reagan's expression after bombarding the country of Granada, the motherland of Malcolm X's mother (*New York Times*, November 4, 1983).

12. Rezende, "A alimentação como objeto histórico complexo."

The oldest Christian baptismal formula (Gal 3:26–28) is bold: it means the end of immigrant criminalization. It is a permanent reminder that God created the world (Ps 24), but the feudal lords, the rulers, the royalty, the bankers, the corporations, and the puppet states created the borders.

The one who lays claim to semantics is believed to have the exclusive right to name reality. Is it by chance that the massive children and adult Mediterranean immigrants are from Muslim countries, where Christian countries are sponsoring dozens of wars?

Instead of *Abya Yalans* immigrants being a threat to the USA, is not the opposite true? In the USA, 50.7 million Abya Yalans form a country within a country, which in itself would be the 14th largest world economy with a purchasing power of over one trillion dollars.

In declaring "America First," Donald Trump is also implying "Christianity First," i.e., the hegemonic Western version of understanding and preaching the Bible. In the same pan, Trump is also re-frying the old doctrine of manifest destiny. For instance, during the 1960 Democratic Convention, John F. Kennedy reclaimed a new frontier right close to the Mexican border in Los Angeles. The entire world was the new limit: "I stand tonight facing West on what was once the last frontier. From the lands that stretch 3,000 miles behind me, the pioneers of old gave up their safety, their comfort, and sometimes their lives to build a new world here in the West. . . . We stand today on the edge of a new frontier." In 1967, the US Ambassador called Vietnam an "Indian Country," where cowboys' missions consisted of "moving the Indians away from the fort so that the settlers could plant corn."[13]

In the Kingdom of God semantics there are no geographical borders, there are no first- and second-class citizens. In the Reign of God, it is a sacramental action to welcome the immigrant, particularly the least of them (Matt 25:31–46). Jesus not only healed a Samaritan at the border (Luke 17), the Galilean affirmed the leprous person's religion and named him Jesus' preacher as well (Luke 17:11–19). In addition, the most meaningful: Greeks do not have to become Jews (Acts 15). Jewishness is fine; Samaritanism is okay (Luke 10:25–37).

Voltear la tortilla allows us to think of Hagar, Sarah, and Abraham, as wandering folks, food seekers, dreamers in pursuit of a promised land, who, by being willing to become immigrants, also turn out to be founders of the religions of Islam, Judaism, and Christianity. All three religions bare the mark of their immigrant Abraham in the creed: "A wandering Aramean was my ancestor" (Deut. 26:5).

---

13. Hedges, "Guns and Liberty, 29."

Still more. Immigration is the occasion to practice the sacrament of hospitality. The sin of Sodom and Gomorrah was hostility towards the foreigners: "*This was the guilt of your sister Sodom: she and her daughters had pride, excess of food and prosperous ease, but did not aid the poor and needy*" (Ezek. 16:49). Liberating homiletics calls things what they are; it reveals how things are and how God intends them to be.

3. Theological Locus: The Reality of Oppression

> *Being women together was not enough. We were different.*
> *Being gay-girls together was not enough. We were different.*
> *Being Black women together was not enough. We were different.*
> *Being Black dykes together was not enough. We were different.*
>
> AUDRE LORDE

Voltar la tortilla (to flip the tortilla) means permanently approaching preaching from the place of oppression. When we flip the corn tortilla, we place ourselves and our crude reality as our point of departure in the Christian pulpit. To arrive to a safe port, let us revisit a couple of methodologies.

3.1 Methodist Quadrilateral

From his Anglican identity, John Wesley handed over to the Methodists three sources for the Christian life of a believer and added a fourth one: Scripture, Tradition, Reason, and Experience.

Western missionaries, sooner rather than later, taught us—as Southern missionized—the "three selves": self-sustaining, self-propagating, and self-governing. *Voltar la tortilla* added the missing self, i.e., "self-theologizing." Instead of copy-and-paste, we do "original" proclamation, namely, from our time and place of origin.

Theologizing instead of mimicking helps us to qualify the Methodist quadrilateral and problematize the order-rank, from the same Latin word, *ordo*. If Wesley added experience in fourth place, we place it in the first while preaching, in tune with our definition of theology: "The critical reflection of the praxis of liberation, in the light of the Bible."

Voltar la tortilla homiletics raises the queries: "Scripture, according to whom?"; "Whose tradition?"; "Whose logos?"; and "Whose experience?"

To put it quite bluntly, it is more accurate to use the plural nouns of experiences, hermeneutics, traditions, and reasons.

From the experiences of male slaves and females in general, Moses delivered only nine commandments since the tenth imperative does not apply to their identity as private property or objects: "You shall not covet your neighbor's wife, nor his male servant." (Exod. 20:10).

From Roman Catholic female, queer, slave, re-married experiences, there were fewer than seven sacraments, given the fact that "the Holy Orders, Eucharist, Marriage, and Last Rites," did not apply to their identity granted to them by the plantocracy. We must never forget that walled-Immigrant-Christianity first landed in *Abya Yala*, literally the "Roman Catholic Church" and the "Church of England." Missionary preaching came later since it was intended for second-class members. Full access to the church for non-Europeans took centuries. Four ways of being church were walled: "The Church and the People," "The Church for the People," "The Church of the People," and "The People's Church."[14] Moreover, the last one is still coming.

From a Caribbean Protestant experience under the *Pax Britannica*, the Native and African *Abya Yalans* did not have access to the sacraments. It was anathema to learn mathematics, to read, and to write. During worship, there always had to be a white person present. The ringing of the bells was aimed at the masters, for them to keep an eye on the time of their slaves on their way from church to the plantation,[15] whereas for Africans' time was not a commodity. From the colonizers' point of view "to be my brother's keeper" (Gen 4:9) meant surveillance via installation of a panopticon (circular prison), or dividing Africans and Indigenous *Abya Yalans* through snitches, infiltrators, and whistleblowers on the order of the Judas Iscariots of the world. No wonder their revolutionary songs and sermons were exquisitely coded, their very lives depended on it.[16]

Experiences, hermeneutics, traditions, and ways of reasoning matter. Some North-Atlantic preachers still stick to their tradition of "be reasonable, do it my way," or worst yet "my way is God's way."

3.2 Church Base Communities Method

In the homilies in which I have participated within church base communities, I have witnessed the epistemological rupture with colonized homiletics. Sermons from these communities are dialogical, rooted in contextual

---

14. Davis, *Emancipation Still Comin'*, 72–73.
15. Pérez-Álvarez, *Gospel to the Calypsonians*, 16.
16. Cone, *Spirituals and the Blues*, 126.

reality, praxis of liberation oriented, biblically driven, self-critical, and close with a fiesta or celebration.

The point of departure of proclamation is experiential, meaning to see and feel the social situation, to listen to what is going on in the everydayness instead of focusing on metaphysical entities. Statistics are taken with a grain of salt since their results are based on how, what, when, why, and who you ask.

To see also demands that we know our world in order to undress magical concepts like meritocracy, which preaches the modernity dogma that everybody can climb economically. The author of 2 Thess. 3:10 claims, "If anyone doesn't want to work, they shouldn't eat." However, translations such as the King James, Living Bible, and others put the stress on laziness as opposed to "inability" or lack of resources. Ignoring structures of inequality, they say, "You are poor because you don't want to be rich," "Where there's a will there's a way," or, worse yet, "Don't give a fish to the hungry, teach them how to fish," even if the lake has been privatized, polluted, or militarized. Meritocracy hides the structural conflicts and globally designed inequality of savage capitalism. One billion go hungry while there is enough food to feed twice the human population even as we read. This simply turns our stomachs!

To see also means to judge, for the ability to judge connotes the critique of the current powers that be in the light of Christian Scriptures, through diverse epistemologies and multiple senses, in order to envision our reality in a holistic way. To judge has to do with how to think instead of what to think. In judging, we always have to keep in mind that privileges should not be our blinders but rather our opportunities to serve the poor. To judge avoids abstractions as an ideological mechanism that prevent us from tackling the concrete suffering of people with first and last names. Mayan sacred scriptures of the *Popol Vuh* is so relevant in this case: "When you have to choose between two ways, ask yourselves which one has a heart. The one who chooses the way with a heart will never be wrong."

To act is the next ingredient after doing social analysis and biblical scrutiny: what strategy are we going to prepare, what we can do, how are we to behave, and which actions will we take to reshape the anti-Reign of God into the Reign of God's justice for all? The immediate needs have to be addressed, but the structural sins have to be confronted as well.

To review our actions is to be self-critical: What did we do wrong? How can we be more effective? What behaviors should we change? What hurdles did our actions encounter? What lessons did we learn from our mistakes? What are we going to do differently next time? How do we feel? To review does not mean going through a checklist but rather is related to our axiology or value system in a time when, as Antonio Machado stated, "Only a fool thinks that the price of something is the same as its value."

To celebrate is linked with the most universal of human rights: *la fiesta*. Whether our concrete praxis achieved the goals of the community, whether it left a bittersweet flavor in our mouths, or even if it experienced a modest win, the celebration is a joyous reminder: *Mañana será mejor*, namely, tomorrow will be better.

3.3 Intersectionality

The particular historical location for Caribbean and Latin Americans is oppression in its many layers. Audre Lorde, daughter of Caribbean immigrants from Granada and Barbados, played a significant role in cooking from scratch the womanist concept of intersectionality, which, according to Kimberlé Crenshaw is "a means of capturing both the structural and dynamic (e.g., active) aspects of multiple discrimination, thus affecting both theory and practice."[17]

Audre herself had a menu of oppressive identity markers. Among them: female, light black (although she chose to be black), lesbian, mute until the age of four, diagnosed blind at birth, and born in Harlem to immigrant parents.

Voltear la tortilla points toward parrhesian homiletics, i.e., delivering the message, not a massage: "*He [Paul] proclaimed the kingdom of God and taught about the Lord Jesus Christ—with all boldness and without hindrance!*" (Acts 28:31).

This Greek word composed of *pan* and *rhema* has to do with *parrhesiazesthati*, that is, "the activity of saying everything" or *parrhesiastés*, namely, the one who says everything. Parrhesian homiletics thus preaches the unsustainability of a "single issue struggle" but the need to approach the multiple oppressions which intersect in our everydayness. Liberating preaching then will address the social evils of classism, patriarchalism, racism, ageism, ableism, militarism, consumerism, patriotism, heterosexism, xenophobia, criminalization of immigrants, linguistic discrimination, and the McDonaldization and Coca-Colonization of our taste.

---

17. Morgan, *Sisterhood is Forever*, 46. See also Crenshaw, "Demarginalizing the Intersections of Race and Sex"; "Mapping the Margins."

4. Social Location: The Community

*The Europeans did not bring the culture;
they brought their culture.*

CARLOS PELLICER

Voltear la tortilla aims to break with the rampant neoliberalism system based on chronic individualism. Caribbean and Latin American homiletics are grounded in the communal subject[18] and marks its distance from the "Robinson Crusoe," "Lone Ranger," or "one man band" capitalistic individualism.

Our collective subjectivity is rooted in communalism as the *sine qua non* of being: "Hispanics insist that the community, or the 'social location,' is not the pantheon but the place of birth of being."[19] God is neither an idea nor a doctrine but rather an encounter that takes place within the family of faith. From the immersion of the individual subject into the communal subject does not follow that the individual is gulped by collectivity. The opposite is true: "In an authentic community, the identity of 'nosotros' doesn't extinguish the 'yo'; the word in Spanish for 'we' is 'nosotros'; which literally means 'nos otros'; a community of *otros*."[20]

4.1 *Nosótrico*

Voltear la tortilla from imperial homiletics is to focus on Southern epistemologies such as the Tojolabal culture. For ages singing in this dialect, one out of the 28 dialects of the Mayan language was banned. They still sing in two voices, very soft and mellow in contradistinction to the Master's thunder voice. Currently, their communities release artists from labor since they sing for the common good and not for resuming a brilliant individualist career. This Chiapas civilization learned their *nosotrico* or we-ness from their Sacred Scripture of the *Popol Vuh*, the Divine Counsel.[21]

The *nosotrificación* (we-ness-ification) preaches co-responsibility. Therefore, when somebody breaks the law, they say "one of us committed a crime" but they still continue to be a part of the community and are held accountable by practicing restorative justice.[22]

18. Scanone, "Religión."
19. Goizueta, "Theology as Intellectually Vital Inquiry," 68.
20. Goizueta, "Nosotros," 57.
21. Lenkersdorf, *Los hombres verdaderos*.
22. Lenkersdorf, *Aprende a escuchar*, 123.

Native *Abya Yala* cultures socialize children in such a way that they learn through the adults' praxis, by observation and incorporation. They also do it by means of the institutions of the *tequio* or communal working and the *milpa*, namely, cultivating a variety of plants while the whole family participates. Togetherness has primacy over the attitude of "how is it going to help my cause?"

Voltear la tortilla connotes taking distance from the Cartesian individualistic *ego* and embracing the Tojolabal *Tik*, i.e., the organizational principle of we-ness, instead.[23] By the same token, not only the Mayans did (and do) philosophy but the Aztecs, too.[24] Nonetheless, the North-Atlantic imperial philosophers keep favoring Greece as the mother of philosophy. Dynnik[25] adds Egypt and Asia but dismisses Africa Sub-Sahara, *Abya Yala* and Australia.

The *nosótrico* finds resonance in Jesus talking to the fig tree (Mark 11:14) since his Mediterranean culture addressed plants and trees as subjects as well. Today, we know the vegetable realm has culinary and musical preferences. Tojolabal philosophy and theology does not consider subjects to be active and objects to be passive as in Western thought. Subjects do not *aprehender* (apprehend, *greifen*), they *aprender* (learn, *begeifren*) from the objects. For instance, this Mayan culture does not torture horses by breaking their spirit through humiliating practices. Instead, they establish a *nosótrica* communication with the four-legged sisters and brothers.

4.2 *Amaútico*

Northern homiletics endorses acculturation, i.e., the imposition of Western culture, whereas Southerners opt for enculturation or treating all cultures as co-equals, since all of them are vehicles of God's grace and, at the same time, all of them are tainted by sin.

The *amáutico* is a legacy from the Andean culture, that is, one of the foundational seven ancient civilizations, together with the Mesoamerican, Nigerian, Egyptian, Mesopotamian, Hindi, and Chinese.

From *Amautismo*[26] follows a "liberating science," a global wisdom that inspires a sacred relationship with the *Pachamama* or Mother Earth. This philosophy and theology have stewed in the *Sumaj Kausay* and *Sumaj Qamaña* spiritualties related with the good living based on a respectful

---

23. Lenkersdorf, *Filosofar en clave Tojolabal*.
24. León-Portilla, *La filosofía náhuatl estudiada en sus fuentes*.
25. Dynnik et al., *Historia de la filosofía*.
26. Ticona, *El indianismo de Fausto Reinaga*.

communion with the entire creation. Fausto Reinga, the greatest *amáutico* thinker in the 1960s, was already unapologetic, proud of being indigenous, and linked being indigenous not with the skin but with the soul.

The Judeo-Christian tradition emptied Goddess-Supreme Mother matriarchy by demonizing women (Gen 3:16) along with her main attribute of wisdom by satanizing the snake (Gen 3:14).[27] *Abya Yalans'* theologies and philosophies, on the other hand, keep matriarchy and their sacred snake alive since she is caressing the mother earth all the time. In an authentic contextual Andean and Mesoamerican Eucharist, it can very well be preached: "This is the snake of God who takes away the sins of the world."[28]

While the Judeo-Christian patriarchalism stigmatizes menstrual blood, *Abya Yala* theology sacralizes it: "Nana, the Creator Mother, created with diverse colors the plants, fishes, snakes, and all the animals, and she gave birth to all of them out of her menstrual blood."[29]

In ancient civilizations, the "blood mystery" was experienced differently in terms of gender. Male hunters and warriors associated the vital liquid with death; while females linked it with "child birth," or life giving,[30] in tune with what the Nicene Creed preaches about the Holy Spirit: "The Giver of Life."

In spite of the fact that Jesus de-stigmatized blood when he touched the bleeding woman (Mark 5:21–34), the prejudice prevailed. During World War II, the US Red Cross did not accept blood from African-North-Americans. Dr. Charles Drew, the director of the blood banks of that country, protested and resigned since he himself was a Black person. In the 1970s, Dictator Anastasio Somoza, being advised by anti-revolution Cubans, bled the miserable by paying them one US dollar per liter of blood and selling it in the States ten times higher. The blood of the queer family and of sisters and brothers with piercings and tattoos is still anathema.

Voltear la tortilla hermeneutics of the Candlemas feast (Luke 2:22–24) breaks with imperial Christianity's institution of quarantine, by instituting a second lent to postpartum women. Protests against the stigmatization of menstrual blood either by Isaiah, "All our righteous acts are like filthy rags" (Isa 64:6), or our current "sanitary" towels propaganda continues even to this day.

---

27. Eisler, *Sex, Myths and the Politics of the Bodies*.

28. Even my professor of the 1970s, Harvey Cox, fails to do justice to matriarchy and snakes. See Cox, *On Not Leaving It To The Snake*.

29. Ibarra, *Cosmogonía y mitología indígena americana*, 82, quoted in Campos, *Gracias a Dios que comí*, 52.

30. Gilman, *His Religion and Hers*.

4.3 I-n-I[31]

Rastafarianism is an Abrahamic religion born in the 1930s in Jamaica but not officially recognized by the government until 2003. Inspired by Marcus Garvey and globally propagated by Bob Marley, the core of its Rastaology is the concept of "I-n-I," pointing towards the relational sense of self and the neighbor, "I am because we are; and since we are, therefore I am."

To dignify ourselves is well rooted in an African sense of aesthetics in dressing-up and in dialogical philosophy by addressing the neighbor as Ms., Mrs., or Mr. with a body language showing plenty of respect and endearment. It has to do with the uplifting of oneness in two persons.[32]

> "Get up Stand up"
> You, preacher man don't tell me
> Heaven is under the earth
> You a duppy and you don't know
> What life is really worth?
> It's not all that glitters is gold
> And half the story has never been told
> So now, we see the light
> We gonna stand up for your rights.[33]

Furthermore, the cosmic notion of I-and-I or oneness links human beings with the ancestors, the entire creation, and with the Divinity. I-n-I embraces "ital" or vital food. Being vegetarians, Rastas do not eat anything with a face. They resist the Babylon system with their mouths, their spirits, and their bodies, fighting for equal rights for the whole creation.[34]

From *voltear la tortilla*, we learn to turn our backs on the hierarchical, elitist medieval doctrine of the great chain of being that advocates ontological supremacy. In its place, liberating homiletics preaches *perichoresis*, or the communion of all beings, the dialogical knot, the dance of love, or the talking circle of everything and everybody who opposes all forms of oppression.

Afro-*Abya Yalans* see the community as the social location as well. "It takes a village to raise a child" is indicative of the primacy of the collective being. The philosophy of Ubuntu humanity or universal bond confesses, "I am because we are."

Mark 8:27–38 portrays imperial Herod as a man of order: first me, second me, and last me (Mark 8:27)! Peter is the first person who names

---

31. A Rastafarian word for "we" or "oneness." In www.urbandictionary.com.
32. Clark, "Sociological Construct of Rastafarian Philosophies."
33. Marley and Tosh, "Get Up Stand Up."
34. Chevannes, *Rastafari*.

Jesus' identity as the Messiah (Matt 16:16). However, Peter had internalized the identity defined by Herod, namely, that of an almighty Messiah who will provide 2800 slaves to every single Israelite and, furthermore, a Messiah who will replace the ruling of Rome with the ruling of the Israelites. That is why when Peter heard Jesus talking about suffering and dying, he had to rebuke Jesus since Peter had already sold his soul to the lords of this individualistic, competitive, and cruel world. No wonder Jesus got mad, called Peter Satan, and proceeded to remind his disciples of their real identity: Jesus: I-n-I (Mark 8:27). Jesus reminded his followers that their identity is grounded in the community, not their personal merits or curriculum vitae. Jesus Christ is the Messiah who lives in community like the African saying warns us: "One finger cannot pick up a grain."

In *Abya Yala*, we say that a person who is self-centered doesn't have a grandmother—namely, that nobody claims him. However, things are changing with the identity granted by the empire, namely, the "selfies": "I take a selfie, therefore I am." From this perspective, the heading "the Lost Sheep" (Luke 15:3–7) does not do justice to Jesus' style of life of togetherness, which points toward the "Incomplete Flock."

When speaking "I," Rastas are embracing their "sistrins, breddins, mother earth, and the Divine." One love, one blood, or "I-n-I." In Mexico some Aztecs created the movement "RasTecs" to show family ties, as the perichoretic poem states:

> *The spirit sleeps in the stone,*
> *dreams in the flower,*
> *awakes in the animal,*
> *feels in the man,*
> *and knows that she feels in the woman.*

5. What Informs Homiletics: Suspicion of Ideology

> *She studies, and disputes, and teaches,*
> *and thus she serves her Faith;*
> *for how could God, who gave her reason,*
> *want her ignorant?*
>
> SOR JUANA INÉS DE LA CRUZ[35]

---

35. Carol in celebration of St. Catherine of Alexandria (1692)

Voltear la tortilla methodology dismisses that kind of magical thinking that allows preachers to believe they can faithfully proclaim the Scriptures while isolating themselves from the powers that be. The unmasking of the imperial ideology is necessary: "In the task of preaching, the messenger includes the economic, political, and social identity of the preacher. The message also takes shape in part through the economic, political, and social identity of the congregation."[36]

The Western paradigm opts for the melting pot as a means to legitimize the neoliberal political and economic system, echoing Margaret Thatcher's infamous TINA (there is no alternative . . . but hers!): "When I was a pre-school child, nobody had spoken to me about the American [sic] society, the melting pot, or the Anglo-Saxon values. It was not necessary. I, and others like me, got the message through a myriad of non-verbal ways: differences in food, dressing, and speaking—a scary feeling indeed."[37]

The suspicion of ideology consists of mistrusting the imposition of a set of dis-values carried out by the imperial pulpit. This hermeneutic of suspicion refers to Hermes, the Greek translator of Olympus's messages to humankind. Little wonder Hermes in Rome's Latin became Mars, the god of war and of lies, or "post-truth" to use a current term.

Paul Ricoeur was of the opinion that there were three Masters of Suspicion: Karl Marx and his Cosmo vision based on the historical materialism; Friedrich Nietzsche and his explanation of hell as the sense of impotence of the *rancidus* (resentment, rotten, lame) people; and Sigmund Freud, for whom God is nothing more than a mere childish fantasy.[38] However, according to one father of Latin American liberation theology, Søren Kierkegaard is the champion of all of them:

> It was characteristic of all previous philosophy to deal with precisely that field of being which does not depend on our free will in order to be what it is. It is a being that does not disturb us, that does not upset us. . . . Nietzsche, Marx, and Kierkegaard rebelled against and broke with it. Of the three, Kierkegaard was the most conscious of the novelty of this method, which was to detect which fields of being can exist only if I make a decision.[39]

Freud, on his own, elaborated three injuries that humankind's narcissism cannot tolerate. First, Copernicus's heliocentric model of the universe, that is, the expelling of our planet from its privileged place. Second, Charles Darwin's

---

36. González and González, *Liberating Pulpit*, 67.
37. Avalos, *Latinos in the United States*, 43.
38. Ricoeur, *Freud and Philosophy*, 32.
39. Miranda, *Being and the Messiah*, 23. See also Pérez-Álvarez, *Vexing Gadfly*.

evolution theory and its ejecting of humankind as the crown of creation. The Anglican scientist went on to affirm that females are the ones who decide with whom to procreate. Additionally, this faithful supporter of Christian missions, contrary to common opinion, pointed out that the most vulnerable species built social networks to face adversity. Finally, Freud self-promoted himself as the third narcissistic injury since, through his psychoanalyses, human beings realize they are not entirely conscious of their behavior.

Voltear la tortilla targets post-colonial homiletics by honoring our own authorities while learning how to pray, "Lead us not into imitation." It is our privilege and our duty to actualize our hermeneutics of suspicion of ideology from *Abya Yala*.

What need have we of our own hermeneutics of suspicion, you might ask? The Honorable Elijah Muhammad stated, "If a man won't treat you right, what would make you think that he would teach you right?" He rightly concluded that, "The same people that enslaved us will never send you a teacher that will free you from their grip." Other very provocative gurus of the suspicion of ideology ilk are Frantz Fanon, Aimé Cesaire, Sojourner Truth, Julia Burgos, Marcus Garvey, Hatuey, the Slave Anastasia, José Martí Pérez, and Jamaica Kincaid's "Hot Casserole." In "Unsolicited Letter," he writes:

> You had always felt people like me cannot run things, people like me will never grasp the idea of Gross National Product, people like me will never be able to take command of the thing the most simpleminded among you can master, people like me will never understand the notion of rule by law, people like me cannot really think in abstractions, people like me cannot be objective, we make everything so personal. You will forget your part in the whole setup, that bureaucracy is one of your inventions, that Gross National Product is one of your inventions, and all the laws that you know mysteriously favor you. Do you know why people like me are shy about being capitalists? Well, it's because we, for as long as we have known you, were capital, like bales of cotton and sacks of sugar, and you were the commanding, cruel capitalists, and the memory of this is so strong, the experience so recent, that we can't quite bring ourselves to embrace this idea that you think so much of.[40]

It is not for nothing that the first feminist of our continent was Sor Juana Inés de la Cruz, who actualized suspicion of ideology. In her *Letter by Sor Filotea de la Cruz* (1690), the Mexican philosopher and theologian put the misogynist Paul in his place. She paved the road for us to do likewise.

---

40. Kincaid, "Unsolicited Letter," 36–37.

Consequently, liberating preaching must dismantle Paul's homophobia (1 Cor. 6:9) by denouncing the way he favored the "list of sins" of Mediterranean cultures and buried Jesus' praxis of welcoming to the table precisely those sinners. Juana, the woman who considered dressing like a man to have access to the university, helps us to undress Paul's culturally bound homophobia. In like manner, today's assertive latria-brides[41] who believe in the power of the cross (1 Cor. 1:23) but who equally refuse to put up with a man's nonsense, will think twice before accepting the stoic preaching that says, "love bears and endures all things." (1 Cor. 13:7). The challenges continue when one considers Paul's Euro-centrism (Acts 16:9); his clericalism, by changing Jesus' laity status (Heb. 7); his sacrificetialism (1 Cor. 11:34) in contrast to Jesus' feeding of the poor (John 6:1–14); and his "churchianity" as opposed to Jesus' communism (Mark 10:45).

Emancipatory homiletics seeks to read between the lines and between images by distinguishing between what happened (ontology) and what people said had happened (epistemology).[42] Such is the case of teología mujerista, which "raises new questions, and often becomes subversive by training Hispanic women to be suspicious of everything we haven't participated in defining."[43]

From the outset, slave catechism was bold in confessing that the "Nigger John or Nigger Mandy were created by God to make a crop."[44] That alone was his sole purpose for existing and his sole worth in the eyes of the Lord. Moreover, if a slave dared to ask the meaning of "Thou shalt not commit adultery," or any of the other commandments, the answer was the same: "To serve our heavenly Father, and our earthly Master, obey our overseer, and not steal anything."[45] The slaves early on resisted this understanding of the Scriptures and refashioned the gospel. *Voltear la tortilla* is to preach from the perspective of the plundered Canaanites and of the Prodigal Son who was forced to leave home due to his queer identity (Luke 15:11–32).

From the heteronormative homiletics, Jesus and the children (Matt 10:13–16) is a mere act of charity; whereas from the margins we contemplate Jesus denouncing hegemonic masculinity by presenting himself as weak and effeminate, sharing with women the chores of taking care of children. In this case, Vodun theology is more merciful: "When you feed the children you feed

---

41. Latria is defined as a smart, assertive young black woman. www.urbandictionary.com

42. Trouillot, *Silencing the Past*.

43. Isasi-Díaz, "Mujerista Theology's Method," 51.

44. Wilmore, "Identity Crisis," 5.

45. Matthews, *Slavery and Methodism*, 87.

the saints." We see Jesus' vulnerability again on display when he converts from xenophobia, thanks to the Syrophoenician woman. (Mark 7:28) The Galilean repents from being an imperialist, thanks to the Samaritan woman words. (John 4:7–26). We perceive Jesus preaching an all-inclusive salvation through feeding, healing the bodies, and fighting the structural sin of the anti-Reign of God, as Martin Luther King Jr. grasped in his sermon, "A Time to Break Silence," delivered at Riverside Church in Manhattan:

> On the one hand, we are called to play the Good Samaritan on life's roadside; but that will be only an initial act. One day we must come to see that the whole Jericho road must be transformed so that men and women will not be constantly beaten and robbed as they make their journey on life's highway. True compassion is more than flinging a coin to a beggar; it is not haphazard and superficial. It comes to see that an edifice which produces beggars needs restructuring.[46]

King's post-colonial pulpit reminds us that as recent as the 1960s, Jericho's roads were all over the US, to the point of needing the survival GPS of the "Green Book."[47] Blacks driving on extended journeys out of town had to take their own food, plan their restroom and gas stops, look for lodging without the infamous sign "bnb"—but no Blacks—and stay away from "sundown towns."

Voltear la Tortilla repudiates the ideology of impotence, of "nothing can be done," to instead preach, "Nothing else can be done." We have the capacity not only to see things for what they are but also to see things for what they can be.

6. Universality & Particularity

Gottes Wort und
Luthers Vergehet
Nun und Niemmermehr.[48]

---

46. King preached this sermon at the Riverside Church in New York City in April 4, 1967.

47. The Negro Traveler's Green Book, published (1936–67) during the segregation era in the United States, identified businesses that would accept African American customers. The Green Book was compiled by Victor Hugo Green (1892–1960), a black postal worker who lived in the Harlem section of New York City. www.britannica.com/topic/The-Green-Book-travel-guide.

48. "God's Word and Luther's doctrine now and never pass away."

From his romantic island, Herder held that the center of the universe was the solar system, the center of the solar system was the earth, and, the center of the earth was Europe. Instead of that mono-centrism of the old paradigm, *voltear la tortilla* preaches a poli-centrism based on the historical praxis of liberation for everybody.

Billy Graham died on February 21, 2018, the same day Malcom X was assassinated (1965), the former with 99 years and the later with 39. The champion of suspicion of African North Americans was cognizant of the evangelist's potent cocktail of Evangelical Christian Nationalism: "I have watched how Billy Graham comes into a city, spreading what he calls the gospel of Christ, which is only white nationalism. That is what he is. Billy Graham is a white nationalist; I'm a black nationalist."[49]

Graham's particularity however, from the very outset, was exported as a universal. Little wonder he transformed the gospel into a global commodity: "We are selling the greatest product on earth. Why shouldn't we promote it as effectively as we promote a bar of soap?"[50]

In the early 1960s, while visiting Disneyland, Billy Graham congratulated Disney for building such a world of fantasy. Mickey's creator immediately reacted: "Billy, this is the real world, fantasy is what is outside."[51]

This Evangelist was good at recycling his sermons. Through his "one size-fits-all" approach, Graham got rid of the sermon's particularity or specific context. What took place was generic preaching, colonialism, the manifest destiny, in short, the crusade of Massa God of the plantations.

Shortly after his death, Graham's remains were given the rare privilege of "lying in honor" in the Rotunda of the U. S. Capitol. The broadcasted message was direct: spreading Graham's version of the gospel ran parallel with spreading the empire's version of democracy. For this millionaire preacher, having a "personal relationship with God" meant a having a personal development through the three Fs, "faith, freedom, [and] free enterprise," or the three Cs of David Livingston, "Christianity, civilization, [and] commerce."

Vine Deloria stated it in cold turkey: "In the political arena, it was impossible to tell Graham from the rest of Nixon's aides. When the president came to the University of Tennessee in 1970—one of the few campuses he dared to visit—to address Graham's revival meeting, a choir of 5,500 voices sang 'How Great Thou Art' as Nixon was seated, awaiting Graham's

---

49. Butler, "Billy Graham."
50. Martin, "Vivid Portrait," 17.
51. Piquer, "Estados Unidos."

introduction. There remains one question as to which 'thou' the choir was trumpeting."[52]

Graham always pointed at the Bible with his mantra, "The Bible says." Nonetheless, it was not what Scriptures spoke but his particular interpretation converted into a universal norm, "My way is God's way." His preaching then comforted the comfortable and sent to hell[53] communists, the queer family, the Vietnamese, unions, Roman Catholics, racial integrationists . . .[54]

Graham's exceptionalism, sense of entitlement, and heteronormative white supremacy, prevented him from learning of Mexican Alfonso Reyes's dictum: "The only way to be usefully national is to be generously universal."

By the entrance of Wartburg Seminary Castle in Iowa, one can read in German: "God's Word and Luther's doctrine now and never pass away." In front of this "protestant infallibility" dogma, let us bear in mind that all doctrines are always mirrors of a particular geography, time, and culture. The same is true for sermons and interpretations of the very authors of the Bible. What remains forever is Jesus's liberating preaching and praxis.

Bibliography

Avalos, David T. *Latinos in the United States: The Sacred and the Political.* South Bend, IN: Notre Dame University Press, 1986.

Butler, Anthea. "Billy Graham and the Gospel of America Nationalistic Christianity." *AlterNet*, March 15, 2018.

Campos, Maximiliano Salinas. *Gracias a Dios que comí; el cristianismo en Iberoamérica y el Caribe s. XV–XX.* Ciudad de México, Mexico: Dabar, 2000.

Chevannes, Barry. *Rastafari: Roots and Ideology.* Syracuse, NY: Syracuse University Press, 1994.

Chidester, David. *Salvation and Suicide: An Interpretation of Jim Jones, the Peoples Temple, and Jonestown.* Indianapolis: Indiana University Press, 1991.

Clark, Hilary. "A Sociological Construct of Rastafarian Philosophies." *University of Vermont*, December 2, 2009. Online. https://debate.uvm.edu/dreadlibrary/Clark.htm.

Cone, James. *The Spirituals and the Blues: An Interpretation.* Maryknoll, NY: Orbis, 1998.

Cox, Harvey. *On Not Leaving It to the Snake.* London: SCM, 1968.

Crenshaw, Kimberlé. "Demarginalizing the Intersections of Race and Sex: Black Feminist Critique of Antidiscrimination Doctrine, Feminist Theory, and Antiracist Politics." *The University of Chicago Legal Forum* 140 (1989) 139–67.

---

52. Deloria, *God is Red*, 346.

53. See the hot reflection on the Devil and Graham according to Jim Jones, in Chidester, *Salvation and Suicide*, 175n64.

54. Hays, *Baby in the Woods*, 50

———. "Mapping the Margins: Intersectionality, Identity Politics, and Violence against Women of Color." *Stanford Law Review* 43.6 (1991) 1241–99.

Davis, Kotright. *Emancipation Still Comin': Explorations in Caribbean Emancipatory Theology*. Maryknoll, NY: Orbis, 1990.

Deloria, Vine. *God Is Red: A Native View of Religion*. New York: Putnam, 2003.

Dynnik, M. A., et al. *Historia de la filosofía*. Vol. 1. Ciudad de Mèxico, Mexico: Grijalbo, 1960.

Eisler, Riane. *Sex, Myths, and the Politics of the Bodies: New Paths to Power and Love*. San Francisco: Harper, 1955.

Fernández, Silvio Castro. "Afrodescendientes." *Aporrea*, May 13, 2011.

García de León, Antonio. *Misericordia; el destino trágico de una collera de apaches en la Nueva España*. Ciudad de México, Mexico: Fondo de Cultura Económica, 2018.

Gates, Henry Louis, Jr. *Black in Latin America*. New York: New York University Press, 2011.

Gilman, Charlotte Perkins. *His Religion and Hers: A Study of the Faith of the Fathers and the Work of Our Mothers*. 1922. Reprint, Berkeley, CA: Altamira, 2003.

Goizueta, Roberto. "Nosotros: Toward a US Hispanic Anthropology." *Listening* 27 (1992) 57.

———. "Theology as Intellectually Vital Inquiry: The Challenge of/to US Hispanic Theologians." *Proceedings of Catholic Theologians Society of America* 46 (1991) 68.

González, Catherine Gunsalus, and Justo L. González. *The Liberating Pulpit*. Nashville: Abingdon, 1994.

Hays, Daniel Alexander. *A Baby in the Woods: Billy Graham, Anticommunism, and Vietnam*. Chicago: Eastern Illinois University Press, 2017.

Hedges, Chris. "Guns and Liberty." *Truthdig*, February, 28, 2018. Online. https://www.truthdig.com/articles/guns-and-liberty.

Hernándes, Eleazar López. "Una misión descolonizadora de nuestras mentes en relación a los indígenas." Speech delivered at Centro Nacional de Ayuda a Misiones Indígenas, Mexico, 2009. Online. http://www.curasopp.com.ar/web/es/teologia-india/75-una-mision-descolonizadora-de-nuestras-mentes-en-relacion-a-los-indigenas.

Isasi-Díaz, Ada María. "Mujerista Theology's Method: A Liberating Praxis, A Way of Life." *Listening* 27 (1992) 51.

Kelly, Kate. "The Green Book: The First Travel Guide for African-Americans Dates to the 1930s." *HuffPost*, March 8, 2014. Online. https://www.huffpost.com/entry/the-green-book-the-first_b_4549962.

Kincaid, Jamaica. "An Unsolicited Letter to Antigua's British Colonizers." In *A Small Place*, by Jamaica Kincaid, 6–37. New York: Farrar, Straus & Giroux, 1988.

Lenkersdorf, Carlos. *Aprende a escuchar*. Ciudad de México, Mexico: Plaza y Valdés, 2011.

———. *Filosofar en clave Tojolabal*. Ciudad de México, Mexico: Porrúa, 2005

———. *Los hombres verdaderos: voces y testimonios tojolabales*. Ciudad de México, Mexico: Siglo XXI, 2005.

León-Portilla, Miguel. *La filosofía náhuatl estudiada en sus fuentes*. Ciudad de México, Mexico: UNAM, 2006.

Luther, Martin. "Heidelberg Disputation." In vol. 31 of *Works of Martin Luther*, edited by Henry Eyster Jacobs and Adolph Spaeth, 40. Philadelphia: Muhlenberg, 1943.

Marley, Bob, and Peter Tosh. "Get Up Stand Up." *Talkin' Blues*. Universal Island Records, CD, 1991.
Martin, Harold H. "A Vivid Portrait of the Famous Revivalist Billy Graham." *Saturday Evening Post*, April 13, 1963. 17–22.
Matthews, Donald. *Slavery and Methodism*. Princeton: Princeton University Press, 1965.
Miranda, José Porfirio. *Being and the Messiah: The Message of St. John*. Eugene, OR: Wipf & Stock, 2006.
Morgan, Robin. *Sisterhood is Forever: "Multiple Oppressions."* New York: Washington Square, 2003.
Pérez-Álvarez, Eliseo. *The Gospel to the Calypsonians: The Caribbean, Bible, and Liberation Theology*. Chicago: Lutheran School of Theology at Chicago, 2004.
———. *A Vexing Gadfly: The Late Kierkegaard on Economic Matters*. Eugene, OR: Pickwick, 2009.
———. *We Be Jammin: Liberating Discourses from the Land of the Seven Flags*. Chicago: Lutheran School of Theology at Chicago, 2002.
Piquer, Isabel. "Estados Unidos regresa al mundo de la fantasía con el centenario de Walt Disney." *El País*, December 6, 2001. Online. https://elpais.com/diario/2001/12/06/cultura/1007593201_850215.html.
Rezende, Marcela Torres. "A alimentação como objeto histórico complexo: relações entre comidas e sociedades." *Estudios Históricos* 33 (2004) 175–79.
Ricoeur, Paul. *Freud and Philosophy: An Essay on Interpretation*. New Heaven, CT: Yale University Press, 1970.
Scanone, Juan Carlos. "Religión, lenguaje y sabiduría de los pueblos." *Stromata* 34 (1978) 25–47.
Segundo, Juan Luis. *The Liberation of Theology*. Maryknoll, NY: Orbis, 1976.
Subcomandante Insurgente Marcos. "La larga travesía del dolor a la esperanza." *La Jornada*, September 22, 1994.
Ticona, Esteban. *El indianismo de Fausto Reinaga*. La Paz: Cima, 2015.
Trouillot, Michel-Rolph. *Silencing the Past: Power and the Production of History*. Boston: Beacon, 1995.
Velázquez, María Elisa. *Mujeres de origen africano en la capital novohispana XVII–XVIII*. Ciudad de México, Mexico: INAH, UNAM, 2006.
Wilmore, Gayraud S. "Identity Crisis: Blacks Predominantly White Denominations." In *Colloquium on Black Religion*, edited by William Howard, 5. New York: Reformed Church in America, 1976.
Wink, Walter. *The Powers That Be: Theology for a New Millennium*. New York: Doubleday, 1998.

The Passion of the Christ?
or
The Passion of Mel Gibson?[1]

Eliseo Pérez-Álvarez

Luke 23:1–49; Deuteronomy 21:23

"May the words of my mind and the meditation of my heart comfort the afflicted and afflict the comfortable."

The *Passion of the Christ*, a movie starring Mel Gibson, seeks to capture Jesus's passion. So let's take a close up look at this film this sunny morning from beautiful St. Croix. The pre and existing sales make this film the most successful religious movie ever produced. We know that when the film business is having bad times, it immediately goes ahead and makes a Bible movie. Nonetheless, in this case, what significantly contributed to the economic boom was the omnipresent anti-Semitic campaign. Is this so? or it is an anti-Africa, anti-women, anti-queer, anti-children, and anti-poor crusade?

Let's have a seat and watch the movie:

---

1. Before the imminent second part of *The Passion of the Christ*, this is my proposal: To revisit my sermon preached at Kingshill Lutheran Church, St. Croix, USVI, on Passion Sunday, April 4, 2004. "Second parts were never good," says the dictum, but in this case I'm sure that "second parts can never be worse than the first part."

The Passions Against Africa

The portentous political emancipation of Jesus' people took place in Africa, prophetically immortalized by Bob Marley's "Exodus" reggae album. The same continent practiced hospitality by welcoming political refugees Baby Jesus, Mary, and Joseph. Herod the Great was powerless before the Wise Men's civil disobedience. That's why it comes as no surprise that in Puerto Rico, January 6 is the most sacred day, with Black Melchior at the center. This was the only day off slaves had during the whole year.

Still more, African Lucius was a leader in the Antiochean Christian community (Acts 13:1). On Pentecost Day, the Holy Spirit descended on people from Cyrene (Acts 2:10). Some folks from this city were members of Jerusalem's Christian congregation (Acts 6:9). Simon of Cyrene's sons, Alexander and Rufus, were wise and bold African disciples in Rome's Christian house (Rom 16:13).

Gibson, on his own, portrays Simon of Cyrene as a renegade who is mad at Jesus. This Australian producer follows the racist interpretation of Simon of Cyrene—and thus all Black people—as the "burden bearer" directly legitimated by the Bible (Luke 23:26). Little wonder a catechism raises the question, "Why were Blacks created?" and the answer is, "To make a crop."[2]

The Passion of the Christ focuses on Herod's deaf-mute slave as being good for nothing. In awe, we watch the way in which his boss enjoys vacationing in the "sun, rum, and fun" of the Virgin Islands! The moral of the story is: "Bear the cross now, wear the crown later."

Yet, the scene of Jesus hanging on Simon's neck was a big achievement. Other than that, Gibson favors the Nazarene suspended on the cross as the most scandalous fact. Nothing further from the truth. Being naked was the most humiliating act. That's why up until the sixth century, Jesus hung without clothes in the crucifixes. Many people mention Dietrich Bonhoeffer's assassination by Hitler, but few realize before the Lutheran theologian— who began to change his theology in Black Harlem New York—was hung in 1945, he was stripped of all his clothes! If Jesus had been incarnated in the Caribbean . . . nakedness was the most natural style!

This white-skinned, privileged filmmaker preferred to listen to the writings of Augustinian nun Anne Catherine Emmerich in "The Painful Passion of our Lord Jesus Christ." He not only doesn't distinguish between Christ the divine and the historical Jesus, he also hides the most terrifying

---

2. Gayraud S. Wilmore, "Identity Crisis: Blacks in Predominantly White Denominations." Lecture delivered at the Second Annual B. Moses James Colloquium on Black Religion, March 13, 1976.

element of being crucified: instead of being buried, the birds and dogs of prey, together with wild beasts, will take care of the remains, preventing the eternal rest of the crucified people.

The Passions Against Women

According to the gospels, Mary was a brave teenager who obeyed God no matter what. She knew what it meant to be a single mother in a town of no more than 400 inhabitants (John 8:41). By the way, this has been the story of three out of four Caribbean women due to the slave trade, slave auctions, slave breeding farms, labor terrorism, immigration, militarism, and so forth.

Gibson's Mary, in contradistinction, is like a goddess that lies beyond any danger. On her way to Golgotha, the Roman soldiers surrender to her and end up as her private bodyguards. She irradiates cleanliness, calmness, impassiveness, and motionlessness, like a statue.

Mary Magdalene is the protagonist of the four gospels. She is the Apostle of the Apostles, the Beloved Disciple, the woman who overshadowed Peter, and the model of gender equity in following Jesus.

The Passion of the Christ, on the other hand, reduced Mary Magdalene to a pale shadow. She is an adulterous woman who was saved by the bell while everybody was ready to stone her to death. The Australian actor dehumanized Mary the mother of Jesus by treating her as a goddess, and, by the same token, sub-humanized Mary Magdalene by silencing her powerful leadership: "You're prettier when you're quiet."

The Passions Against the Queer

The gospel of Mark calls our attention to Jesus' disciple who carried a water jar on his shoulder, à la womanish style (Mark 14:13). This story evokes another one, when the Galilean took care of the children (Mark 10:16), which broke the patriarchal law that prevented men from dealing with infants and "becoming effeminate."

Jesus didn't care what people said about him! That reminds us of the boxing match of March 24, 1962, between Emilie Alphonse Griffith and Benni Paret, alias the Kid. While being weighed the day before, the Cuban Kid touched St. Thomian Griffith's butt and called him "mariquita," that is, the diminutive of Mary, or "fag" in English. Needless to say Emilie was boiling with anger, and in the 12th round of their 15 round fight, he sent the Cuban Kid to the hospital in a coma. The Cuban boxer fought during ten days to come back but it never happened. He passed away. Griffith declared his bisexuality 40 years after that episode, only to face a media firestorm and lynching. The St. Thomas USVI boxer replied:

> Me no know nothing. When me killed a man, people forgave me; today me showing my love for a man and my people repudiate me![3]

Gibson's queerphobia preaches that the transgender, bisexual, intersexual, or gender diverse are soul-less. People may argue that he was trying to be inclusive in picturing Satan as an intersexual person, that is, a female-male individual. In that case, why didn't the film director choose an inter-gender sister or brother to personify Jesus? Did Mel betray his own repressed gender orientation as he did in "Braveheart," when he showed his butt while walking alongside muscular, handsome, undefeatable, and immortal male warriors?

In any case, some queers are more equal than others. In Nazi Germany, queer Germans killed queer Jews. In the Virgin Islands, if you are poor, you are "maricón" or "anti-man"; whereas if you are well to do, you are gay! St. Croix people know what I'm talking about.

The Passions Against Children

Jesus's lips mentions the "Reign of God" ninety times, and the gospels record the phrase around 110 times, "counting children and women," the last and the least (Matt 11:5).

Gibson's script is closer to Augustine's idea of a childless heaven where there is no one younger than 30 years old. No wonder the Council of Carthage established limbo—children who pass out of this life unbaptized continue to live in happiness—in the year 418 to alleviate Augustine's psychological war on children. There was a time when unbaptized kids had to be buried in different cemeteries.

The Passion of the Christ is more at home with the children's crusade of the year 1212 CE, which was in fact an immigrant event to get rid of the superfluous little ones while plundering Jerusalem. Or what about the more than 100,000 Native North American offspring who were uprooted from their parents and swallowed by White supremacists? Or, bringing things more to home, let us remember how, when the Black human flesh business and chattels became unsustainable, the abolition took place to give room for "breeding farms," i.e., factories of Black children.

3. This paragraph was added for the published version.

Well, this movie ignores the children's rights issued in 1989 by the United Nations, which embraces the hundreds of thousands of children that, even as we worship, are incarcerated, working in agricultural fields, and in the army, crossing seas and deserts, being objects of organ trafficking, rape, prostitution, and, above all, starvation.

While Jesus dignifies children, Gibson associates them with demons that torture Judas until the extreme. Mel links infants with monsters possessed by the androgynous Devil. The Australian producer was disappointed when his film was rated as Restricted in Mexico. Was he expecting that children will watch themselves in the big screen to celebrate their satanization? Thanks, but no thanks!

The Passions Against the Impoverished

Jesus was killed for mingling and sharing the table with outcasts, folks with disabilities, the impoverished, and the dregs of society, who were considered non-persons. The Nazarene was crucified because he favored the excluded persons in detriment of the hundreds of clean and holy rules of the dominant classes.

Gibson is very selective in choosing scenes of the Galilean life which don't do justice to his prophetic ministry. Mel reduced the three years of Jesus' pastoral work to his last twelve hours hanging from the cross. In the Hollywood star's opinion, those bloody and sweaty last hours were the price "the Christ" had to pay for human sinfulness. Gibson filmed his own hands as those being nailed since: "It was me who placed Jesus on the cross. It was my sins." Bankers got the message: "If God didn't forgive his own Son; we won't forget personal, national, or continental external debts at all, because the Bible tells me so."

The Gospels tell us that the Nazarene was crucified by the Roman empire and the religious Jewish leaders whose economic interest were jeopardized. In Gibson's mind, Pontius Pilate and his first lady are simply saints, and Jesus was tortured, tortured, and tortured because he was paying humanity's debt . . . including his . . . in the first place!

To Make the Film and Sermon Short

Today is Palm Sunday also known as Passion Sunday. This morning, we celebrate God as the passionate, sensitive, feeling Liberator, whose sacrifice is to eradicate all unnecessary and innocent sacrifices: "I have come that they may have life to the fullest" (John 10:10).

Consequently, Jesus lived a life consecrated to fight all human suffering caused by the earthly empires. Gibson, quite the opposite, glorifies violence as an end in itself in a morbid and sadomasochist way. He filmed the seven falls and the unending, jet-propelled blood, captured in slow motion, with disgusting close ups, which are Hollywood's bread and butter.

We agree that this movie may help to undermine Docetism, namely, the heresy that affirms that Jesus' body was a mere appearance. Nonetheless, isn't Gibson divinizing Jesus' body by making his torturing so unbearable, so invulnerable, à la semi-gods like Rambo, Wonder Woman, or Captain America? Isn't Gibson adding fuel to the movie genre known as the "White Savior"?

This Passion Week, we'll see Jesus followed by crowds who have been fed, healed, and dignified by him. We'll see the Galilean prophet assaulting the fortress-butchery-IRS-bank-temple and expelling the greedy business parties who exploit the impoverished pilgrims. We'll see the Road-Opener (Heb 6:20) denouncing the civil and religious authorities which worship the emperor and devour the widows, the orphans, and foreigners. We'll see a prophetess anointing him and therefore politicizing the meal in Simon the Leper's house by declaring Jesus the only King (Mark 14:3–9). We'll see our Liberator inaugurating a new community, where his blood will be the end of the menstrual blood stigma and will experience a definitive rupture with the lucrative religious system based on "cleanliness," like current "sanitary towels"! We'll see the arrest of Jesus in the middle of the night—due to fear of the people—as a subversive politician (Mark 14:48) and hanging between two political prisoners.

The Passion of the Christ's antagonistic view presents a sadistic god that doesn't care about his Son's life mimicking Abraham's and Isaac's human sacrifice (Genesis 22). It presents a meek Palestinian who, in the Sermon on the Mount, preaches blind submission to the oppressors. It presents a clown Barabbas who gets the amnesty since it hides his radical nationalistic subversiveness (Luke 23:19). It presents Jesus as an "industrial designer," high tech savvy, whose idleness allows him to invent new models as an antidote of boredom for his select customers. It presents a baby Jesus whose rosy childhood was sweetened by Mary's upper middle class etiquette. It presents a servant Master who, by washing his disciples' feet without any nuances, is providing a blank check for submissiveness, servanthood, and slavery. It presents Jesus' sharing bread with his disciples without denouncing the cannibal system that swallows people, countries, and entire continents.

"Popes" John Paul II and Billy Graham have praised *The Passion of the Christ*. What a coincidence! They just happened to be the champions of anti-people of color, anti-women, anti-queer, anti-children, and anti-poor movements.

Pontius Pilate complained to Jesus: why do you always answer with a question? Jesus' reply was: why not?

"What Would Jesus Do?" is the question. Are we talking about the Jesus of Mel Gibson or the one of the gospels? This is the counter-question.

Preaching in Brazil and the Formation of Brazility

Experience and Vulnerability as Homiletical Locus

ABDRUSCHIN ROCHA

INTRODUCTION

IN GENERAL, DISCOURSE THEORIES agree that as a set of memories, experiences, expectations, and perspectives, discourse is more than language, albeit discourse presupposes language. In an etymological sense, discourse evokes the idea of a course, a path, movement, etc. In this sense, it has to do with the word in movement, with the practice of language, and with the very production of human existence.[1]

The processes and conditions from which the production of language takes place take the human being in their history into account; after all, there is a relation between the language, the subjects who speak it, and the circumstances in which communication is produced. That is, far from treating the language in a "sanitized" way, closed in on itself, it must be related to its exteriority, to conceive it in transit. It is with this perspective that the preaching in Brazil is treated in this text: not only as a preaching communicated in a certain space of time, in the context of a certain liturgy, subject

---

1. The so-called "Discourse Analysis," as a field of knowledge, does not treat language as an abstract system but rather treats "language in the world," assuming that the production of meaning is part of human life.

to a general objective analysis, or even to be merely classified by denominational styles and origin; rather, as the result of memories, experiences, expectations, and perspectives—in short, such preaching presupposes subjects whose language is deeply determined by historical-social conditions, whether such production is liberating or oppressive. It is the intent of this article to look at preaching as performed by subjects affected by their own history and the possibilities that this relation suggests.

It is in this sense that the article is divided into three sections: the first one seeks to demonstrate the plurality and ambiguity from which the Brazilian identity is constructed; the second proposes to measure this same plurality and ambiguity present in the discourse that sustains the preaching that is practiced in Brazil, highlighting different types of preaching and the influence of colonial thought in this discourse; and the third objective is to show the inadequacy of postcolonial discourse and to propose a decolonial preaching, in which experience and vulnerability become a homiletic *locus*.

1. PLURALITY AND AMBIGUITY IN THE CONSTRUCTION OF BRAZILIAN IDENTITY

A good way to start a text that intends to discuss preaching in Brazil is to identify its *locus*, that is, the context from which the sustaining discourse develops. Although we still live with epistemological perspectives that affirm knowledge is universal, we start from the assumption that all knowledge is the fruit of its locale and, therefore, must be evaluated from parameters that arise from the context itself. No knowledge should be imposed as a universal parameter since, despite this recurrent desire to universalize it, the marks of the place from which it is constructed are always striking. In fact, knowledge could only be universalizable if it were the exact representation of the world. However, since we assume that knowledge is not a mirror of objective reality but rather a process by which the world itself is being constructed—a consciousness that has been formed from the so-called Linguistic Turn and all traditions which followed it—it follows that this space of subjectivity, called "context," is sufficient to justify that emerging forms of knowledge be marked by the place that engenders them. Therefore, we start from the Brazilian context, its peculiarity, its culture and religiosity, and its ambiguities and contradictions, in order to better understand the preaching in Brazil and the discourse that supports its many nuances.

Identity and Brazilian religious context

There was a time when identity was thought of as something static, cohesive, and solid; therefore, it seemed obvious to think of it from its etymological perspective—that is, as a quality that refers to the same, the identical. Identity also appears in literature as a category through which it is possible to think of anything. For example, thinking of a given text from the category of identity would mean, roughly speaking, that it will always manifest itself as the same thing, a position that would deny, for instance, any possibility of polysemy. This, of course, also indicates the type of hermeneutics that would be established there: a "maintenance hermeneutics," concerned with the consolidation of worldviews intended to be hegemonic. As such, identity differs from another category: that of alterity. The latter, in turn, refers us to the other—to the diverse, to the different. Similarly, to think of a text from the category of alterity would mean presupposing a certain polysemy, that is, the possibility that the text may always be read from another perspective, from another place, or from other demands.

Identity, as a set of characteristics and traits that are characteristic of an individual or community, faces another fundamental problem: there is no identity of a person or even a people that builds from itself. That is, there is no identity that is built from identity. It also means that it cannot be thought only in terms of permanence, stability, or continuities. In other words, the self-consciousness of an individual or a people will always be established in comparison with the other, with the different, with the strange, from identifications but also by means of fractures, ruptures, and blows. Moreover, the ambiguity resulting from the construction of the identical from the other is unresolvable. Just as human subjectivity is constructed from intersubjective relations, so will the subjectivity of a community or nation. This means, then, that even the identity, which shows that we are unique, is in constant construction. In this sense, one cannot fail to consider Zygmunt Bauman's warning that even our identities are, in a sense, liquid.[2] For the Polish sociologist, in the context of a liquid modernity, we do not inherit our own identity but are led to create it. In other words, fewer and fewer identities are built on the basis of the community, the nation, or even the political movement to which one belongs. Happiness, lifestyles, values, meaning and purpose of life—important elements in building an identity—are now redefined by ourselves, and such redefinitions accompany the person throughout his or her life. This is an issue that has been on the radar of academic discussions for some time, as the other is closer and closer to us, whether

---

2. Bauman, *Identidade*.

this is noted through the phenomenon of globalization, the shortening of distances made possible by the Internet, or even from the phenomenon of immigration.

Therefore, thinking the identity of one individual or a people is not possible without taking otherness into account—one is built on the assumption of the other. This is particularly significant when we consider Brazilian identity. Perhaps few countries in the world are characterized by such a great diversity of ethnicities, socioeconomic conditions, political perspectives, religious matrixes, customs, flavors, colors, values, etc. The problem of proximity and exchange of cultures, a phenomenon that is increasingly present in Europe, is already a reality that has been lived in Brazil since its foundation. That is, such proximity is, in fact, part of the DNA of Brazilian culture. In this sense, the very miscegenation that is on the horizon of European culture, defying it more and more, will certainly invalidate the assumption—still held by many—that there is a pure, universal identity and knowledge, patronized by the Global North. North and South are gradually approaching one another, even to the detriment of some who defend ethnic purity, and this certainly has serious implications for cultural identities.

Starting from the assumption that identities are not ready, it makes room for them to be thought of in the perspective of mutual affection. The complete "sanitization" that keeps people free from being affected by one another is not a component of human nature. The same will be said of cultures and societies. On the contrary, as long as humanity is not ready, understanding humanity is possible only when we consider it an affectional being (*páthos*), and in that sense, it may be said that it is a *being-with-others*.

In addition, one cannot think of the identity of a people without considering aspects of their religious context. In the case of Brazil, it is necessary to ask about the main elements that have been amalgamated in the constitution of the Brazilian religious matrix. When one considers the historical formation of nationality, it is perceived that the miscegenation delineated the Brazilian identity. Both Iberian Catholicism and European magic came with the settlers and found the indigenous religions here. Subsequently, the religions of the African matrix were brought by the Africans, victims of slavery, and articulated in a significant syncretism. In addition, in the nineteenth century, European spiritism and some fragments of Roman Catholicism expanded. As far as Catholicism is concerned, two aspects emerge from the outset: a more popular, festive, carnivalesque, and syncretic one and a more Romanized, intimate one, which gained strength from the nineteenth century with the separation of Church and State on the occasion of the Proclamation of the Republic in Brazil.

It is also in the nineteenth century that the denominations of Historical Protestantism arrive that, unlike popular Catholicism, identified "native religious values with evil, sin and heresy. . . . Such rejection has become a constitutive element of Brazilian evangelical identity and has enriched their apologetic, which is a viscerally anti-Catholic discourse." Although the first Portuguese who began the process of establishing European Christianity in Brazilian land also revealed difficulties in dialoguing with the other forms of culture and religion that were already present here, in the case of popular Catholicism, syncretic forms have developed further.

Although there is a process of secularization in the West, especially in the European context, this process is still very timid in Latin America and in Brazil. Our context is still markedly religious, with strong characteristics of plurality, ambiguity, and syncretism. In Brazil, religion is already present and mixed with the ideals of conquest, which guided the first explorers. It is enough to consider that the first action of the Portuguese in Brazilian lands, around 1500 CE, was to say a mass. Moreover, the whole process of colonization, legitimized by the patronage regime, is supported by religion. Therefore, religion and conquest are intertwined, and this imbrication added to the inability to dialogue with the experiences and perspectives of others still seem to endure to this day. This certainly impacts the understanding of Brazilian culture and also the discourse that underpins preaching in Brazil.

1.2 Plurality and Ambiguity in the Formation of Brazilianness

Ambiguity is inherent in human identity, insofar as it is constructed in the permanent comparison with the other, as we have seen so far. We refer to the other as a category—the category of difference. But when this other that affects us permanently is human, then we speak of others, we speak of a plurality of others. Our identity is formed by a plurality of others! This does not mean that we only construct an identity from the otherness. That also means that the constructed identity itself is ambiguous. Or rather, ambiguity is present in one's own identity, which means that it is far from being homogeneous and singular. We would like to gauge this in the cultural fabric that forms Brazilianness. To do so, we will quickly see some perspectives that have been proposed by Brazilian authors who have been seeking to answer the following questions: who is the Brazilian? What is Brazil? They have helped us understand what it means to be Brazilian and in what sense this identity is built. With this information in mind, we will be in a better position to identify the implications of this construction for the discourse that sustains preaching in Brazil.

Undoubtedly, Gilberto Freyre was one of the first interpreters of Brazil that used anthropological and sociological categories to understand Brazilian identity. He wrote many books, but is known for his work, *The Masters and the Slaves* (1933),[3] which, besides being a watershed in the study of Brazilian society, is perhaps the first anthropological study of a historical society altogether. His importance lies in the fact that he is the first person who, opposing racism, says that miscegenation is a good thing. More than that: miscegenation is a distinctive feature of Brazilianness. Many believe that this was the main contribution of *The Masters and the Slaves*. Freyre's thesis stands out even more at a historical moment in which Brazil resented its mixed-race condition and in an international context that breathed the rumors of the emergence of a pure race. It must be remembered that in 1933, when Freyre's work was launched, Hitler assumed the leadership of the Nazi party and since then, these ideas of purism about the race circulated. Gilberto Freyre demystifies such an idea when he asserts that it is precisely in the experience of racial mixture that the importance of race lies; it was exactly that which made a different kind of Brazil possible. He, for example, separates "race" from "culture," thereby breaking the idea that there is a superior race and an inferior race.[4]

The Masters and the Slaves stands out from other sociological approaches (especially approaches of the time) because it is a work about private life and intimate life. So, too, it is an extremely sexualized work. It was the first work to treat sexuality as a trait of Brazilianness in such an open way. In Freyre's narrative, there is a sexual freedom, a renegade (as compared, of course, with the morals brought from Portugal) that shows in very clear terms the genesis of this mixture that forms Brazil. And one of the presuppositions of the book is the theory that sexual depravity, very common among slave masters and their slaves, originates the miscegenation and, consequently, is the base of the construction of the Brazilianness. For him, slavery no doubt generates all sexual depravity.

For Freyre, relations such as the plasticity of the Portuguese (between their European culture and Africa), the influence of the milkmaid on the creation of the children of the sugar planters, and the change in eating habits and the way food is prepared, among other things, provoke a cultural interpenetration that will be important for the establishment of this

---

3. Cf. Freyre, *Casa-grande e senzala*.

4. Freire will be criticized for many things, especially for the so-called "racial democracy myth," which is the idea that Brazil—unlike the United States and South Africa—escaped racism and racial discrimination due to miscegenation. Often considered the theorist of the oligarchies, he will be criticized for allegedly succumbing to this false idea, although he was also the first to break with so-called "scientific racism."

miscegenation. Throughout *The Master and the Slaves*, there is a constant reading of the Brazilian society in the terms of an intense intercultural dialogue that sustains a certain fluidity in the culture. Freyre, in fact, rejects the view of a pure culture, which celebrates continuity and permanence. For him, there is a certain fluidity that engenders the Brazilian identity. Although Freyre considered slavery a horror, in his opinion, there would not be such a cultural mixture, that distinctive feature, had it not existed.

Who are the Brazilians and what is Brazil? As Brazilians, what sets them apart from other peoples, what makes them the way they are? These questions also determined the work of another important interpreter of Brazil: Sérgio Buarque de Holanda. For Sérgio Buarque, to a great extent, the answer to such questions needs to take the historical relationship that Brazilians have with the family into account. In all their social relations, Brazilians are those who seek intimacy, familiarity, proximity, etc. Therefore, this affective search for the other, for the familiarity with the other and with things, is a distinguishing mark of the Brazilian people. On the other hand, Brazilians have difficulties with everything that is bureaucratic and impersonal, and that is why they are more affectionate to charismatic figures, figures with whom they identify affectively, than with those who are only competent. In Brazil, for example, state leaders who are more charismatic than competent have a greater chance of being elected than those who are competent but uncharismatic. The same can be said with regard to preaching: the discourse of preachers who are just charismatic is also more likely to be welcomed by the people than that discourse that is uttered by people who are only competent. Although this may represent some truth when we consider other countries, in Brazil this is exacerbated.

In his main work, *Roots of Brazil*,[5] Sérgio Buarque uses a kind of "ideal type" to characterize this affability of Brazilians: for him, the Brazilians are a "cordial man." That is, it is someone dominated by the heart, someone extremely affable, who opens the doors of his house easily, who makes friends easily. However, it is necessary to make an important observation here: "Cordial," for Buarque, derives from "cordes" (heart). In that sense, it is precisely because it is overwhelmed by the heart and the impulse that it can also become very violent. Brazilians, then, embody the two characteristics at the same time, and pass from one condition to the other without any transition. That is, even affable, receptive, and hospitable people, when they feel harmed, can respond to this in a significantly violent way. So for Sérgio Buarque, such contradiction is part of Brazilianness.

---

5. Holanda, *Raízes do Brasil*.

The Brazilian anthropologist is able to identify a proximity of opposites in the structure of Brazilian society—such as wealth and poverty—and interprets this as a mark of Brazilian cordiality. The social contradiction itself, revealed in the geographic proximity between rich and poor, is related to the contradiction of Brazilian identity. That is, for the Brazilian, light and shadow are very close realities: in the light we can identify this hospitality and this affable character, but the dark side of this affability means that Brazilians can also hide a great indifference to social inequality. There is, therefore, an emotional ethic that allows realities to blend; the horror of distances is a mark of this Brazilianness, of that which we call Brazilian identity.

Another important thinker who interprets Brazil is Roberto da Matta. He draws on his experience of anthropological research among tribal societies to analyze Brazilian society. Tribal societies have no record of social memory, such as the more westernized and urban societies. In fact, the social memory of these societies is much more fluid and complex and is recorded in another way. Roberto da Matta uses this methodology to understand Brazil, appropriating Brazilian daily materials, that is, the most important rituals in Brazilian society: Brazilian carnival and also their rites that denote authority; the Brazil of the complex relations between State and society; the Brazil of narratives that are told and that weave their history; the Brazil of hierarchies but also of equalities; the Brazil of diversified cooking, etc.

Roberto da Matta deepens the relation between the public and the private, already thematized by Sérgio Buarque, from the metaphors of "street" and "home." For him, there is a difference between what happens on the street and what happens at home. Street and home are not two geographical and urban spaces but rather two social spaces that represent society. What you do at home is almost the opposite of what you can do on the street.[6]

For Roberto DaMatta, Brazilian culture is also the pull rank culture,[7] that is, a culture of, "You know who you are talking to?" This, for example, characterizes our difficulty in dealing with the public space to a great extent. But it should be borne in mind that this is an authoritarian ritual aimed at establishing identities. That is, people who consider themselves important cannot stand impersonality and anonymity. People who consider themselves important believe their position requires differential treatment. People who consider themselves important come to their position as inherent in their identity, so some are keen to be called by the title because it

---

6. For example, an individual who make sure their homes are kept clean, but who do not hesitate litter the streets when walk the streets.

7. Translator's note: This refers to the practice of attempting to gain privilege by showing one's social or economic position.

differentiates them from others. This goes from the politician, passing by the famous artist, to the evangelical pastor or priest of an important parish. For many of these, the title is important and defines the importance of him or her in society. In a Christian context, obviously, such a posture implies serious consequences for the discourse that underpins preaching in Brazil.

In the perspective of Roberto da Matta, Brazil is also explained from what could be called a culture of "jeitinho"[8] and "transgressions." For Brazilians, there is always an easier way—peripheral to the rules—of doing something. That is, from the perspective of Brazilians there are always reasons (however personal) that justify the breaking of rules and laws: haste justifies the decision not to queue; high taxes justify evasion; the bureaucracy justifies the payment of tips, etc. This logic in which a public and collective rule can be broken due to a greater private and personal force is a mark of Brazilianness, according to Roberto da Matta.[9]

Many other authors also contributed with their perspective on the formative elements of Brazilianness. There is some unanimity in the approaches—with respect to this plurality, ambiguity, and contradiction—that characterize our culture: approaches that work from the aspects related to meztiçage, such as Darcy Ribeiro in his book, *The Brazilian People*, to aspects related to the political-economic context, as approached by the sociologist Francisco de Oliveira in his book, *Crítica à Razão Dualista / O Ornitorrinco*.[10]

2. PREACHING IN BRAZIL: PLURALITY AND AMBIGUITY IN DISCOURSE

2.1 Plurality and Ambiguity Represented in Distinct Types of Preaching

It is necessary to consider all diversity and ambiguity in the fabric of Brazilian culture and religion in order to understand preaching in this context. When it comes to Christian tradition, there are at least four denominational traits

8. "Jeitinho" or "jeitinho brasileiro" can be described as a way of finding solutions to problems by attempting to bend the system in order to gain a personal benefit.

9. Since "jeitinho" is a specific way for the Brazilian to improvise solutions, such a posture can have a positive or negative connotation. Positive when it manifests creativity in the face of some problem and is contextualized in the scope of the interpersonal relations of the Brazilian; negative when it arises in the institutional context, in the peculiar way of dealing with the laws and, therefore, it is linked to the notion of corruption. In one way or another, the "way" is part of the national identity.

10. Cf. Oliveira, *Crítica à Razão Dualista*.

that, permeated by all syncretism and religious hybridity, affect preaching in Brazil. We refer to the Roman Catholic Church, the Protestant churches, the Pentecostal churches, and the neo-Pentecostal churches. The religious syncretism and hybridism that pervade each of these Christian followings in Brazil are striking: Catholicism influences and is influenced by African-born religions; the Protestant identity was influenced by the Catholic Church and by African and indigenous religions and other religions;[11] and Neo-Pentecostalism is influenced by Pentecostalism and African religions and religiosity.

This hybridity can also be seen in the preaching practiced in most of these very followings. However, although elements of one following are determinant of the identity of the other, the discourse that underpins preaching in Brazil is of an exclusivist character. Such exclusivism, in addition to exposing this significant contradiction, prevents any possibility of dialogue as well as sustaining a highly proselytizing preaching. Protestant, Pentecostal, and Neo-Pentecostal pulpits, for example, are spaces for true proselytizing campaigns, with an emphasis on the individual conversion, above all, of Catholics and adherents of African-born religions. Even churches originating from the Protestantism of immigration (or transplantation), historically maintained by their headquarters in Europe, are rethinking their strategies for the inclusion of new adherents due to the end of the financial resources coming from outside—such is the case, for example, of the Evangelical Church of Lutheran Confession in Brazil (IECLB).

Luiz Carlos Ramos, in his attempt to examine the horizons of homiletics for the Church of the future, offers us some interesting reflections to understand different types of preaching present in Brazil. While metaphors or "ideal types," it is worth considering the three horizons proposed by Ramos: (1) horizon of the Middle Ages; (2) horizon of the Media Age; and (3) horizon of the Human Age. As the third horizon is Ramos's proposal, we will emphasize the first two, because we believe that they predominate in the models of preaching in Brazil.

The first horizon, called the Middle Ages, is a model that goes beyond the limits of the medieval period. The possible kind of preaching from this horizon has become classic both in the context of the Protestant Reformation and in the scope of the Roman Catholic counter-reformation. This preaching is characterized by extreme concern with dogmatic, doctrinal, and catechetical content. In this model, preaching has the function of reproducing a certain content, above all, by oral-verbal and literary means. Taking as reference the discussion about the relationship between identity

---

11. See Hahn, *História do culto protestante no Brasil*.

and otherness, proposed at the beginning of this article, it can be said that preaching in the horizon of the Middle Ages is significantly marked by identity. That is, in this model, no discourse is admitted that departs from the set of dogmas that has already been established in the context of a given denominational following. Such a horizon imposes the need for a "maintenance hermeneutics"—the hermeneutic activity becomes a tool for maintaining the tradition and the status quo, being restricted to the offer of methods and techniques that would give us access to the supposed secrets of the Word of God. In terms of the Protestant tradition, for example, the sermon took on a professorial, highly rationalistic, and apologetic tone (after all, it is assumed that the Word of God is fully and objectively revealed in the Scriptures). It can be said that, to a large extent, Protestant identity was built from these elements. And this is precisely why the so-called horizon of the Middle Ages must be seen as a metaphor or "ideal type," since it brings together elements of both the medieval Christian tradition and modern rationalism.

The second horizon—the horizon of the Media Age—contrasts with the excessive preoccupation with content by emphasizing the form of the message, its "packaging." As a model that is currently in rapid expansion, it is worth noting the significant technological dazzle that characterizes this horizon. There is, in this sense, a shift from the verbal-oral-literary to the visual-iconic imagery. This horizon is consolidated from a new generation protagonist of an information society—also called the Society of the Spectacle—from which a new way of dealing with the information is constructed. For example, the non-linearity in information flow, multitasking behavior, and speed and access to information are highlighted. In this model, rationality gives way to emotions; after all, media communication is more emotional than rational, and this makes preachers adapt to a generation that prefers concise imaginative narratives rather than abstract and extensive verbal discourses.

The horizon of the Media Age emphasized form to the detriment of content; rather, content was co-opted by form, much as Marshall McLuhan envisioned in the 1960s. McLuham was noted for his famous phrase, "The medium is the message."[12] Such a finding, for example, can be perceived in Pentecostal preaching. In a classical Pentecostal worship service, it is common practice for people to evaluate the quality of preaching in light of the aesthetic effects it produces, even if they do not remember the content of preaching. That is, the way preaching happens; the preacher's own performance is often already a message for the community of faith. Although the Media Age horizon further characterizes those segments connected with

---

12. See McLuhan, *Os meios de comunicação como extensões do homem*.

Pentecostalism and Neo-Pentecostalism, it can also guide certain more contemporary expressions of historical Protestantism and even determine the preaching of Catholic priests, who are considered more mediatic. Due to their emphasis on form, the preaching models that are constructed from this horizon tend to focus the content as something simply given. It can be said that it is predominantly marked by a hermeneutic of alterity since the content becomes more negotiable from the point of view of its interpretation.

In general, one notices that the various models of preaching stand somewhere between identity and otherness. There are those models based on identity, that is, on the assumption that the revelation of God is already definitively established and therefore nothing new could appear on this horizon. There are those models that establish themselves from otherness and, in this case, it is assumed that the revelation is inscribed in the horizon of the advent and the novelty. On the other hand, there are also models that in practice are based on alterity—after all, the preachers who represent this approach deal with the text more fluidly—but when it comes to considering the institution and the dogmas it defends, it is the logic of identity that rules. In this, the Brazilian contradiction is perceived as well.

2.2 Colonial Thought as Determinant of Discourse

One aspect that characterizes practically all denominational followings is the tendency to import from the North almost everything that configures Christianity, in its Catholic as well as its Protestant side. From sacred music to theological literature, through ecclesiological models, we import almost everything. Similarly, the preaching of the North (Europe and, above all, the United States) has been imported and adapted to our context. In terms of Protestantism, much of the homiletical literature that was used in Brazil for decades, especially in theological seminaries, was translated from the North since there was initially no specialized literature written by Brazilians. For that reason, the model of preaching adopted was the classic and expository, as used by the Protestant churches of the North. More than that, a logic was imported from the North since it was not only a homiletical model but also a broader discourse that determined not only the type of sermon but also a way of being a church.

To a great extent, this preaching is based on the idea of conquest, a remnant of times of colonization, and it is marked by the American discourse of success. It is good to point out that the term "conquest" is extremely derogatory when we consider its links with Western history. In other words, conquest has always been associated with force, genocide, intolerance, and ethnocentrism, but in some way this expression has been sanctioned, legitimized, sacralized, and used in most of the pulpits of the churches with motives not unlike those that inspired all Northern colonialism. And here is another contradiction: at the same time that Brazil inherits the violent discourse of conquest from the North, which is a platform for any and all colonialist projects, Brazil is also the victim of its own discourse in the condition of subaltern people. In other words, although we are referring to a Global South country, one cannot deny the existence of "pockets" of the North that survive here through their highly colonialist and exclusive discourse. Boaventura de Souza Santos, in justifying the use of the metaphor "Epistemologies of the South," mentions this relative overlap between global North and South:

> The South is here metaphorically conceived as a field of epistemic challenges, seeking to repair the damages and impacts historically caused by capitalism in its colonial relation to the world. This conception of the South overlaps in part with the geographical South, the set of countries and regions of the world that have been subjected to European colonialism and which, with exceptions such as Australia and New Zealand, have not reached levels of development similar to the global north (Europe and North America). The overlap is not total because on the one hand, within the geographical North, very large classes and social groups (workers, women, indigenous, Afro-descendants, Muslims) were subjected to capitalist and colonial domination, while on the other hand, in the interior of the geographical South, there have always been the "small Europas," small local elites who benefited from capitalist and colonial domination and who, after their independence, exercised it and continued to exercise with their own hands the subordination of social classes and groups.[13]

Colonialism has not only occurred in the political and economic sphere, as we normally understand it; we must also speak of colonialism as an epistemological domination, which was expressed both in an unequal relationship of know-how—suppressing many forms of knowledge belonging to the colonized peoples—as well as psychological effects that make subaltern social groups buy the dominant discourse and act on it. This explains why religious groups in Brazil nourish themselves from the discourse of the North without any criticism, imposing on their countrymen the same violence that historically victimized their own people. And in that sense,

---

13. Santos and Meneses, "Introdução," 19.

it is not enough to argue, as many do, that we have nothing to do with the processes of violence and domination that were imputed to our parents for at least two reasons: first, because in a more subtle way, this domination still permeates our way of being Brazilian; second, because the human being, while *being-with-others*, is defined not only by other contemporaries but also by those who have preceded us in history and by those who will come.[14]

Not unlike all the millenarianisms that have taken place in the history of Western Christianity, there is an expectation shared by a good part of the Brazilian evangelical population that Brazil belongs to evangelicals and must be governed by evangelicals or someone who commits themselves to their vision of world. On the verge of unprecedented political chaos in the history of Brazilian democracy, there are many who hold out hope that God will raise a ruler whose principles align with the evangelical ideology. In this eagerness to take power in the name of God, many soon identify the Kingdom of God with politicians, political parties, or even political ideologies. So much so that there are those who believe there is no liberating Christianity possible on the left; those who demonize the left believe that the Kingdom of God can only come from the evangelical, political right.

One of the implications of this discourse aimed at conquest is the attempt to sanitize life. That is, the discourse that inspires preaching in Brazil is to a large extent selective about the realities it addresses and about the biblical readings that underlie it. In this regard, it is of particular importance to heed Lévinas's warning about what he called the "models of satisfaction" of our time:

> According to the models of satisfaction, possession commands the search, enjoyment is better than necessity, triumph is truer than failure, certainty is more perfect than doubt, the answer goes further than the question. Search, suffering, and question would be simple diminution of the finding, of joy, of happiness, and of the answer: insufficient thoughts of the identical and of the present, indigent knowledge or knowledge in an indigent state. Once again, it's good sense. It is also common sense.[15]

The models of satisfaction identified by Lévinas also determine this preaching highly committed to the logic of conquest. Possession, joy,

---

14. As to this constitutive relation we have with history, it is noteworthy a mention of the Russian concept of *sobornost*, "which affirms that each human being is the singularization of all human history. In each person, there is the encounter between the ancestors, the contemporaries and those who will still come (Safra, "A fragmentação do ethos no mundo contemporâneo").

15. Lévinas, *Entre nós*, 111.

triumph, certainty, response, etc. are the themes present in the discourse that most succeeds in connecting to the wishes of the people, and both function as "tour guides" for those preaching engaging in entertainment as well as being part of the artillery homiletics for those preaching highly committed to conquest and proselytism. Such discourse, it is worth mentioning, pervades both evangelical preaching and political rhetoric in Brazil, and the more it moves the crowds, the more it can sell the ideal, even at the expense of the real. That is, from this perspective, so many preachers who humanize the Gospel fail by admitting that "in the world we will have afflictions," as well as those politicians who admit the complexity of Brazilian problems and the need for a broader and longer-term reform project. And that is why these models of satisfaction also translate into what we have come to call charisma in Brazil: a charismatic is one who can skillfully and aseptically select and mobilize themes that translate into a "strong" and conquering Gospel. Let us not forget that the interpreters of Brazil, some of whom are listed in the first part of this article, emphasize charisma as a national preference over ethics and competence.

Christian discourse, therefore, has largely panned the ground of life and separated only the nuggets, rejecting all the gravel that materializes in the hardships and imponderable existence. Such a discourse is extremely selective in that it focuses on the ideal and rejects the real, thus determining the preaching that ends up fulfilling the task of shaping the consciences and outlining a way of being a church. As ambiguous as it may seem, one must reflect on how colonialist this conquest discourse is. Apparently destined to empower, it is in fact highly proselytizing and incapable of dialogue—just a different way of colonizing consciences.

3. FROM POSTCOLONIALISM TO THE DECOLONIALIZATION OF PREACHING

As we have seen so far, there is a highly colonialist discourse that sustains a way of being a church and, consequently, is distilled in the preaching that is practiced in the pulpits of Brazilian churches. That is, one cannot speak of preaching in Brazil without taking into account this epistemological colonization that leads to the reproduction of the same domination of which we are victims as a subaltern people. On the other hand, it should be emphasized that just as there are implications of colonialist discourse in preaching, the same will be said of postcolonial and decolonial critiques. There is a path that leads from coloniality to decoloniality capable of generating much reflection. It is necessary to pay attention to the implications of this discussion for the construction of the discourse that guides the preaching. Our intention in this part of the article is to show this course and to propose a decolonial discourse as the basis of preaching, which draws from what Latin America has produced best in terms of experience.

3.1 The Insufficiency of Postcolonial Discourse

When speaking of postcolonialism, from a descriptive perspective, two issues are usually involved. Firstly, the temporal question, predicted in the prefix "post." This is a time that goes back to the processes of decolonization in some countries, such as those in Africa and Asia, which took place in the middle of the twentieth century. Added to this are some events, such as the fall of the Berlin Wall and the end of the dictatorship in Latin America, which contributed to the modern project of colonization of those subaltern peoples being put in check, becoming a target for postcolonialist critique. This time is characterized by the liberation, independence, and emancipation of countries and societies exploited by imperialism and neocolonialism.

A second question also arises when we consider postcolonialism, which goes far beyond the temporal question. This is how Stuart Hall expresses himself:

> The term "postcolonial" is not restricted to describing a particular society or epoch. It relays "colonization" as part of an essentially transnational and transcultural global process—and produces a decentralized, diasporic, or "global" rewriting of the great imperial narratives of the past, centered on the nation.[16]

Due to the historical changes described above, many theoretical contributions—influenced by the literary and cultural studies that have rocked some American and British universities since the 1980s—have established themselves as a criticism of colonialism and neocolonialism. In addition to its merely temporal significance, postcolonialism, as a theoretical critique of colonialism and neocolonialism, has brought many contributions to the formation of an awareness of the epistemological ties that make the nations of the South dependent on the nations of the North. It was sought to understand, for example, how the identity of the colonized is constructed in the measure in which it assumes the discourse of the colonizer; it was also sought to understand how, in the perspective of the colonizer, the colonized world was structured discursively. From the manifestation of the history and ideas of the colonized "dwarfs," a kind of "colonial wound" began to be

---

16. Hall, *Da diáspora*, 109.

denounced. Referring to this wound, Walter Mignolo proposes the concept of "locus of enunciation" in order to designate the asymmetry of places from which the relation between colonizer and colonized arises:

> Damages are defined by the colonial wound, and the colonial wound, be it physical or psychological, is a consequence of racism, of the hegemonic discourse that calls into question the humanity of all those who do not belong to the same locus of enunciation and to the same geopolitics of knowledge of who creates the parameters of classification and gives himself the right to classify.[17]

These wounds were opened, above all, due to slavery, racism, supposed male superiority, religious preferences, etc. As a consequence, there is a transformation of geopolitics related to borders, languages, or aesthetics, but there is also the transformation of the geopolitics of knowledge and that which refers to the memory of those excluded from the "official" history. Postcolonialism, therefore, promotes discussion around this wound, and this geopolitical transformation can now be narrated by various followings, such as art, historical research, and the sciences. Worthy of note is the fact that the cultural production that is built on this new epistemology is significant.[18]

However, in spite of the undeniable theoretical contributions and the inclusion of intellectuals of the so-called global South, postcolonial critiques generally came from theorists of the North or even Southern theorists who eventually undertook their criticism from the North. It was noted, for example, that many Latin American academics lived in the United States and, despite struggling for alternative and radical knowledge, actually only reproduced the hegemonic epistemic scheme that permeated Regional Studies in the United States. They wrote about the subaltern perspective, but not from the subaltern perspective.[19] That is, the theory was built in the North while the subjects studied remained in the South. In the theoretical basis, there

---

17. Mignolo, *La idea de América latina*, 34 (my translation).

18. As to some examples related to this cultural production that tries to narrate the wound mentioned by Walter Mignolo, see Cunha, *Provocações decoloniais à Teologia Cristã*, 57.

19. It was Gramsci who initially used the term "subaltern," with the aim of referring to the subaltern classes, especially the rural proletariat (Cf. Gramsci, *Cadernos do cárcere*). However, in the context of the so-called "Subaltern Studies," the sense of "subaltern" underwent modifications, inasmuch as it came to designate the historical subject that responds to the categories, not only of class, but also of gender and ethnicity. If on the one hand subaltern identifies with the colonized subject, on the other hand, this new understanding concerns an active subject.

was an underestimation of the ethnic-racial perspectives coming from the region and a privilege of Eurocentric thinkers such as Foucault, Derrida, and Gramsci, a position that was also understood as betrayal of the objectives of producing subaltern studies.[20] Moreover, from the perspective of the critics of postcolonialism, it is necessary to differentiate and even oppose subalternity as a postmodern critique of subalternity, as a decolonial critique—that is, to oppose the mere Eurocentric critique of Eurocentrism to the criticism of Eurocentrism from the silenced and subalternized knowledge.[21]

3.2 Preaching and Decolonial Discourse: Experience and Vulnerability in the Latin American Tradition

As we saw earlier, the postcolonial discourse, although it has made contributions, proved insufficient in its critique of hegemonic thinking. Therefore, it is the denunciation of the Eurocentrism present in the silenced and subalternized knowledge—in general, a criticism that opposes the speaking about the subaltern when speaking from the subaltern—that is denser in some theorists and marks the transition from postcolonial thought to that which was conventionally called "decoloniality." That is, there is a radicality in decoloniality that predicts the construction of an epistemology from subaltern ethnic-racial places.[22] The distinction between postcolonialism and decoloniality suggests that it is not sufficient merely to recognize subaltern status and effective critical reflection from outside; rather, it is necessary to empower subalternized peoples to assume their responsibilities to think their own condition and produce knowledge from their own places. That is, decoloniality presupposes that subalternized peoples also have the right to contribute to the multifaceted web of knowledge that is woven by civilization and the consequent dignity of all peoples. Decoloniality, therefore, supposes a deeper project which is set in motion beyond the mere historical overcoming of colonialism and neocolonialism. It manifests itself as a kind of epistemic disobedience, without which "epistemic unlearning will not be possible and therefore we will remain in the domain of internal opposition to modern and Eurocentric concepts, rooted in the categories of Greek and

---

20. It is extremely important to know the history of post-colonial discussions from the presence of the two Subaltern Studies Groups that represented it: the South Asian Group of Subaltern Studies, which began in the 1970s, led by Ranajit Guha, a dissident of Indian Marxism, and the Latin American Group of Subaltern Studies. For more information, see Grosfoguel, "Para descolonizar," 115–16.

21. Mignolo quoted in Grosfoguel, "Para descolonizar," 116.

22. Grosfoguel, "Para descolonizar," 118.

Latin concepts and the experiences and subjectivities formed of these bases, both theological and secular."[23] That is, decoloniality presupposes a more surgical treatment in the identification of alternative forms of coloniality in addition to the anticolonial struggles that generated the independence, especially political, of the former colonies. As Mignolo says, it is necessary and urgent "to untie the knot, to learn to unlearn, and to learn to relearn at every step."[24]

As a deeper project of knowledge production from subaltern ethnic-racial places, decoloniality has a spectacular and sufficient set of experiences capable of constituting it as a category from which to construct a new discourse capable of sustaining a preaching more liberating, more dialogical, and more connected with the demands of our own place. Considering this set of experiences, a first element here must be highlighted: the very relation between experience and language in Latin America (and, in particular, in Brazil) is peculiar. That is, the assumption in Brazil that revelation is inextricably experience and language acquires sharper contours. The Brazilian cultural configuration favors the understanding that Christianity does not manifest primarily as a message in which one should believe but rather as an experience of faith that later becomes a message. And it is for these and other reasons that the Latin American tradition favors the construction of a theology that goes beyond the written texts and translates into a theology of living texts. A theology of the person values human experiences, although these are sometimes not supported by the normative parameters that are established from the current theological descriptions. That is, in addition to the "normative" texts and the truth that derives from it, there are people of flesh and blood who, as such, should be considered in theological formulations as well as become presuppositions for them. Although genuinely Latin American, this perspective does notoriously depart from the hegemonic discourse of the North, including that which was imported to the South by Southern intellectuals.

Another characteristic of the Latin American experience that must be emphasized is vulnerability as a trait of identity. The Latin American tradition left us a hermeneutic whose propulsive force not only materializes in the legitimization of the weak and oppressed but also, much more than that, in the construction of an epistemological project that is based on decolonization. This project includes identifying those subjects in history who deserve the position of protagonists, although they have been obscured in front of the subjects carried by the culture of the North. In a special way,

---

23. Mignolo, "Desobediência epistêmica," 288.
24. Mignolo, "Desobediência epistêmica," 305.

it has to do with the task of adding the element of human vulnerability to its own hermeneutics, presupposing it as constitutive of the human being: being human is being vulnerable. In addition, vulnerability is the foundation of all *sensitivity, compassion,* and *community*. This also means that the non-recognition of vulnerability impairs the recognition of the vulnerability of the other and the ethical demand that results from it. The dream of invulnerability, central to modern design and desired by historical and present empires, is an immoral dream since it dehumanizes.[25] The critique that is built from the Latin American tradition assumes that hegemonic thinking prevents us from representing the world as our own and makes us objects, not epistemological subjects. If we cannot represent the world as our own, neither can it be transformed, and such subservience keeps us exiled in our own home. In view of what has been said, it is not very difficult to perceive the profound implications of this discussion for preaching in Brazil. We have a rich tradition from which to rethink preaching, but we are still hostages of the colonialist discourse that continues to oppress people, regardless of social class or religious denomination. With this in mind, let's take a look at the two ideas we suggested earlier and see how they can inspire a new preaching, more sensitive to the Brazilian context as well as more liberating.

The idea that experience precedes the language of the Christian message has not yet been sufficiently explored in terms of preaching in Brazil. One possible reason lies in the Protestant tradition itself, in which the Scriptures and the discourse that evokes them predominate over tradition and human experience. That is, in the Protestant tradition there is little room for human experience and the contingencies of history. However, the statement of Carlos Mesters, that "the main concern of the people is not to interpret the Bible but is to interpret life with the help of the Bible" (albeit against the Protestant tradition that comes to Brazil in the nineteenth century), should be the parameter not only for biblical hermeneutics but also for preaching in the Brazilian context. This would be tantamount to affirming that "the revelation of God, once happened and recorded in the text, becomes alive to the community of faith in this new context of life."[26] A biblical reading that starts from reality—that is, from the human "ground," from the concreteness of life, from the place of joys and sorrows, victories and defeats, dreams and dislikes, from where the Word of God interweaves and articulates—must also inspire a speech that supports a preaching in the same terms. Such a preaching, of course, from the ground of experience in which the listener stands, would no longer be guided by the models of satisfaction as

---

25. See Stalsett, "Vulnerabilidad," 145–57.
26. Mesters quoted in Libânio, *Teologia da revelação*, 98–99.

narrated by Lévinas (those who privilege possession, joy, triumph, certainty, the answer, etc.). After all, reality also includes the search, the need, the loss, the doubt, the question, etc. It seems very obvious to think of the Scriptures as a parameter of human experience when it is overlooked that they were also the result of human experience. A discourse that ignores the experiential place of the listener can only produce a preaching highly centered on the rules of faith, on dogmas and doctrines, a linear and homogenizing discourse that says very little about the complexity of life. Brazil is a place where plurality also manifests itself in distinct and contradictory realities and this obviously requires thematic plurality. The same Bible that reveals some so-called "heroes of the faith," celebrated and carried out in preaching that emanates from the Brazilian pulpits, also provides the story of ordinary people, which, despite being an auxiliary in the "official" theological systematizations, has the power to connect in a deeper way with the history of the many listeners.

The second idea that we would like to explore here is constitutive vulnerability, which is further evidenced in LA. The non-recognition of vulnerability makes one always look at the system with extreme parsimony and consider the other in an extremely critical way, a very common, present posture in the constitution of the sermons in Brazil. The plurality and ambiguities of life also make them vulnerable, which is why fundamentalism builds its discourse in such a way as to shield people from the inevitable results of this plurality and ambiguity. In other words, plurality and ambiguity threaten the stability of the sense system of people, and, in response to this, linear and homogenizing discourse is used instead. Moreover, the search for this stability as a cure for vulnerability lays against Brazil in its best sense.

To assume vulnerability in preaching would be to give up the ideal of conquest and proselytism, which are expressed as assimilation of the other by force; to purify all the violence present in the discourse, even when it is an absolute truth; and an evangelization more aesthetic than rational, in which the beauty of incarnate Christian life, expressed above all in love, prevails over mere communication of "truths." In short, it would consist of a message that valued the Brazilian pathos more, in which the recurring strategy of wiping the tears of the people did not lose sight of the initiative of crying with those who cry.

Therefore, considering the traits of our Brazilian identity and the best of the Latin American tradition implies assuming, in the context of plurality and ambiguity, our own experience and vulnerability as a place of discourse and preaching.

Bibliography

Adam, Júlio César. "Preaching in Transition: a Homiletic Perspective from Latin America and Brazil." *International Journal of Homiletics* 1.1 (2016) 1–10.

Bartz, Alessandro, et al. "Conversão ou trânsito religioso?" In *Religião e sociedade: desafios contemporâneos*, edited by Iuri Andréas Reblin and Rudolf von Sinner, 231–68. São Leopoldo: Sinodal, 2012.

Bauman, Zygmunt. *Identidade: entrevista a Benedetto Vecchi*. Rio de Janeiro: Zahar, 2005.

Bittencourt Filho, José. *Matriz religiosa brasileira: religiosidade e mudança social*. Petrópolis: Vozes/Koinonia, 2003.

Cunha, Carlos Alberto Motta. *Provocações decoloniais à Teologia Cristã*. São Paulo: Edições Terceira Via, 2017.

DaMatta, Roberto. *A casa e a rua: espaço, cidadania, mulher e morte no Brasil*. 5th ed. Rio de Janeiro: Rocco, 1997.

———. *O que faz do Brasil, Brasil?* Rio de Janeiro: Rocco, 1986.

Debord, Guy. *A sociedade do espetáculo: comentários sobre a sociedade do espetáculo*. Rio de Janeiro: 1997.

Freyre, Gilberto. *Casa-grande e senzala: formação da família brasileira sob o regime da economia patriarcal*. 48th rev. ed. São Paulo: Global, 2003.

Gramsci, Antonio. *Cadernos do cárcere*. Vol. 5. Rio de Janeiro: Civilização Brasileira, 2002.

Grosfoguel, Ramón. "Para descolonizar os estudos de economia política e os estudos pós-coloniais: transmodernidade, pensamento de fronteira e colonialidade global." *Revista Crítica de Ciências Sociais* 80 (2008) 115–47.

Hahn, Carl Joseph. *História do culto protestante no Brasil*. São Paulo: ASTE, 1989.

Hall, Stuart. *Da diáspora: identidades e mediações culturais*. Belo Horizonte: Editora UFMG; Brasília: UNESCO, 2003.

Holanda, Sérgio Buarque de. *Raízes do Brasil*. 26th ed. São Paulo: Companhia das Letras, 1995.

Lévinas, Emmanuel. *Entre nós: ensaios sobre a alteridade*. 2nd ed. Petrópolis: Vozes, 2005.

Libânio, J. B. *Teologia da revelação a partir da modernidade*. 6th ed. São Paulo: Edições Loyola, 2012.

McLuhan, Marshall. *Os meios de comunicação como extensões do homem*. 20th ed. São Paulo: Cultrix, 2011.

Mesters, C. *Flor sem defesa: uma explicação da Bíblia a partir do povo*. 5th ed. Petrópolis: Vozes, 1999.

Mignolo, Walter D. "Desobediência epistêmica: a opção descolonial e o significado de identidade em política." *Cadernos de Letras da UFF—Dossiê: Literatura, língua e identidade* 34 (2008) 287–324.

———. *La idea de América latina: colonialidade, saberes subalternos e pensamento liminar*. Belo Horizonte: Editora UFMG, 2003.

Oliveira, Francisco de. *Crítica à razão dualista / O ornitorrinco*. São Paulo: Boitempo, 2003.

Ramos, Luiz Carlos. *A pregação na idade mídia: os desafios da sociedade do espetáculo para a prática homilética contemporânea*. São Bernardo do Campo: EDITEO, 2012.

Ribeiro, Darcy. *O povo brasileiro: a formação e o sentido do Brasil*. São Paulo: Companhia das Letras, 1995.

Safra, Gilberto. "A fragmentação do éthos no mundo contemporâneo." In *Espiritualidade e saúde: da cura d'almas ao cuidado integral*, edited by Sidnei Vilmar Noé, 7–15. 2nd ed. São Leopoldo: Sinodal, 2004.

Santos, Boaventura de Sousa, and Maria Paula Meneses. "Introdução." *Epistemologias do Sul*, edited by Boaventura de Sousa Santos and Maria Paula Meneses, 19. São Paulo: Cortez, 2010.

Stalsett, S. J. "Vulnerabilidad, dignidade e justicia: valores éticos fundamentales em um mundo globalizado." *Revista Venezolana de Gerencia* 9.25 (2004) 145–57.

How Are They to Hear without a Preacher?

Homiletics from a Cuban Protestant Perspective

CARLOS EMILIO HAM

Introduction

CUBA IS A *sui generis* Third World country. Its Revolution, which triumphed in 1959, adopted a Socialist system with a strong atheist policy, inherited from the former Soviet Union, very early, causing many pastors and members of the churches to abandon the country.[1] Theodore A. Braun analyzes this period in a positive and constructive way, saying:

> But soon a new situation began to unfold. As Christians who remained in Cuba began to see the hungry being fed, the naked being clothed, [and] the poor being lifted (all of it by the government, outside the aegis of the church), they were filled with surprise. Here was God fulfilling the prayers and aims of the church through the instrument of a secular "Cyrus," but there was a big difference—the needs of the people were now being solved by structural changes in society and not the needs of individuals by Christian charity. That brought a new question to challenge the church: what was its mission if there were no longer poor people to help? The answer came down to the

---

1. The Presbyterian Church lost 70 percent of its pastors, and 80 percent of graduates from the Evangelical Seminary of Theology left as well, mainly to the USA.

basic hermeneutical calling of the church: to interpret what God is doing in the world and to join God there. Thus, Christians began to play an increasingly active role in the unfolding revolutionary society.[2]

The churches that were more open to the revolutionary process experienced quite a dilemma. On the one hand, they recognized that an atheist regime was serving the people from a philosophical standpoint,[3] and yet, at the same time, they had to acknowledge that this political system was trying to promote (in words and deeds) the values of the gospel of God's kingdom. One can imagine the homiletical challenge that this meant for these mainline Protestant historical churches. They were trying to be "salt" and "light" in a Marxist society while being faithful witnesses of the Risen Lord, to be incarnated in the new society. In the midst of this quandary, others were preaching hope in the exodus (from the country) and the Fundamentalists were preaching "opium" from the pulpits.

At the same time, Cuba has suffered one of the longest embargoes, imposed by the US Government, which has been condemned by the great majority of the world's nations and by various United Nations General Assemblies. There was, however, a positive side to this isolation. Since our missional relationships with our "mother churches" in the US were suddenly cut, the remaining pastors in the Cuban churches had to be very creative with their theological approaches as they sought to be more "indigenous" and closer to the Cuban culture.

The negative aspect, of course, is that the embargo created economic shortages which damaged the quality of life of the Cuban population. Nevertheless, even with these hostile practices of different US administrations towards our people, in contrast, our brothers and sisters of the churches in that country have accompanied us by pursuing "mutuality in mission," which has benefited churches in both countries. In this regard, we quite often preach and hear messages of reconciliation, love, and mutual support in our pulpits, from both Cuban and American preachers.

After the collapse of the Berlin wall in the late 1980s and since the country's secular constitution was adopted in the early 1990s, the churches were no longer confined to carrying out their mission within the four walls

---

2. Braun, *Perspectives on Cuba and Its People*, 75.

3. In 1976, a Socialist Constitution was approved by a referendum which acknowledged that the socialist state "bases its educational and cultural policy in the scientific materialist concept of the world, established and developed by Marxism-Leninism" ("Constitución de la República de Cuba" art. 38.2.a).

of the sanctuaries, now extended throughout Cuban society.[4] In a public referendum that took place on February 24, 2019, a new Constitution of the Republic was adopted in which its secular nature was reaffirmed.[5]

There have been signs of changes taking place as the churches recover their important role in the society. The social involvement of these churches has gained a new momentum, primarily for the following reasons: (a) the growing improvement of the relations between the state and the churches, by which the latter now have more freedom to carry-out their mission (which includes preaching in the public sphere); (b) the needs of the population have increased as a result of the economic crisis (which lately has worsened further due to the tightening of the US embargo, the world economic crisis, and our own mistakes); and (c) as a consequence of the decentralization of the economy by the state (which challenges the civil society in general).[6]

These critical conditions have generated a crisis of ethical and moral values, which, in turn, have led to many new persons attending Christian churches (and other religions as well). They are trying to find an answer, not only to their existential and spiritual needs but to their material ones as well. In current times, the challenges are great for Christian communities, especially now that we are able to preach the gospel beyond the walls of the sanctuaries for the first time in forty years. These new opportunities to preach more broadly and openly gained greater currency after the pastoral visit to Cuba of Pope John Paul II in January 1998.[7] This was also the case following the visit of the two Popes—namely, Pope Benedict XVI in March 2012 and Pope Francis in September 2015.

A year after the latest papal visit, four rallies were organized on the island called "The Cuban Evangelical (Protestant) Celebrations." They promoted love, peace, and unity among the Evangelicals in Cuba as well as among the white Cuban people. All four celebrations were televised, allowing millions of Cubans to see and listen to the proclamation of the gospel in the public square. In the following decades the churches have had increasing access to the media (TV, radio, Internet) and to public spaces (e.g., theaters, stadiums, in the streets) to preach the gospel, particularly on the special occasions of the Christian calendar (e.g., Holy Week and Christmas). But,

---

4. Ham, "Empowering Diakonia," 190.

5. "The State recognizes, respects and guarantees religious freedom. The Cuban State is secular. In the Republic of Cuba, religious institutions and fraternal associations are separate from the State and all have the same rights and duties. Different beliefs and religions enjoy equal consideration" ("Constitución de la República de Cuba" Art. 15).

6. Ham, "Empowering Diakonia," 190.

7. Ham, "Empowering Diakonia," 4.

to quote the Apostle Paul, "*How are they to hear without a preacher?*" (Rom 10:14).

Homiletics, as the "art of preaching" (from the Greek word *homilian*, which refers to a person talking to a crowd), is gradually gaining momentum in the public sphere of our country, as it embraces a wide variety of topics, such as sources, doctrinal and ethical content, structure, illustrative materials, language, and preparation for the pulpit and delivery.

Throughout more than forty years of ordained ministry, I have been motivated by the blessing and privilege of preaching. This is true not only in the more than fifteen congregations of the Presbyterian-Reformed Church I have served as a pastor but also in other churches and denominations in Cuba, the USA, Canada, Central America, South America, the Caribbean, Europe, Asia, the Middle East, and the Pacific. While serving as program executive for evangelism in the World Council of Churches in Geneva (2001–2013), I had the opportunity of preaching in many of these places worldwide.

The current article will focus primarily on the topic of homiletics from the perspective of the mainline Cuban Protestant ecumenical churches. Most of them were founded in the 1890s by the "Patriot Missionaries,"[8] who lived out their Christian faith incarnated in their patriotic commitment.

Around fifty denominations were founded on Cuban territory from the end of the nineteenth century until 1963. Historic Protestantism was mostly tied to the middle class. It encouraged a North American lifestyle among its faithful and was known to the general population through good works, mainly by founding schools, homes for the aged, and student hostels.[9]

The Biblical Text

Thomas G. Long highlights the importance of Scripture for preaching when he points out:

> Preaching is biblical whenever the preacher allows a text from the Bible to serve as the leading force in shaping the content and purpose of the sermon. More dynamically, biblical preaching involves telling the truth about what happens when a biblical text intersects some aspect of our life and exerts a claim upon

---

8. Expression coined by Rafael Cepeda, a Cuban Presbyterian-Reformed pastor and church historian, referring to the patriots who we persecuted because they were fighting the Spanish Colony, had to flee the island to the USA. In that country they were converted to the Christian faith according to the Protestant tradition.

9. Cepeda et al., *En La Fuerza Del Espíritu*, 95–96.

us. Biblical preaching does not mean merely talking about the Bible, using the Bible to bolster doctrinal arguments, or applying biblical "principles" to everyday life. Biblical preaching happens when a preacher prayerfully goes to listen to the Bible on behalf of the people and then speaks on Christ's behalf what he or she hears there. Biblical preaching has almost nothing to do with how many times the Bible is quoted in a sermon and everything to do with how faithfully the Bible is interpreted in relation to contemporary experience.[10]

For the past fifty years, the Cuban Council of Churches has imported millions of bibles into the country for Protestant and Roman-Catholic churches and for the population in general. Quite often, preachers in Cuba "use the Bible to bolster doctrinal arguments," as mentioned in the previous quote. We have seen this recently when a Reform of the Constitution of the Republic of Cuba was debated very passionately. One of the main issues was a proposal to change the definition of marriage from the union of a man and a woman to a union between two persons, paving the way for the marriage of gays and lesbians. Even after this Referendum took place and a new Constitution was adopted on February 24, many Fundamentalist preachers, quoting the Bible, still argue for the importance of "natural marriage" (i.e., between a man and a woman) today. So today, more than ever, we need to pursue homiletics in Cuba as a way of interpreting the Bible "in relation to [our changing] contemporary experience."

In the nineteenth century, the upsurge and development of scientific and technological thought, together with the French and Russian Revolution and the rise of the United States of America as a world power, accelerated the movement towards secularism and created a crisis, calling into question many traditions and increasing doubt about the book which most Christians accepted as authoritative in matters of belief and conduct. The fundamentalist's response was to preserve as inviolable Calvin's view of inspired Scripture as the authoritative revelation of the will of God. Therefore, the words themselves have been set down by the Holy Spirit so that we have the pure Word of God free from human admixture. Their accent is laid on obedience to Scripture literally construed. On the other hand, the liberal's response was to continue to affirm that the Bible is authoritative for faith and life while adopting a critical view that emphasized the ideas of progressive revelation and inspiration. They attempt to reconcile an authoritative view of the Bible with the human and historical side of its composition.[11]

---

10. Long, *Witness of Preaching*, 48.
11. Mackenzie, *Authority in the Reformed Tradition*, 104–5.

In other words, the latter recognize the authoritative value of the Scriptures while showing in their approach a more open, broad-minded, and tolerant attitude towards them. This example can also be applied to the hermeneutic and homiletical approach of the Cuban mainline Protestant ecumenical churches.

Hence, the significance of the Holy Scripture for preaching is particularly important in the tradition emerging from the Protestant Reformation, starting with Martin Luther. In fact, a "Protestant is a Pope with the Bible in his/her hand."[12] For the Reformer John Calvin, the Bible is authoritative, and it is so because it is authenticated and enlightened by the Holy Spirit. "We ought to speak our conviction," he says, "in a higher place than human reasons, judgments, or conjectures, that is, in the secret testimony of the Spirit."[13] In Cuba we experience similar understandings.

In contrast with other contemporary approaches to the authority of the Bible, the Swiss Theologian Karl Barth took up the study of Scripture with a new seriousness. He understood the Word of God in three forms: preached, written, and revealed. He denied that the Word of God proclaimed or written had an inherent divine power. "The Bible *becomes* the word of God," he says, "whenever God makes it the vehicle of his speaking to us." Only the free decisions of God produce the event in which the Bible and revelation become one: to speak of the Word of God is to speak of the work of God—hence authority presupposes obedience.[14]

Ross Mackenzie, in his article "Authority in the Reformed Tradition," says:

> In summary, the following would generally be accepted by Reformed theologians and teachers who have been influenced by Barth, and would regard themselves as neither Fundamentalist nor Liberals: First, the Bible is a witness to revelation and is not itself the Word of God. The witness is always different from that to which it witnesses. We therefore have to hear what the Bible as a human word has to say. Second, inspiration means the act of revelation, in which the prophets and apostles in all their humanness became the witnesses they were, and in which alone they in all their humanness can become for us the witnesses they are. Third, as the authority of Scripture does not lie in its indefectibility or infallibility, so the assailability of the

---

12. This quote is borrowed from Nicholas Boileau (1636–1711), a French poet and author of *Satires, Epistles, Poetic Art*. It is taken from his *Satires XII*, published in *El Protestantismo de A a Z*, 3.

13. Calvin, *Institutes of the Christian Religion* I.VII.4.

14. Mackenzie, *Authority in the Reformed Tradition*, 105–6.

human word in the Bible is no ground for rejecting its authority. The authority of Scripture lies beyond the words of the page of Scripture in the free and sovereign act of God.[15]

The Latin American and Caribbean Theologians of Liberation have also contributed substantially to biblical hermeneutics and have had an impact on some of our preaching in Cuba. Pablo Richard, for example, emphasizes the three meanings that should be found in the study of Scripture: (1) the textual meaning, which looks at the text as such, as an independent literary structure; (2) the historical meaning, which is determined by the history from which it emerges; and (3) the spiritual meaning, which is decided when the text is read to discern and communicate the Word of God in our current reality. Therefore, the Bible finds its meaning when we interpret the text as such, when we interpret it in the past history in which it was formed, and finally, when the text is interpreted in our own reality and transforms it in a "great revelation of God."[16]

On the other hand, Clodovis Boff suggests the following considerations when the Bible is being read from the point of view of the poor and from their liberation perspective:

> First, it is a hermeneutic which privileges the application over the explanation. . . . It tries to find in the Bible its textual meaning but connected to its current meaning. The most important matter here is not so much to interpret the text of the Scripture, but to interpret the book of life "according to Scripture." Second, the liberating hermeneutic seeks to discover and activate the transforming energy of the biblical texts. "It is difficult to make a Revolution without the Bible." Fourth, the theological-political reading of the Bible highlights the social context of the message. It places the text in its historical context in order to make a proper translation, not literal but historical. And finally, the liberating hermeneutic is developed among the poor, incorporating the contributions of the "popular reading of the Bible," at the level of a hermeneutical mediation, benefited by the popular wisdom in the socio-analytical mediation. This way, the poor, or even better, the church of the poor, expressed by the "church community bases," appears as the privileged "hermeneutical subject" in the Biblical reflection.[17]

---

15. Mackenzie, *Authority in the Reformed Tradition*, 107–8.
16. Richard, "Teología En La Teología de La Liberación," 219.
17. Boff, "Epistemology and Method," 108–9.

But in order to accomplish a liberating reading of the Bible by the poor—according to Carlos Mesters—it is necessary to stress a careful balance between the three readings, which should be critical—namely, the ones of the pre-text, of the con-text, and of the text. This way he analyzes the hermeneutical procedures described earlier with a new nomenclature:

> (1) The pre-text is the global reality in which the community of believers is located. God created the world and in the world is where we ought to find God reflected. . . . If God is not known in the reality where we live and struggle for life, he simply is not known. . . . The critical reading of God is necessary in order to find the reality of God in it, promoting the kingdom on earth. (2) The con-text is the community of believers, which read both its own reality (the pre-text) as well as the Bible (the text). In order for God to speak from the pre-text and from the text, they must be read in the community. And the community is forged in the reading which seeks to face the challenges of the reality. (3) The text (the Bible) also must be read critically from its own historical context, respecting the distance that separates us from the ancient centuries in which it was written. Here the problem is double: on one hand (a) the relation of the reading in the community, with the results of the biblical sciences, which is indispensable to respect the distance mentioned, and on the other, (b) the permanent relationship of the popular reading with the pre-text and the con-text. The living God which rules today ought to speak to the community, this concrete community, through the reading of the Bible.[18]

The Cuban Professor and Theologian, Adolfo Ham, in his article "Hermeneutics and Revolution," explains the ways in which this science has guided the reflection and action of the Cuban Church in the beginnings of the revolutionary process of our Country:

> For us there is an intimate conjunction between the hermeneutical problem, that is, the approach to the Word of God in the Biblical text and the larger and wider text composed of history and historical commitment, that is, the political militancy as well as the evangelizing action (the credibility of the church and the efficiency in communicating the liberating message) . . . For us hermeneutics, far from the academic discussions with their philosophical, idealistic presuppositions, is the technique of reading out of the concrete situation in the light of Scripture. A hermeneutic exercise starts from the liberating praxis of the

18. Mesters, *Flor Sem Defesa*, 3–4.

Christian which allows the re-reading of the Bible in the larger Bible: the historical process.[19]

Ham goes on to say that "two categorical elements of the Biblical and Hebrew concept of the word can help us. There is no contradiction between word and action. It means that the word is subversive by its nature. Also, that the word manifests itself in the midst of history, it is a creating word and therefore is a liberating word." So, the Bible is word/event which liberates more than a written word in the dead code of letters. We also refer to what the theologians of liberation have called "the re-contextualizing of the Bible." It means that the true sense of the word cannot be discovered unless it passes through the difficult procedure of the liberation of the word itself, and the discovery of its subversive and liberating character for those Christians which are within the political commitment of the revolution. No hermeneutics stands without this re-contextualizing of the word. The radical iconoclastic character of Scripture in Exodus: "You shall have no other gods before me" (Exod 20:3) sounds more important as the revolutionary character of the life and message of the prophets and the OT emphasis on the dignity of the human being: no person should be enslaved or have their share in the benefits of creation taken away. In the Old Testament, the central motivation is the community sense (brother-sister-*chesed*), keeping law (*mishpat*) and justice (*tsedeqá*) means to prevent authentic relations from being disturbed (*mishpat*) and to maintain the full integrity of each person (*tsedeqá*).[20]

So, for the Cuban Christians, Biblical hermeneutics is not just an academic exercise but rather a question of survival. The abrupt collapse of the European Communist bloc, a deeper imposition of the trade sanctions by the United States of America's Government, and internal mistakes thrust Cuba into a deep economic crisis at the beginning of the nineties, undoing the higher standard of living Cuba had enjoyed since the Revolution, with free health care, education, etc. The people are now paying the price of that crisis, mainly the elderly and the children. Biblical paradigms can help us to be faithful in the midst of crisis and offer hope for the future of not only the Church but also the Country.

---

19. Ham, "Hermeneutics and Revolution," 112.
20. Arce et al., *Cristo Vivo En Cuba*, 111–12.

Our Context

As stated above, the fact that we believe that Scripture "is not itself the Word of God" is a homiletic challenge since the preacher is called to reveal it as the Word of God through the sermon. In other words, the Scripture's message becomes the Word of God when it is interpreted and applied to the life of the congregation and lived by the community. So, revelation comes not only to those who wrote the Bible, furthermore, it is completed by the preacher who is bridging this message and applying it to the life of the community in its own context. For example, when Jesus says to his disciples, "But whoever wishes to become great among you must be your servant, and whoever wishes to be first among you must be slave of all" (Mark 10:43b–44), it can be read as his call to invest our time, resources, and gifts in accompanying and assisting those in need, who, in the Cuban context, are mainly the elderly. So, if "the Son of Man came not to be served but to serve, and to give his life a ransom for many" (Mark 10:45), we are urged to do the same!

In the Cuban context, a theology of preaching is closely connected to the people. Carlos Camps, professor in the Matanzas Seminary, says in the preface to one of his books:

> It is a theology that originates from the reflection of the people of God, here in Cuba, especially during these interesting years for us Cubans; it is a theological task which establishes a feedback that goes from the people to the theologian and from the theologian to the people.... What is being preached is and has been, the result of the dialectic relationship between the Word of God, which challenges us in our context, becoming flesh, provoking the expectations to live within our realities and struggles.[21]

When the preacher goes to the Bible, s/he does not go with a blank tablet but rather with a set of categories and expectations already in place. In this regard, Thomas G. Long says:

> It would be impossible to describe everything that a preacher brings to the interpretation of a text, but at least three of these important frames of understanding deserve our special attention. First, a critically informed view of Scripture. We know that the Bible contains a set of writings produced by human beings caught up in the circumstances of particular times and places, people that wrote both with a faithful vision and a culturally conditioned mind-set. This means that the Church must not

---

21. Camps, *Desde Un Púlpito Para Un Pueblo*, 13.

only listen obediently to the words of the Bible, it must also interpret those words of human product for their own age.[22]

Second, Long points to a Theological Heritage:

> Preachers go to the Bible not as "universal Christians" (there is no such a thing) but with a particular theological heritage and viewpoint.... A theologically informed interpreter of Scripture enters the text guided by a map drawn and refined by those who have come to this place before.... As we prepare to preach, we go to Scripture not just as individual believers but as practicing theologians on the frontlines of the church, seeking to hear the gospel today in continuity with the theological memory of the whole church.[23]

And finally, an awareness of the circumstances of the hearers.

> The biblical word does not come as a disembodied word, speaking timeless verities to all people everywhere. The Bible speaks to particular people in the concrete circumstances of their lives. ... It is not the word of God in the abstract but of God who is for us, of God who is against us in order to be truly for us.[24]

For our mainline Protestant churches in Cuba—particularly those that prepare their pastors at our Evangelical Theological Seminary in Matanzas—these three categories are valid, and I would say, challenging, as well. We definitely make an effort to see that our "view of the Scripture is critically informed." This is dealt with further down in the section on *Elements to Take into Consideration for Biblical Exegesis and Hermeneutics*. Our Seminary is ecumenical; therefore, we work with different, diverse "theological heritages" which make our sermons (at our chapel and, of course, at our churches) richer and more diverse, even dealing with the same biblical text. Finally, lifting the "awareness of the circumstances of the hearers" is where I think we need to work more intentionally. This is true not only in our Seminary but in others in Latin America and globally as well. At our Seminary, I believe that—in general terms—as in other Protestant seminaries we are good in biblical sciences (in exegesis and hermeneutics of the Bible), but we need to be more intentional in other sciences in order to pursue more in-depth exegesis and hermeneutics of the contexts to which we are applying the Biblical message. In other words, we need to be more intentional in the interdisciplinary approach of theology informed by other sciences,

22. Long, *Witness of Preaching*, 51.
23. Long, *Witness of Preaching*, 53–54.
24. Long, *Witness of Preaching*, 55.

such as economy, psychology, sociology, ecology, and anthropology, among others.[25]

When the Bible is read in church, the congregation is listening in on a communication originally intended for readers long ago and far away. Thus, preachers are charged with two important tasks: exegesis and hermeneutics—I would add of both the biblical text and of the context—on one hand, and proclamation on the other.[26]

With regard to the interpretation of the congregation's context, Thomas G. Long shares the following thought:

> The preacher goes to the Biblical text for the congregation and, indeed, with the congregation. . . . Exegesis is a work of the church enacted through the preacher as its chosen representative. . . . So, the move from the text to the sermon begins not with a decision about how to inform the congregation about the results of the preacher's personal exegesis of the text but rather a decision about what aspect of the congregation-text encounter will be carried over into the sermon itself. The bridge the preacher must now cross is the one between the text-in-congregational-context and the sermon-in-congregational-context.[27]

In his or her homiletical task, the preacher ought to develop a "close reading" of the world of the text (Bible) and the text of the world (the congregation). Richard B. Hays says, "The preacher should begin to ask questions concerning the significance of the text for theological reflection and for the congregation." Hays then poses the following questions in this regard, which will bring Scripture into a critical dialogue with the congregation's world:

> What understanding of God, Jesus, the church, and the world is presented in the passage?; what would it mean for the community of faith to treat this passage as normative for its life and witness?; at what points will the community find itself already in agreement or disagreement with the teaching of the text?; and how are the points of tension to be interpreted or acted upon?[28]

Leonora Tubbs Tisdale also addresses the importance of taking into consideration the congregation for the sermon design, from the very beginning. She says:

25. Ham, "Empowering Diakonia," 17.
26. Hays, "Exegesis," 122.
27. Long, *Witness of Preaching*, 79.
28. Hays, "Exegesis," 127.

Good preaching not only requires its practitioners to become skilled biblical exegetes. It also requires them to become adept in "exegeting" local congregations and their contexts, so that they can proclaim the gospel in relevant and transformative ways for particular communities of faith. . . . Unfortunately, however, homiletical texts and courses have not always attended as carefully or thoughtfully to the exegesis of contexts as they have to the exegesis of the texts. While preachers have been provided with detailed methods for biblical interpretation, congregational interpretation has frequently been left to the intuition and the hunches of the local pastor. . . . Indeed [we] may well find that a gap exists between the pulpit and the pew—a gap [we] need help understanding and bridging."[29]

We have been observing, how important it is for *contextual theologies*—such as a Theology of Liberation—to identify linkage between the biblical message and the community of believers in a way that the former transforms the latter. So, says Tisdale, "[A] way to bridge this gap is to view preaching as an act of constructing 'local theology'—that is, theology crafted for a very particular people in a particular time and place."[30] She goes on to say, "Sermons of local pastors, preached in their own unique congregational contexts, provide real-life examples of contextual theologizing in action."[31] Finally, she observes, "The 'interpretation,' or hermeneutical stage, necessarily involves a dual focus: interpretation of the *listeners*, including their contexts: personal, domestic, social, political, economic, and interpretation of the *biblical text* in its context—historical, theological, and literary."[32]

This is certainly our experience in Cuba regarding homiletics. Quite often we argue that in order to be a good theologian, one does not necessarily need to hold a PhD. As pointed out above, each preacher is a theologian in the sense that he or she constructs a 'local theology' which is grounded in both the biblical message and in the reality of the congregation. Therefore, I believe that we ought to be more intentional in publishing all sermons that contain an excellent practical and contextual theology.

Cuban Christians are supported by the fact that the same God who liberated the people in Egypt in extremely difficult conditions is with us now. People are confident that the same Christ who inaugurated a new Covenant, opting for the poor of his times and helping to liberate us, is also with the poor, helping to dignify the people of Cuba. His glorious and

---

29. Tisdale, *Preaching as Local Theology and Folk Art*, xi–xii.
30. Tisdale, *Preaching as Local Theology and Folk Art*, xii.
31. Tisdale, *Preaching as Local Theology and Folk Art*, xiii.
32. Tisdale, *Preaching as Local Theology and Folk Art*, 25.

victorious resurrection is a certainty that for God and all those who trust him, all things are possible. The two books that God wrote—quoting Saint Augustine—the book of life and the Bible, confirm an eschatology based in the hope of the coming of the kingdom here and now, a kingdom of "righteousness and peace and joy in the Holy Spirit" (Rom 14:17). This is the way the con-text—the community of believers—is inspired in the Biblical Text. It is also the way it challenges the current times, to be critical protagonists in the pre-text of the Cuban situation in order for the kingdom to be a reality in our world. This is the message that the Lord invites us to proclaim and to live in Cuba today.

Exegesis and Hermeneutics

The word "exegesis" means simply "interpretation." Every close reading of a text—any text—is an act of exegesis. It is an explanation of a biblical text in its own context. The preacher's task of exegesis, however, is made more challenging by the historical distance between the present time and the biblical one. These documents were written in the Hebrew and Greek languages in ancient cultures, for communities whose customs and assumptions differed dramatically from our own. Preachers must understand the historical and literary contexts of the biblical text and then reflect imaginatively on the way in which that text might speak to a congregation in a very different historical setting. The more precise the exegesis, the more focused the proclamation will be.[33]

In other words, René Castellanos, our Professor of Greek in the Evangelical Seminary in Matanzas, Cuba, defines biblical exegesis, as the process by which we analyze and explain a Biblical text (*Explicatio*) in order to apply it (*Applicatio*), under the guidance of the Holy Spirit, to discover the meaning of the text to our particular situation.[34]

Another important concept to consider in studying the Biblical text is hermeneutics. The word hermeneutics comes from the name *Hermes*, a god from Greek mythology, son of Zeus, who served as a messenger and interpreter of the gods. Consequently, hermeneutics is the art of translating or interpreting a text or ancient message in our own context (here and now). In Karl Barth's words, "It is to see what the Biblical author saw and to retell it in our own language."[35]

---

33. Hays, "Exegesis," 122.
34. Castellanos, *Notes from Greek Exegesis Classes*.
35. Alsup, *Notes from Greek Exegesis Classes*.

"Hermeneutics in general terms is the art of understanding," says James A. Sanders,

> More specifically it refers to the method and techniques used to make a text understandable in a world different from the one in which the text originated.... It pertains to the world of communication among humans and with the divine. Speech is the act of formulating thoughts coherently and expressing those thoughts in a way that communicates them to another or others orally or in writing. Hermeneutics is the art of understanding such an expression in the world of the hearer or reader. The hermeneut, engaging in the act of understanding, is also a text, as it were, and the encounter between the two is an act of intertextuality. Every text read or heard is already an interpretation of earlier texts incorporated into it, exhibiting its own hermeneutics of understanding those earlier texts.[36]

René Castellanos often referred to what he called the "Hermeneutical Circulation," moving from the "Biblical World" to "Our World," and from "Our World" to the "Biblical World." I would rather use the notion of "Hermeneutical Spiral," pointing to a dynamic, ascendant movement between both "worlds," out of which the content of the sermon is conceived, preached, and—hopefully—lived.

The *formula* 1+3+1, taught by René Castellanos in our Evangelical (Ecumenical) Theological Seminary, can illustrate these concepts better:[37]

ELEMENTS TO TAKE INTO CONSIDERATION FOR BIBLICAL EXEGESIS AND HERMENEUTICS:				
1	3			1
CONVICTION	APPROACHES			DECISION
THE WORD OF GOD FOR US	THE T[EXT] IN ITSELF **Text** (textile) WHAT DOES THE T[EXT] SAY? PHILOLOGICAL EXEGESIS	THE AUTHOR AND HIS/HER CIRCUMSTANCES **Context** WHAT DID THE AUTHOR TRY TO SAY? HISTORICAL EXEGESIS	WE AND OUR CIRCUMSTANCES **Recontextualization**. WHAT DOES THE T[EXT] ACTUALLY TELL US? THEOLOGICAL EXEGESIS	TO LIVE WHAT WE HAVE RECEIVED

---

36. Sanders, "Hermeneutics," 175–77.
37. Ham, *Trípode Homilético*, 32.

A—**Philological Exegesis:**

1) Knowledge of the language (OT: Hebrew or NT: Greek) or, at least, use of different Biblical versions is recommended.

2) Clarify the phrases or words of difficult meaning.

3) Define the class (genre) of the text (prose or poetry).

4) In order to facilitate the work the use of dictionaries, biblical commentaries, and concordances are recommended.

B—**Historical Exegesis**:

1) To place the text in its historical context (author, date, recipients, motivations, and objectives).

2) **Types of contexts**:

   a) Immediate: verses before and after the pericope;

   b) Thematic: analysis of the passages of the OT and NT which deal with the theme by using Biblical references and parallel passages;

   c) Historical-Social: investigations on the social, political, economic, and historical conditions in the time of writing of a particular book in the Bible. For example, when the Gospel of Luke relates the birth of Jesus, it describes the historical and political context of those times through these words: "And it came to pass in those days that a decree went from Caesar Augustus that all the world should be registered. This census first took place while Quirinius was governing Syria" (Luke 2:1–2); and

   d) Universal: the place that this text occupies in the *History of Salvation*. In other words, to consider God's project with humankind as revealed in Scripture in relation to "secular" history.

C—**Theological Exegesis or Hermeneutic Bridge** (from the biblical world to ours):

This is the moment for applying the biblical paradigm to the current reality, confronting the text with us and our circumstances. It is useful to raise the following questions:

1) What does the text mean to the contemporary reader?

2) What cultural factors need to be contextualized?

3) What is the theological significance?

Now that we have studied this exegetical and hermeneutical method, let's analyze a practical example to gain a better understanding of the whole process:

> *"Jesus went throughout Galilee, teaching in their synagogues and proclaiming the good news of the kingdom and curing every disease and every sickness among the people."* (Matt 4:23)

1. The very first question that we raise concerning a pericope is: What does the text say? (Philological exegesis). It is helpful to read this verse in different versions or translations in order to get a broader picture of what the text says. The next step would be to clarify the phrases or words of difficult meaning. For example, let's choose the word *kingdom*. What does this word or concept mean since our political understanding has changed? Here we can look to the "thematic context," to the analysis of the passages of the OT and NT that deal with the theme, by using Biblical references and parallel passages. We find that the proclamation of the *good news of the kingdom* was the very center of Jesus' preaching, which, according to the Apostle Paul, "Is not food and drink but righteousness and peace and joy in the Holy Spirit" (Rom 14:17).

2. It is also helpful to "place the text in its historical context." Many study Bibles provide an introduction to each book, where we read that the "Gospel according to Matthew is the Gospel written by a Jew, to Jews about a Jew. Matthew is the writer, his countrymen are the readers, and Jesus Christ is the subject. Matthew's design is to present Jesus as the King of the Jews, the long-awaited Messiah" and this is Matthew's great message! This information helps us to understand better why Jesus went out "teaching in their synagogues" and points to the fact that we, as Christians, have a very rich Jewish heritage. We belong to a Judeo-Christian tradition, which many persons tend to forget. It is also helpful to know that the author of this book was formerly a tax collector, which was a very unpopular profession at that time, and that Jesus himself chose him as one of his disciples (Matt 9:9–13). It was that same Matthew, who exploited his own people and was rejected by them, who now gives life to the people by writing this Gospel (around the year 58–68 AD, maybe in Palestine or Syrian Antioch). It is also very helpful to see all these places on the map, including Galilee, which enables us to understand better the Biblical message.

3. Let's also look to the "immediate context." We find that Jesus was already baptized, he was tempted by the devil in the wilderness, and now he begins his ministry in Galilee, calling his first disciples. So this verse is a summary of Jesus' earthly ministry! And what does the text actually tell us? It is one of the most helpful paradigms for the Church's mission today: to carry on Jesus' mission and to do it Jesus' way. Acknowledging that the verse is written in prose (in a "direct language" or ordinary speech), here we are ready to build our "hermeneutical bridge" for the recontextualization of the text, finding in this passage Jesus' *four great verbs or actions*, which guide the Cuban Church in its ministry to its people:

   a) ***Jesus WENT through Galilee.*** Jesus' Ministry was not limited to a specific place, he was always "on the road," which reminds us of Leslie Newbegin's definition of the Church not as an institution, but rather as an EXPEDITION. In the Sixties, Seventies, and Eighties the Church in Cuba had to limit its work to the Church buildings. Now there is a new opportunity for the Church to carry on social projects, to preach by radio and to "go through Cuba" in its mission. Now we can be witnesses of the Lord "in Jerusalem, and in all Judea and Samaria, and to the ends of the earth" (Acts 1:8).

   b) ***TEACHING in their synagogues.*** Jesus visited these institutions to teach the Jewish people all about his concerns, thoughts, and a new vision of the world. An important task of the Church in Cuba today is to teach, to not only inform but also form and even transform the society through the power of the Word read and proclaimed. In current times, thousands and thousands of Bibles are being distributed by the Cuban Council of Churches, so it is also important for us to teach hermeneutics, to teach people to read, interpret, and live the biblical teachings. This is an important aspect of the formative task of the Church.

   c) ***PROCLAIMING the good news of the kingdom.*** This, as we saw earlier, is the core of Jesus' message, and this is exactly what people are looking for: a message of peace and joy in the Holy Spirit, in moments in which there is great skepticism, insecurity, and uncertainty in the population.

   d) ***CURING every disease and every sickness among the people.*** The contribution of the Church in the present Cuban situation is not only from the theoretical point of view. Jesus was very consistent in what he said and did, and therefore is appointing us "to go and bear fruit, fruit that will last" (John 15:16). If we are not living messages, our messages will not be alive. This is the great challenge for lay preachers.

This is a very difficult moment for the Cuban people, but it is also a *Kairos*, a moment of opportunities for the Church to serve the people. That is why the Christian communities are distributing humanitarian aid (from the National Council and Churches of Christ, Pastors for Peace in the USA, and from other countries) among hospitals, daycare centers, homes for elderly people, etc.

Consequently, we are called to build a new community *(koinonia)* based on the teaching *(didache)*, preaching *(kerygma)*, and serving *(diakonia)* ministries. We could, therefore, graphically represent Jesus' (and our) "wholistic" ministry the following way, which is an excellent resource to prepare the sermon:

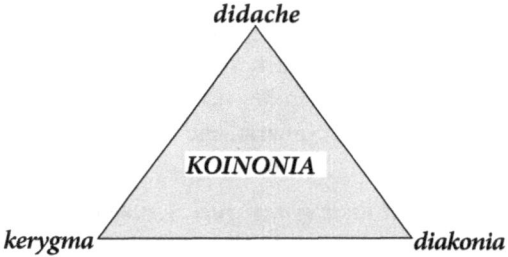

Conclusions

So, the soil is ready for the seed of the word of God to continue to be planted. As we have analyzed earlier, it is easier to accomplish this from the point of view of the Cuban socialist state. But it is also the case that it is more needed in this moment in which there is a readjustment of values in our society. Furthermore, it is critically needed in times when material poverty is increasing in our population. Before going to his Father, our Lord Jesus Christ left to his disciples the "Great Commission" with these words: "All authority in heaven and on earth has been given to me, therefore go and make disciples of all nations, baptizing them in the name of the Father, the Son, and the Holy Spirit, and teaching them to obey everything I have commanded you, and surely I am with you always, to the very end of the age" (Matt 28:18–20).

These verses, which are the conclusion of the Gospel of Matthew, confirm that mission belongs to the Lord himself and that he shares it with us. He co-missions us to work along with him—expressed symbolically with the vertical dimension of the cross—but the mandate refers also to the call to work for each other—represented by the horizontal dimension. In this way, our ministry has been commissioned by our Lord in favor of his kingdom here on earth and with the full conviction of the Holy Spirit's permanent accompaniment.

Today, in Cuba, we are living in a very difficult and challenging moment as a result of the strengthening of the US embargo, the breakdown of the European Socialist countries and the Soviet Union, the international economic crisis, and our own mistakes (as we have seen earlier), but this moment is very creative as well, a time not only to analyze the role of Christianity in Cuba but also enquire as to how it meets with the Marxist context for the benefit of the Cuban Society. In this regard, I appreciate Giulio Girardi's remarks:

> The affinity between the history of Marxism and of Christianity not only involves their deformation due to their alliance with the empires, but also their renewal in their efforts to break down those ties, liberating themselves from those dependencies and rescuing their original projects. In the heart of these projects is, both for Marxism and for Christianity, the identification with the oppressed and the need to militantly take their side. To rescue their original inspiration is, therefore, both for Marxism and for Christianity, to break down the wall that historically has divided them, to discover their fundamental convergence and together commit themselves, on the side of the oppressed people of the world, in the construction of a new history.[38]

For the churches in Cuba, the phrase attributed to the Swiss Reformed Theologian Karl Barth is more relevant than ever, namely, that to become a faithful witness, we must hold the newspaper in one hand and the Bible in the other.[39] Precisely in that interrelation, between the Scriptures and our context, is where the Christian witness becomes real.

In conclusion, the Cuban churches are empowered by God to preach the *good news* of the gospel of the kingdom by words and deeds, to not only serve the most vulnerable people but also be proactive in prophetic engagement, going ahead, discerning God's will for the nation, discovering and showing the way towards God's kingdom. This role is to be with the people, particularly with the "least of these"—not as a political party but rather

---

38. Girardi, *El Ahora de Cuba*, 257.

39. The actual phrase is: "Take your Bible and take your newspaper and read both. But interpret newspapers from your Bible" (*Time*, May 1, 1966).

offering care and building bridges for communication, dialogue, and reconciliation. This is a "treasure in clay" (2 Cor 4:7), the utopia of the gospel. It is what the churches bring to the Cuban society in order to seek transformative justice and build communities.[40] The central *kerygma*, the key message, is hope, certain that even when we do not know what the future holds, we know who holds the future!

Bibliography

Alsup, John. Unpublished notes from Greek Exegesis Classes. Austin Presbyterian Theological Seminary, Austin, TX, 1997.

Arce, Sergio, et al. *Cristo Vivo En Cuba. Reflexiones Teológicas Cubanas*. San José, Costa Rica: Departamento Ecuménico de Investigaciones (DEI), 1978.

Boff, Clodovis. "Epistemology and Method." In *Mysterium Liberationis: Conceptos Fundamentales de La Teología de La Liberación*, edited by Ignacio Ellacuría and Jon Sobrino, 108–9. Vol. 1. Madrid: Editorial Trotta, 1990.

Braun, Theodore. *Perspectives on Cuba and Its People*. Edited by the National Council of Churches of Christ in the USA. New York: Friendship, 1999.

Calvin, John. *Institutes of the Christian Religion*. Edited by John T. Mcneill. Translated by Ford Lewis Battles. Louisville: Westminster John Knox, 2006.

Camps, Carlos. *Desde Un Púlpito Para Un Pueblo*. Quito: Departamento de Comunicaciones del Consejo Latinoamericano de Iglesias (CLAI), 1997.

Castellanos, René. Unpublished notes from Greek Exegesis Classes. Evangelical Theological Seminary, Matanzas, Cuba, 1980.

Cepeda, Rafael, et al. *En La Fuerza Del Espíritu*. Edited by Benjamín Gutiérrez. Mexico City, Mexico: Alianza de Iglesias Presbiterianas y Reformadas de América Latina (AIPRAL), 1995.

"Constitución de la República de Cuba." *Granma: Official Voice of the Communist Party of Cuba Central Committee*. 1976. Online. http://www.granma.cu/file/pdf/gaceta/Nueva%20Constitución%20240%20KB-1.pdf.

Dockery, David. *Preaching and Hermeneutics: Contempary Preaching*. Philadelphia: Broadman, 1992.

Girardi, Giulio. *El Ahora de Cuba, Tras El Derrumbe Del Comunismo y Tras La Visita Del Papa*. Madrid: Editorial Nueva Utopía, Consejo de Iglesias de Cuba y Caminos, 1998.

Ham, Carlos. "Empowering Diakonia: A Model for Service and Transformation in the Ecumenical Movement and Local Congregations." PhD diss., Free University of Amsterdam, 2015.

———. "The Homiletic Tripod: A Guide for Cuban Lay Preachers." Project Presented to the Faculty of Austin Presbyterian Theological Seminary, Austin, TX, 1995.

———. *Trípode Homilético. Una Guía Para Predicadores Laicos*. Quito: Departamento de Comunicaciones del Consejo Latinoamericano de Iglesias (CLAI), 2003.

Hays, Richard. "Exegesis." In *Concise Encyclopedia of Preaching*, edited by Richard Lischen and William H. Willimon, 122–28. Louisville: Westminster John Knox, 1995.

---

40. Ham, "Empowering Diakonia," 202.

Long, Thomas. *The Witness of Preaching*. Edited by Richard Lischen and William H. Willimon. Louisville: Westminster John Knox, 1989.

Mackenzie, Ross. *Authority in the Reformed Tradition: A Pope for All Christians?* Edited by Peter McCord. Mahwah, NJ: Paulist, 1976.

Mesters, Carlos. *Flor Sem Defesa: Uma Explicaçao Da La Biblia a Partir Do Povo*. Petrópolis: Vozes, 1983.

Richard, Pablo. "Teología En La Teología de La Liberación." In *Mysterium Liberationis: Conceptos Fundamentales de La Teología de La Liberación*, edited by Ignacio Ellacuría and Jon Sobrino, 12. Vol. 1. Madrid: Editorial Trotta, 1990.

Sanders, James. "Hermeneutics." In *Concise Encyclopedia of Preaching*, edited by Richard Lischen and William H. Willimon, 175–77. Louisville: Westminster John Knox, 1995.

Tisdale, Leonora T. *Preaching as Local Theology and Folk Art*. Minneapolis: Fortress, 1997.

The Hermeneutics of African Caribbean Homiletics

Carol Tomlin[1]

THE PURPOSE OF THIS chapter is to explore the meeting points of African Caribbean homiletics through hermeneutical lenses. It will identify the distinct characteristics of African Caribbean Pentecostal homiletics and its shared features with global Pentecostalism. The chapter will first contextualize African Caribbean Pentecostalism situated in Britain and then draw attention to the theological and educational background of the clergy as a backdrop for the analysis.

The exportation of Pentecostalism from North America to the Caribbean, especially Jamaica, is critical in charting African Caribbean Pentecostalism in Britain. It landed on the shores of Jamaica by 1910 but did not make a huge impact until after the Second World War, when it became the fastest growing religious movement. The religious landscape of Jamaica up until that time saw historic denominations in the form of Anglican churches and other spiritual expressions—such as Myal, Cumina, Revival Zion, and Pocomania—that bring together elements of African and European religious traditions. The rise of Pentecostalism was paralleled with the decline of groups such as Cumina, etc. In general, white American missionaries in Jamaica were instrumental in its initial development, but since the early 1950s, its rapid growth was in the main due to the leadership of indigenous ministers who became Pentecostals whilst working in the United States. When these ministers returned to Jamaica, they established indigenized Pentecostal

---

1. Carol Tomlin's essay was previously published as chapter 4 in Tomlin's *Preach It: Understanding African Caribbean Preaching* (London: SCM, 2019) and is used with permission.

churches, which combined the status of Christian denominations with revivalists and indigenous cults. Morrish gives an insightful account of the syncretistic cults in Jamaica, postulating that the African-European roots of these cults were even more evident than the bicultural origins of American slave religions.[2] Pentecostalism was particularly amenable to indigenisation because of its syncretistic nature.

Significantly, Pentecostalism from Jamaica to Britain can be traced to the mass migration of the Caribbean population during the post-war period. The early migrants, commonly referred to as the Windrush generation, were instrumental in developing African Caribbean Pentecostal churches in Britain. It is relevant at this point to briefly explain that African Caribbean churches are a part of what is currently referred to in Britain as black majority churches (BMCs). These churches tend to be Pentecostal or Charismatic and delineated by two groups: The first comprise congregants predominantly from an African background, and the second, Caribbean, also referred to as African Caribbean. Though similar in some respects, the latter generally has a longer history in Britain, both ecclesiastically and in academic texts. Recent scholarly writing in the field of African Caribbean Pentecostal churches can be seen, for instance, in the work of Beckford, Aldred, Adedibu, Reddie, and Muir;[3] however, the hermeneutical framework for preaching in these churches are relatively under-researched.[4]

The early migrant Caribbean preachers in Britain were largely uneducated and untrained in homiletics, and they tended to present sermons from memory and extemporarily without the aid of written notes. The Bible as the "written word" was very often the only source with which reference was made. Individuals with the ability to preach could be "called upon" without prior notice to "deliver/bring the word" and there was the view that one should be ready to "bring the word" at any time, presumably based on the Apostle Paul's invocation to Timothy to "Preach the word! Be ready in season and out of season" (2 Tim 4:2). This practice is virtually outdated in Britain, particularly with the younger generation, many of whom, are increasingly becoming educated theologically through attending courses at institutions of higher education, such as Queens Foundation, Birmingham, and the Universities of Birmingham and Roehampton. Some aspiring ministers have also attended institutions in North America that link to their denomination, such as the Church of God's, Lee University in Cleveland,

---

2. Morrish, *Obeah, Christ, and Rastaman*.

3. See Beckford, *Dread and Pentecostal*; *Documentary and Exorcism*; Aldred, Respect; "Holy Spirit"; Adedibu, *Coat of Many Colors*; Reddie, *Black Theology*; Muir, "Theological Education."

4. See Mullings, "Reading Black."

Tennessee. Others have attended bible schools or courses established by their own local denomination or church. A case in point is Ruach City Church, who have developed their Certificate in Practical Theology. Despite these promising trends, there still remains a paucity of rigorous theological education.

Muir suggests that the reason for the lack of theological training among Pentecostals in general is historical and equally applicable to blacks and whites as they often share similar concerns regarding theological education.[5] He explains that in the formative years of the Pentecostal movement there was reluctance to "privilege education." Indeed, in many quarters there was outright antipathy and animosity towards the emergence of liberal theology from the nineteenth century that questioned the inerrancy of Scripture, the God of miracles, and the dynamic power for missions evidenced in Spirit baptism. For Pentecostals who maintain a fundamental view of Scripture, this resulted in a "dead church," powerless to reach the "unsaved" and spiritually ill equipped for the "end time" mission to usher in the Kingdom. Muir also believes that this challenge continues in Pentecostal/Charismatic practice to the present day.[6] This issue has implications for the hermeneutics of Pentecostal preaching, which shall be discussed with reference to African Caribbean homiletics in the remainder of this chapter.

African Caribbean Pentecostal Homiletics

The shared framework in the liturgy of African Caribbean Pentecostalism provides a platform for its convergence in preaching. The preaching event is the most prominent feature of African Caribbean Pentecostal ecclesiology and one which also plays a pivotal role in Pentecostalism generally. Inevitably, African Caribbean preaching mirrors aspects of global Pentecostalism, but there are distinct characteristics as well. It must be stressed that attempts to posit a matrix of preaching has to consider its multifarious nature for preaching is also dependent upon individual personalities and proclivities, which diverge from mere reductionist analyses. However, we will outline African Caribbean Pentecostal homiletics, especially contemporarily, by focusing on the following ten broad areas:

1. Expressive and performative nature of preaching.
2. Deductive versus inductive sermons.
3. Approaches to sermonic preparation and delivery.

---

5. Muir, "Theological Education," 3.
6. Muir, "Theological Education," 2.

4. Pentecostal hermeneutics and theological education.
5. Plenary view of the Bible and interpreting biblical texts.
6. Preaching in context.
7. Worldliness themes in preaching.
8. Attire as signifiers.
9. Life situation and serial preaching.
10. Influence of prosperity theology.

1. Expressive and Performative Nature of Preaching

The premier homiletician, Fred Craddock, makes an important point that both the content and method of preaching are pertinent to theology.[7] This is useful to bear in mind when analyzing any type of homiletic model, including those in the Pentecostal tradition. Focusing on the early Pentecostals, MacRobert states that Christianity was expressed in narrative theology, the shout, the song, the dance, and distinctive African motor behaviors, accompanied by the polyrhythmic clapping of hands, stamping of feet, and swaying of bodies.[8] He further explains that such worship is found among Jamaican Pentecostals and replicates the patterns found in West Africa. In black Pentecostal preaching in general, there is a high display of expressive behaviors and a "certain license of freedom in the preaching moment."[9] Interestingly, MacRobert's earlier work centered on the British context, drawing attention to the degree of culturally expressive behaviors dependent on the denominational affiliation.[10] African Caribbean churches under the leadership of white Pentecostals in North America (for example, New Testament Church of God) appear to be more restrained compared with Oneness groups headed by African Americans, where there is no pressure to conform to the norms and expectations of white Pentecostals.[11]

Equally, while cultural manifestations are demonstrated cross-generationally, at times, some of the second and third generation seem to be more reserved in their worship compared with their forebearers; but this still depends, to some extent, on the type of church they attend. This variance may also be attributed in part to the hybridity of their culture, which can

7. See Craddock, *As One Without Authority*.
8. See McRobert, "Black Pentecostalism"; "Black Roots of Pentecostalism."
9. LaRue, *I Believe I'll Testify*, 89.
10. See MacRobert, "African and European Roots."
11. MacRobert, "African and European Roots," 11.

be considered a fusion of aspects of both British and Caribbean. However, the expressive behaviors described by MacRobert are prevalent in preaching and can be seen cross-generationally, irrespective of denominational affiliations. Ministers that are highly rated seem to be those who are outstanding communicators with the ability to utilize distinctive African communicative styles, such as call-response, whereby an audience either echoes or adds to the utterance of a speaker or performer.

Preachers who communicate biblical texts are expected to bring "the word" to life, and, in this sense, preaching can be seen as performative. Writers such as Thomas explain the performative nature of sermons.[12] The preacher is expected to embody the word of God, including head or rationality, heart or emotionally, and body or physically. The word is embodied and brought to life or incarnated in the total being of the preacher, not solely confined to the rational part of his or her being; hence, the preaching act can accurately be described as performative.

2. Deductive Versus Inductive Sermons

In terms of both its exegetical undergirding and sermonic structure, deductive preaching has been established as normative practice. Based on the Enlightenment's rationalistic, hermeneutical paradigm, this homiletic mode seeks to filter biblical texts into propositions, irrespective of their original form or genre. Meanings of texts are conveyed to listeners in a linear fashion, and sermons progress sequentially, with clear argumentation, concluding with specific applications for the listening audience—a seemingly mono-logic sermon style which affirms the authoritarian role of the preacher, disconnected from the audience. Commenting on Craddock's work, Cosgrove and Edgerton state that he recognized that the traditional, deductive, three-point sermon was rapidly losing ground in the early 1970s and that this led to his new method.[13] Craddock's New Homiletic proposal of the "inductive model" engages listeners from passive recipients into active participants. This heightens the listeners' role in the preaching event and transfers the making of meaning of the text from solely the preacher to that of the listener. In this way, the preaching event becomes dialogic, unlike (as he sees it) the flat, lacklustre, and passive listening of deductive

---

12. Thomas, *Introduction to the Practice*, 88.
13. Cosgrove and Edgerton, *In Other Words*.

sermons,[14] diverging from the old, traditional, and kerygmatic preaching of Karl Barth.[15]

LaRue contends that Craddock's concerns regarding the deductive, three-point sermons are justifiable but primarily addressed to white preachers in mainline churches and that in the black church, the deductive, three-point sermon did not have the same negative impact as it had on some white congregations. Even though LaRue writes about African American sermons, his ideas are equally applicable to African Caribbean Pentecostals. As LaRue states:

> The idea of a boring preacher or an overly authoritarian preacher thundering broadsides to a disconnected, discontent audience is not what the three-point sermon wrought in the best of black preaching. Not then, not now. The three-point sermon in the black church is clothed in imagination, humour, playful engagement, running narrative, picturesque speech, and audible participation on the part of the congregation.[16]

LaRue advocates that the three-point sermon is not the issue but rather that the *boring* three-point sermon that must be rejected. He rightly affirms that black preachers must be exposed to other methods of preaching.

Jiménez argues that the deductive style often found in Pentecostal preaching in the Caribbean, with its stress on individualism and authoritarianism, is a relic of colonialism.[17] During the colonial times, it invested certain individuals with authoritative powers that maintained the social order—including slavery. He calls for the deductive preaching style to be deconstructed, aimed at liberating people, and for a critical dialogue with the New American Homiletic school.

3. Approaches to Sermonic Preparation and Delivery

It is important to return to the theme of orality, discussed in the introduction of this chapter, to underscore the act of Pentecostal preaching among African Caribbean clergy as it is critical to spiritual formation, consigning significance to orality. Hollenweger asserts that Pentecostal theology

---

14. Craddock, *As One Without Authority*, 55.
15. For further discussion on the New Homiletic, see Gibson, "Defining the New Homiletic."
16. LaRue, *I Believe I'll Testify*, 97–98.
17. Jiménez, "If You Just Close Your Eyes."

emerged out of the African American oral context.[18] It can be argued that the early Pentecostals' emphasis on orality has continued globally, well into the twenty-first century. As Alexander states:

> This orality held important implications for the development and spread of Pentecostalism, which for the most of its own history has been conceived of as largely an oral tradition. Even today the global Pentecostal movement has seen its greatest growth within cultures that incorporate an oral communication mode.[19]

Martin confirms the critical role that preaching played in the Pentecostal movement and opines that Pentecostalism's oral nature may have been diluted to some degree in the West as a consequence of education, but he confirms that preaching still remains a dominant aspect of Pentecostalism.[20] The inherent oral nature of Pentecostal preaching is sometimes viewed as a somewhat distant relative to the more formal, homiletic practice found in historic churches and inconspicuous by its absence in mainstream literature. This is also similar to the perceived superiority of written over oral literacy. It must be stressed that all sermonic approaches are equally valid and there is much to learn from differing approaches.

A popular method for sermon preparation and delivery in mainline denominations—such as the Anglican tradition—is to preach by way of a lectionary, where there is a predetermined, structured cycle of the liturgical year with associated Scripture readings, starting on Advent Sunday, at the end of November or beginning of December. The cycle of readings takes place over a three-year period, and there are typically four types of readings from the Bible. The first is taken from the Old Testament, the second is usually a Psalm, the third is from the New Testament, and the final reading comes from one of the four Gospels. The sermon is usually the theme for that Sunday or provides an explanation of the reading. The lectionary is invaluable in helping ministers prepare sermons and provides a basis from which they can work. Many lectionary preachers tend to execute their sermons in a thematic way, drawing from the texts, the Christian year, and the particular time and circumstances of their congregation's life. In contrast, a thematic approach for Pentecostals does not rely on a structured cyclical year, time, etc., as they do not subscribe to a lectionary approach. According to Thomas, whose findings are from his research of the homiletic practices of twelve black Pentecostal churches in the South London area,

18. Hollenweger, "Critical Tradition of Pentecostalism."
19. Alexander, *Black Fire*, 43.
20. Martin, "Introduction."

the lectionary can serve as a hermeneutical framework to provide a more systematic approach to preaching.[21]

Lectionary preachers believe in the role of the Holy Spirit, reflecting the ideals of Christianity globally, but sermons tend to be tied to the liturgical year. African Caribbean clergy, however, maintain that the Holy Spirit should be at liberty to change the direction of the sermon completely, including the topic, theme, or actual content, which sometimes happens minutes before the actual delivery of a sermon. This author has observed some excellent sermons that were unprepared beforehand. On the one hand, as Thomas asserts, the Holy Spirit should be present in sermon preparation, and one should not have to wait until mounting the pulpit to gain inspiration. On the other hand, he contends, the lectionary preachers should be conscious of the Holy Spirit's role to change the direction of the sermon or topic if necessary, and the lectionary should not be strictly adhered to when mounting the pulpit to deliver the homily.[22] Clearly, there is much to glean from each method of sermon presentation.

A common approach to preaching in general is the expository method, deriving from the Latin word "setting forth" or "making accessible," where the content and theme of the homily progresses in a linear way. The aim of this kind of sermon is to faithfully illuminate a message from scripture by making it accessible to contemporary hearers. There are two central principles in expository preaching. The first is that the authority of scripture in the pulpit is paramount. In other words, the preacher's message must authenticate the scripture. The preacher or expositor attempts to understand the biblical text on its own merit, apart from personal inclination or doctrinal principles. The second relates to the clarity of the preacher's message, in that it should be clearly expressed in language using simple logic, comprehensible to everyone.

There are two principal types of expository preaching: verse-by-verse exposition and thematic exposition. In verse-by-verse expository preaching, the preacher selects a passage, divides it into smaller, consumable units of thought, and then proceeds with an exposition of each verse in a systematic manner. The exposition of each verse reflects a coherent biblical theme or spiritual truth through the interrelationship and application of ideas. In thematic expository preaching, the preacher draws the sermon's theme from the biblical text but reveals that theme in whatever mode seems relevant to making the message coherent to congregants. It is distinguishable from verse-by-verse exposition in that the expositor moves in and out of the

---

21. Thomas, "Has the Lectionary a Place," 3.
22. Thomas, "Has the Lectionary a Place," 4.

biblical text in a way that is not necessarily verse-by-verse.[23] It would appear that the preaching most revered by white British Pentecostals historically and presently tends to be expository with a sequential exegetical approach.[24]

In general, a basic approach to preaching is the developmental one, where the sermon contains one central idea or main aim that is worked out through a series of a few progressive stages by which the idea or purpose reaches to its climax. In contrast, the homiletic approach of the first-generation Caribbean Pentecostals does not follow this modus operandi but is extemporaneous and without notes, as briefly mentioned at the beginning of this chapter. It is also episodic. According to Graves, the episodic approach to preaching is based on a series of vignettes, stitched together like a quilt.[25] David Buttrick's seminal book, *Homiletic*, informs current thinking on episodic preaching. Rather than viewing the sermon as consisting of an introduction and three points, Buttrick conceives the sermon as a sequence of moves which combine to communicate an idea or evoke a response in the listening audience. He articulates that there should be no more than six different topics in sequence. The sermons of the Windrush generation are episodic both in terms of the Buttrick's conception and the actual style of preaching. In some cases there are several "moves" that appear at times to be unrelated. Links between topics tend to be marked by intonation, and coherent strategies connecting points are not always explicitly stated. This type of organizing principle in verbal texts represents an African construct and as Draper and Mtata eloquently state, "The collective representation of oral tradition in performance is what constitutes African religious worldviews, which are usually implicit and assumed to be known rather than explicitly stated."[26]

Implicit themes are inferred from a series of concrete anecdotes. This episodic style of preaching, a departure from the linear homiletic model, has led to criticisms by some of the second generation: that the content and exposition of sermons by the first generation are unstructured and lacking in thematic clarity. The second and third generations still retain an episodic approach to a great extent, but due to enhanced education and theological training, it is combined with a more developmental method. A few individuals preach from memory and without notes, whilst many depend or at least utilize notes as an aide-memoire. Within this framework of preaching, there is a great deal of improvisation and spontaneity.

23. Newton Jr., "Implications of Harry Emerson Fosdick."
24. Kay, "Ecclesial Dimension of Preaching."
25. Graves, *Fully Alive Preacher*, 15.
26. Draper and Mtata, "Orality, Literature, and African Religions," 1.

It is useful to mention that contemporary preachers will sometimes encourage congregations to take notes if they are explaining certain theological concepts, such as justification. Both young and middle-aged congregants sometimes make notes based on the sermon. This is indicative of a more literary approach to biblical learning, which was not undertaken by the first generation, many of whom only had basic literary skills and therefore relied on memory to engage with sermonic texts. Alternatively, note-taking is conducted when congregants consider the sermonic discourse to be more didactic, which they are able to gauge from the presentation of the homily.

Within the African Caribbean preaching genre, there is a significant amount of sound and motion, where spiritual energy is released in a synergy of movement between the minister and congregants.[27] Preachers who demonstrate a high level of intensity in their discourse, often marked by this synergy, are viewed as more "anointed" or spiritual. Congregants base sermonic satisfaction on the delivery of the text engaging the African communication framework as well as the content of the actual homily. Sometimes there is insufficient theological engagement through study and an over-reliance on the enabling "power" of the Holy Spirit. Pentecostals may well heed the often quoted advice of the Apostle Paul, "Study to shew thyself approved unto God, a workman that needeth not to be ashamed, rightly dividing the word of truth" (2 Tim 2:15, KJV). Nevertheless, for Pentecostal preachers, the Divine (the Holy Spirit) hermeneutics must mediate insights of Scripture.

4. Pentecostal Hermeneutics and Theological Education

The primacy of the Bible is the cornerstone for the Christian faith. Ecclesiastic leadership would concur with Long's description that normative biblical preaching should be where the Bible is the major text.[28] In Pentecostalism, the interpretation of the text is coupled with supernatural and experiential spirituality. Cox observes the underlying mystical elements of Pentecostalism compared with established denominations.[29] The belief in the supernatural reflects the underlying hermeneutics of Pentecostal homiletics and the supernatural phenomenon of speaking in tongues in Acts 2 is not merely seen as an historical account. In the African Caribbean faith community, the supernatural is unconsciously translated through the lens of the African worldview, with a tendency to see spirituality in every aspect

27. Sutcliffe and Tomlin, "Black Churches."
28. Long, *Witness of Preaching*, 6.
29. Cox, *Fire from Heaven*, 92.

of life. For Caribbean Pentecostals, spiritual battles and the demonic realm are very real, given credence by the popular biblical verse, "For we wrestle not against flesh and blood, but against principalities, against powers, against the rulers of the darkness of this world, against spiritual wickedness in high places" (Eph 6:12, KJV). The battle between righteousness and evil is seen as a constant one. Whilst Pentecostals in general berate the "wiles" or "schemes" of the devil, in African Caribbean Pentecostalism, evil can also be seen in "obeah" (Jamaican term for witchcraft) and individuals being "set upon" through the medium of obeah or witchcraft, seen as an integral fabric of the spirit world practiced by a few non-Christians. The belief in satanic conflict and the Christian's ability to be "victorious" in conquering demonic onslaught is revealed in some of the "old time" choruses and even contemporary songs. Take the following choruses:

> *Move satan move, let me pass, move satan move let me pass*
> *Move satan move, let me pass*
> *For I am born again*
> *I'm saved and sanctified.*
> *Move satan move let me pass*

(Jamaican chorus).

> *In the name of Jesus, in the name of Jesus, we have the victory.*
> *In the name of Jesus, in the name of Jesus, satan will have to flee,*
> *tell me who can stand before us when we go in Jesus' name, Jesus,*
> *Jesus, precious Jesus, we have the victory*

(Origins unknown).

Regarding doctrine, Pentecostals globally tend to focus on historical books rather than didactic works, often seen in their preference for the books of Luke and Acts. Pentecostal preachers tend to read the New Testament through Lukan eyes, especially through the lens focused on the book of Acts. One of the reasons for the over-emphasis on the Luke/Acts frame amongst Pentecostals, including African Caribbean, could be due to the missionary character of the Pentecostal movement from its beginning, following Jesus' charge to preach the gospel to everyone (Mark 16:15).[30]

Throughout the varied Christian denominations, the tools to exegete and clearly present scriptural truths by clergy are seen as keys for enhancing the spiritual depth of congregants. For many African Caribbean Pentecostals, the degree of spiritual insight is not simply measured by biblical hermeneutics but rather as indicated by the presentation of those ideas. Speaking

30. Adedibu, *Coat of Many Colors*, 142–43.

of African American preaching, which, in this sense, can be equally applicable to the British Caribbean context, Larue says that although it has its imperfections, it continues to be regarded in many circles "as the most vibrant, imaginative, and communicatively effective preaching on the scene today."[31] But there is plenty of "questionable antics" and even "heresy" as well. The latter point is especially significant as laity tends to regard the clergy as authoritative interpreters of Scripture.

Pentecostal preaching in general can be charged with being a site for indiscriminating hermeneutics. Asamoah-Gyadu identifies "proof-texting" as an approach to preaching whereby biblical texts are often taken out of context, which may produce erroneous views on theological matters.[32] Consequently, Pentecostal hermeneutics has been disparaged, and writers such as Fee claim that Pentecostals are known for their weak hermeneutics.[33] Pentecostal ministers globally sometimes misinterpret the meaning of certain biblical texts due to a lack of proper grammatico-historical exegesis, which takes into account the common rules of grammar, syntax, and historical context.

Nonetheless, many Pentecostals, including African Caribbean clergy, will not want to accept reductionist hermeneutics, focusing on grammatico-historical exegesis, to the exclusion of a pneuma-centric one. Any robust application of hermeneutics will not obliterate the major tenets of Pentecostalism. As Adedibu states, "In recent years there has been much exegesis from the pens of black majority churches in Britain, but this is a reflection of a global renaissance amongst Pentecostal scholars."[34]

The accusation levelled at Pentecostals of having an uncritical theology is not without merit, however, and reticence about certain types of theological education is undoubtedly a factor (although in America this is not necessarily the case, evidenced by the plethora of seminaries and institutions such as Oral Roberts University). As previously mentioned, some Pentecostal ministers in Britain are theologically untrained, but increasingly, many are gaining relevant qualifications. For African Caribbean Pentecostal clergy, the lack of theological education impacting their hermeneutics must be seen in light of the wider debate surrounding the academic performance of black Caribbean students, particularly males. Many of the first generation were, by and large, uneducated, and many of the second fared little better

---

31. LaRue, *I Believe I'll Testify*, 418.
32. Asamoah-Gyadu, "African Charismatics."
33. Fee, *Gospel and Spirit*, 83.
34. Adedibu, *Coat of Many Colors*, 139.

in compulsory education.³⁵ Fortunately, some acquired academic qualifications as young or mature adults.³⁶ Given that many of the first-generation preachers, overwhelmingly male, did not possess formal theological literacy skills, this led to a dependence on oratorical ability rather than systematic theological knowledge. It can be argued that despite increased theological educational provision for the second-generation, they are very often not in a position to sustain courses of study due to financial constraints. Furthermore, African Caribbean people as a group tend to be at the lower end of the social strata economically, irrespective of their academic credentials. Another important factor is that these ministers invariably lead churches in deprived urban areas, thus affecting their remunerations and thereby impeding higher education aspirations.

5. Plenary View of the Bible and Interpreting Biblical Texts

Regardless of the extent of theological education, hermeneutically, Pentecostals tend to have a plenary verbal inspiration view of the Bible—a belief that every word is inspired by the Holy Spirit of God. Even though Pentecostals believe that the Scripture is divinely inspired, it can be argued that human beings do not always interpret it accurately, irrespective of the theological persuasion. African Caribbean Pentecostals have an extremely high view of the Bible, and Sturge points to the pre-eminence of Scripture for black Pentecostals who see the written Word as having similar characteristics to the incarnate Word, Jesus Christ (1 John).³⁷ Sturge highlights the supremacy of Scripture for this group, substantiated by a key verse in 2 Timothy, stating, "All Scripture is given by inspiration of God" (2 Tim 3:16, KJV/NJKV).³⁸ The view of the Bible as infallible or inerrant does not imply that various versions of Scripture are error free. It is precisely this reason why many Pentecostals globally place the Authorized Version of the Bible, popularly referred to as the King James, as the foremost text, viewed by some as the version that is least contaminated. This was also the version that was first introduced historically around the globe. Some contemporary African Caribbean ministers, including the present writer, often encourage congregants to read other versions, but in most churches, preachers tend to quote from King James during sermons. The communicative patterns of

---

35. See Rampton, "West Indian Children."
36. See Rhamie, Eagles Who Soar.
37. Sturge, *Look What the Lord Has Done!*, 132.
38. Sturge, *Look What the Lord Has Done!*, 132.

African Caribbean interlocutors, utilizing metaphoric and symbolic language, make certain texts from King James that sound poetic in nature easier to retain and recite, corresponding to the lyrical quality of their speech.

LaRue confirms that black preachers view the Scriptures, although composed of different materials, as the revelation of the narrative of the history of salvation.[39] God is believed to be the author of the Bible, and the Scriptures, though written by several authors, speak in some direct way on God's behalf. Thus, by extension, God may be seen as the real author. The idea that certain texts can be relegated is abhorrent to the majority of African Caribbean Pentecostal preachers. LaRue rightly asserts that black preachers believe that the attentive interpreter can hear God speaking directly through the text and there is often convergence between the preacher and the events of the text. He goes on to state that:

> Blacks are often not given credit for the nuancing they do in this paradigm. To say that one expects to be addressed by God through Scripture is not to suggest that Scripture must be taken literally in all its parts. Instead, the search that drives the desire to understand and interpret the Scriptures grows out of the belief that somehow, in some manner, God is speaking through a particular text. The finds of historical-critical research are of immense benefit to blacks in their quest to hear the voice of God. Blacks simply refuse to relegate that voice strictly to the historical past.[40]

Sturge argues convincingly that an all-powerful God has the divine ability to communicate his thoughts and wishes to his children. Although this view should not be incredulous, it can, as he points out, create a "self-generating hermeneutic," according every verse with the same worth.[41] Unfortunately, the fundamentalist position adopted by Pentecostals has too often been synonymous with indoctrination and lack of criticality, confused with non-negotiable, essential Christian beliefs that, as Sturge rightly states, should be the basis for those professing the Christian faith.[42] The Pentecostal tendency to imbibe a literalist approach in their hermeneutics can lead to selectivity of certain biblical texts without insufficient consideration for the context of the passage, but African Caribbean Pentecostals, as Sturge articulates, are not literalist, theologically speaking.

---

39. LaRue, *I Believe I'll Testify*, 123.
40. LaRue, *I Believe I'll Testify*, 123–24.
41. Sturge, *Look What the Lord Has Done!*, 133.
42. Sturge, *Look What the Lord Has Done!*, 133.

The nature of their culture has created a heightened sense of symbolism and metaphor. There is no doubt when Scripture speaks about "break[ing] up your fallow ground" (Jer 4:3), this is understood to mean "preparing our hearts for a renewed fruitful and living encounter and relationship with God." . . . Some preachers rely heavily on allegory.[43]

It must be emphasized that exegesis of the biblical text is not culturally neutral or objective, and within African Caribbean Pentecostalism, it can be identified by culturally-embedded practices that inform hermeneutical frames. In that sense, employing contextual theology could enhance our understanding of the homiletic practices of African Caribbean Pentecostal clergy.

It is helpful to invoke Ukpong's inculturation hermeneutics, postulating the role of the Bible reader's context in the hermeneutical approaches to the African Caribbean social cultural context.[44] Writing about African biblical scholarship, Upkong advocates that epistemological privilege should be given to the ordinary reader and ordinary Pentecostal clergy. Hence, "The primacy of the reading activity is located not among theologians working in isolation but [rather] among theologians working among communities of ordinary people—it is the ordinary people that are accorded the epistemological privilege."[45] It could be argued that a hermeneutics grounded in theology, drawing on other relevant disciplines, such as history and sociology, and coupled with robustly documenting the voices of African Caribbean Christian and their interpretation of the sacred text might be beneficial for both ministers and biblical scholars.

To that end, writers such as Beckford advocate that theologians must consider black experiences to engage with theology.[46] Adedibu explains that black Pentecostals approach the Scripture with various pre-understanding and suppositions that are inextricably linked with prior experience, which might implicate the interpretation of the text.[47] Personal experience qualitatively impacts on how we all interpret the Bible. Mullings presents an innovative framework and argues that given the primacy of the Bible for African Caribbean Christians in Britain, it is important that a critical reading of biblical texts should be undertaken through the lens of their experiences.[48]

---

43. Sturge, *Look What the Lord Has Done!*, 133.
44. Ukpong, "Inculturation Hermeneutics," 19.
45. Ukpong, "Inculturation Hermeneutics," 20.
46. Beckford, "Dread and Rhatid."
47. Adedibu, *Coat of Many Color*, 138.
48. Mullings, "Teaching Black Biblical Studies," 86.

She introduces black biblical hermeneutics by invoking the work of African-American Hebrew scholar Randall Bailey, who outlines the ways in which the Bible has been interpreted from a dominant, colonial perspective. She utilizes and makes a plea for the Jamaican vernacular and vernacular hermeneutics for critical engagement of the Scriptures "through an assessment of the Bible Society of the West Indies' work, 'A Who Run Tings?'—translated passages of the Gospels into Jamaican (otherwise known as patois)."[49] The relevance of the Jamaican language or voice in preaching and how it represents biblical themes are critical in understanding the hermeneutics found in black Caribbean Pentecostal churches.

6. Preaching in Context

Preaching in context refers to the circumstances out of which preaching emerges. Preaching does not operate in a social, cultural, or theological vacuity but rather is appropriated in particular contexts, and African Caribbean Pentecostal preaching has to be seen within the broader spectrum of Pentecostalism historically. Scholars such as Robert Mapes Anderson view early Pentecostalism as arising from the extreme social tensions among the poor and dispossessed caused by the shift from an agrarian to an industrial society.[50] He argues that their belief in the imminent, apocalyptic return of Jesus Christ brought order to chaotic lives and alleviated social pressures. Similarly, the first generation of Caribbean Pentecostals, who inherited a heaven-bound theology, experienced arduous circumstances resulting from the post-slavery and post-colonial societies from which they came. This theology is also reflected in many of the Jamaican "old time" choruses demonstrated by the examples below—apart from the fourth one, which can also be found in the African American context:

> *My home is in heaven, just waiting for me*
> *And when I reach there, how happy I'll be*
> *My home is in heaven, no rent to pay*
> *My Jesus paid it, paid it all for me.*
>
> *I know where I am going, I know*
> *I know where I am going, I know*
> *Joy bells are ringing, happy children are singing*
> *I know where I am going, I know.*

---

49. Mullings, "Teaching Black Biblical Studies," 87.
50. Anderson, *Vision of the Disinherited*, 49.

> *I'm on my way to heaven's land, and I know I never will turn back*
> *By the grace of God, march until I win, I know I never will turn back...*
> *And when I reach that home above, what a happy time that will be*
> *Angel gonna bow their wing and saints are gonna sing around the throne of God*
> *I'm on way to heaven's land...*
>
> *We'll soon be done with troubles and trials*
> *In that home on the other side*
> *I'm gonna shake my hands with elder*
> *I'm tell God's people good morning*
> *I'm gonna sit down beside my Jesus*
> *I'm gonna sit down and rest a little while.*

The second generation preachers are attempting to reconcile the heaven bound thinking of their forebears with living in the here and now of contemporary society. For example, the Black Theology forums organized by The Queen's Foundation, Birmingham, explore a range of topics evidenced in a recent paper, "Preparing the Black Church for the Twenty-First Century," presented by Rev Dr Paul C. Stewart, a pastor from the Church of God of Prophecy.[51]

7. Preaching Against Worldliness

In preparation for the return of Christ, early Pentecostal preachers expressed disapproval of activities considered to be worldly—and thereby sinful—such as consuming alcohol, smoking tobacco, or attending bars. Instead, they encouraged the pursuit of sanctification, holiness, and uncompromised devotion to God. African Caribbean Pentecostal clergy remain committed to these ideals, and members are advised to refrain from "worldly" or social entertainment such as "clubbing."

A popular "old-time" chorus that is sung in contemporary African Caribbean Pentecostal churches illustrates this view.

> *Good-bye world. I'll stay no longer with you*
> *Good-bye pleasures of sin. I'll stay no longer with you*
> *I've made up my mind to go God's way for the rest of my life*
> *I've made up my mind to go God's way for the rest of my life.*

Increasingly, among the younger generation, there is a certain amount of liberality pertaining to participating in certain social activities. It is not unusual for African Caribbean Pentecostals to attend the cinema, which was

---

51. Stewart, "Preparing the Black Church."

viewed with disdain some thirty years ago. However, the holiness roots of Pentecostalism, with its emphasis on being "separated from the world," has been maintained, reflected in the often quoted biblical verse by preachers to "come out from among them and be ye separate" (2 Cor 6:17, KJV).

8. Attire as Signifiers

Moreover, the first Pentecostals at Azusa Street and the successive generations also believed that sanctification was not only displayed inwardly, by the Spirit, but also outwardly, by the clothing worn—especially by women. Restrictions relating to dress have their antecedents in the Holiness dress codes of the nineteenth century. In several white Pentecostal/Charismatic churches in Britain there no longer appears to be an emphasis on female attire, but this is not the case for African Caribbean Pentecostals, evidenced by the numerous discussions and reference in preaching on the topic. According to Beckford attire is another way that black Pentecostals inscribe sanctification on church culture.[52] Both formal and casual wear is a "visual sign" of the sanctified life.

It was only some twenty years ago that during main worship services in churches such as New Testament Church of God, female members had to cover their hair by wearing a scarf or hat. Hat wearing remains a requirement in churches such as First United Bethel Apostolic church, based on the Pauline injunction concerning head covering for women in public worship (2 Cor 11:3–16). It can be argued that this is a misreading and misapplication of the cultural context of the scripture. In some churches, the clergy and church "mothers" (a term used to describe elderly women) still discourage women from wearing certain clothes—such as trousers, cosmetics, and jewellery—so that they can be distinguished from their non-Christian counterparts. Much of this has changed in many African Caribbean contemporary churches; the dress code is now a lot more relaxed. There remains, however, an unwritten code that one should not wear provocative or revealing clothes if one professes to be a committed Christian. It is not unusual for both male and female preachers to remind women of how they should be dressed based on 1 Timothy 2:9, which states that women should dress modestly. In a recent Facebook post, the popular African American female preacher, Prophetess Dr Junita Bynum, forcefully expressed her distaste for some Christian women who wear "tight clothes" in sacred spaces.

---

52. Beckford, *Documentary as Exorcism*, 122.

Several black Pentecostals globally applauded her comments, yet, as Aldred points out, these Pentecostal churches are sites for "ostentatious" dressing.[53]

Reference to attire in preaching is codified for the "sanctified woman," reflecting the commonly held view that a Christian woman should be distinguished from an "unsaved" woman by their dress. Butler's brilliant historical study of African American women in the Church of God in Christ (GOCIC) in North America highlights that dress reveals theological inclination, particularly towards sanctification.[54] Sanctified dressing is perceived as discouraging unwanted male attention and symbolizes sexual purity and consecration. Clothing represents two functions: the first being a disjuncture from the world and the second embodies the idealized "holy" woman. The discourses on women's clothes can be interpreted as sites for oppressive patriarchal practice, which is plausible, but authors such as Toulis draw attention to the complex gendered relationships in the African Caribbean community, where women wield some influence.[55] Furthermore, the ascribed low status of black women in mainstream society on both sides of the Atlantic, relatively speaking, possibly heightens—for some—the modelling of holiness through dress and deportment.[56] Perhaps the discussion could also be viewed from another angle, in that some women's fashion in modern societies are often represented in ways that objectify women, fuelling a hyper-sexualized consciousness, and, in this sense, reference to women's clothing in preaching can also be interpreted as a counter culture to this pervasive, normative phenomenon.

9. Life Situation and Serial Preaching

In the latter years of the twentieth century to the present times, the focus in Pentecostal preaching has shifted away from an over-emphasis on end-time messages and worldliness to some extent. This is possibly to deflect from the charge that Pentecostals were "so heavenly minded they were of little earthly use." Within the African Caribbean context, there have been vociferous calls for African Caribbean preachers to respond to contemporary social-economic and political challenges facing their community. Though the otherworldly messages encoded in Pentecostalism still informs preaching, it is remodelled in life situation and serial preaching. Life situation preaching is associated with the work of Reverend Harry Emerson Fosdick, who

---

53. Aldred, *Respect*, 17.
54. Butler, *Woman in the Church of God*.
55. Toulis, *Believing Identity*.
56. Butler, *Woman in the Church of God*.

regarded preaching and personal counselling as a means to address issues that are "disrupting lives, troubling minds, and burdening consciences."[57] While attempting to address personal issues, it runs the risk of not preaching the Bible as a whole. Serial preaching, on the other hand, is based on a series of themes or topics—such as the kingdom—and is expedient as congregants are informed of the subject in advance. Homilies in several African Caribbean churches inculcate both life situation and serial preaching, and a vast array of topics are presented, ranging from money to the family and relationships, pertinent to living in the here and now. There appears to be a lack, however, of lucid, expository preaching on issues impacting on the African Caribbean community, such as the high rates of teenage pregnancy, the increase in gang culture, and the preponderance of single women, especially in the church. Though areas of concern to ministers, there is a need for a lucid biblical theology to address some of these matters.

10. Influences of Prosperity Theology

Significantly, some of the second and third generation preachers are influenced by the North American prosperity theology or gospel.[58] The prosperity gospel, whose origins are in the Word of Faith movement, has had a profound impact on the global Pentecostal/Charismatic tradition, including African Caribbean Pentecostalism. Critics often portray the prosperity message as preying on marginalized groups with the purpose of financially benefitting its advocates. The "name it and claim it" identification of prosperity theology reveals the disdain meted at this position. Sturge makes a valid point by explaining that this message should not be totally disregarded, despite some of its unsavory aspects, such as the excessively opulent lifestyle of some of its promoters.[59] It does respond to a fundamental human question—what does God, who is all-powerful, have to say to the poor and socially marginalized? In that sense, according to Sturge, prosperity is similar to liberation theology in its intent, but where the two differ is in their responses to social, economic, and political structures. Whereas followers of prosperity theology lean towards the view that capitalistic systems can be utilized for individual transformation, liberationists tend to identify with the poor and attack the system which breeds oppression.[60]

---

57. Newton Jr., "Implications of Harry Emerson Fosdick," iv.
58. Bowler, *Blessed*.
59. Sturge, *Look What the Lord Has Done!*, 138.
60. Sturge, *Look What the Lord Has Done!*, 138–39.

The preaching discourse found in some independent African Caribbean churches attempts to replicate the prosperity theology of African American and Euro-American Pentecostal-type mega churches established by charismatic preachers such as Creflo Dollar and Rod Parsley. These churches provide a fertile ground for the germination of the American "seed sowing," harvesting "abundant blessings" of prosperity in health and wealth, and more so as many well-known Televangelists are often invited to Britain as guest speakers. It could be postulated that the future generation of African Caribbean Pentecostal clergy may become immersed in the "prosperity gospel," and only time will tell. Based on the observations of this writer, it is unlikely to be the case, as prosperity theology appears to be rooted in the "American dream." In Britain, there is no direct equivalent. In addition, social mobility in the United States, resulting in a sizeable and distinct African American middle class population, is in contrast to reports of British Caribbean professionals, who express "reluctance" and "ambivalence" about occupying a dual position of being both black and middle class, despite their emergence.[61] Similarly, the limited career opportunities afforded to working class African Caribbean people may well stem the full tide of the prosperity gospel within the British context in spite of the prosperity themes within preaching.[62]

Summary

The origin of Pentecostal preaching is located in part to the African American context ensuing from the African oral tradition. The present author identifies ten major areas in the homiletics of African Caribbean preaching, including: expressive and performative nature of preaching; deductive versus inductive sermons; approaches to sermonic preparation and delivery; Pentecostal hermeneutics and education; plenary view of the Bible and interpreting biblical texts; preaching in context; worldliness themes in preaching; attire as signifiers; life situation and serial preaching; and influences of prosperity theology.

Preachers communicate theological themes through a range of expressive behaviors that are culturally familiar to congregants. Sermonic preparation, combining a linear and episodic method, provides opportunities for flexible engagement with the scriptures and interaction with the Holy Spirit. The hermeneutical approach of some African Caribbean Pentecostals—congruent of some Pentecostals—can sometimes result in biblical texts being

---

61. See Rollock et al., *Color of Class*.
62. Clark and Drinkwater, *Ethnic Minorities in the Labor Market*.

taken out of context. The preference for the Authorized Version of the Bible by these clergy ties to the metaphoric language of African Caribbean interlocutors. In this Pentecostal sphere, preaching in context historically centers on the challenges experienced by the Windrush generation, who came from post-slavery and post-colonial societies with its attendant challenges. This has led to an eschatological or other worldly view reflecting the theology of the founding fathers of Pentecostalism. Preaching on worldliness and clothes as signifiers of sanctification are inherent, but contemporarily, there has been a shift to life situation and serial preaching. The prosperity message has infiltrated the theology of African Caribbean Pentecostalism, but whether or not it will be fully realized in Britain is yet to be seen.

Bibliography

Aldred, Joe. "The Holy Spirit and the Black Church." In *The Black Church in the Twenty-First Century*, edited by Joe Aldred and K. Ogbo, 45–62. London: Darton Longman Todd, 2010.

———. *Respect: Understanding Caribbean British Christianity*. Peterborough: Epsworth, 2005.

Alexander, Estrelda. *Black Fire: One Hundred Years of African American Pentecostalism*: Downers Grove, IL: InterVarsity, 2011.

Asamoah-Gyadu, Johnson K. *African Charismatics: Current Developments Within Indigenous Pentecostalism in Ghana*. Studies of Religion in Africa 27. Leiden: Brill, 2004.

Babatunde, Adedibu A. *Coat of Many Colors: The Origin, Growth, Distinctiveness, and Contributions of Black Majority Churches to British Christianity*. London: Wisdom Summit, 2012.

Beckford, Robert. *Documentary as Exorcism: Resisting the Bewitchment of Colonial Christianity*. London: Continuum, 2013.

Bowler, Kate. *Blessed: A History of the American Prosperity Gospel*. Oxford: Oxford University Press, 2013.

Butler, Anthea D. *Women in the Church of God in Christ: Making a Sanctified World*. Chapel Hill, NC: University of North Carolina Press, 2007.

Buttrick, David. *Homiletics: Moves and Structures*. Minneapolis: Augsburg Fortress, 1986.

Clark, Ken, and Stephen Drinkwater. *Ethnic Minorities in the Labor Market: Dynamics and Diversity*. Abingdon: Policy, 2007.

Cosgrove, Charles H., and W. Dow Edgerton. *In Other Words: Incarnational Translation for Preaching*. Grand Rapids, MI: Eerdmans, 2007.

Craddock, Fred. *As One Without Authority*. 4th rev. ed. St. Louis, MO: Chalice, 2001.

Draper, Jonathan A., and Kenneth Mtata. "Orality, Literature, and African Religions." In *The Wiley-Blackwell Companion to African Religions*, edited by Elias Kifon Bongmba, 97–111. Malden, MA: Blackwell, 2009.

Fee, Gordon D. *Gospel and Spirit: Issues in New Testament Hermeneutics*. Peabody, MA: Hendrickson, 2006.

Gerloff, Roswith. *A Plea for British Black Theologies: The Black Church Movement in Britain and Its Transatlantic Cultural and Theological Interaction with Special Reference to the Pentecostal Oneness (Apostolic) and Sabbatarian Movements.* Studies in the Intercultural History of Christianity 2.77. Frankfurt: Peter Lang, 1992.

Gilbert, Kenyatta. *The Journey and Promise of African American Preaching.* Minneapolis: Fortress, 2011.

Gillborn, David. *Racism and Education: Coincidence or Conspiracy.* London: Routledge Falmer, 2008.

Graves, Mike. *The Fully Alive Preacher: Recovering from Homiletical Burnout.* Louisville: Westminster John Knox, 2006.

Hollenweger, Walter. "The Critical Tradition of Pentecostalism." *JPT* 1 (1992) 7–17.

Jiménez, Pablo A. "If You Just Close Your Eyes: Postcolonial Perspectives on Preaching from the Caribbean." *Homiletic* 40.1 (2015) 22–28.

Johns, Cheryl Bridges. *Pentecostal Formation: A Pedagogy among the Oppressed.* Eugene, OR: Wipf & Stock, 2010.

Kay, William, K. "The Ecclesial Dimension of Preaching." In *Toward a Pentecostal Theology of Preaching*, edited by Lee Roy Martin, 200–215. Cleveland, TN: CPT, 2015.

LaRue, Cleophus, J. *I Believe I'll Testify: The Art of African American Preaching.* Kindle ed. Louisville: Westminister John Knox, 2011.

Long, Thomas G. *The Witness of Preaching.* Louisville: Westminister John Knox, 2016.

MacRobert, Iain. "African and European Roots of Black and White Pentecostalism Britain." Paper presented at the Research Conference on the Pentecostal and Charismatic Movements in Europe, University of Birmingham, April 27–28, 1984.

———. "Black Pentecostalism: Its Origins, Functions, and Theology." PhD diss., University of Birmingham, 1989.

———. "The Black Roots of Pentecostalism." In *African American Religious Thought: An Anthology*, edited by Cornel West and Eddie Claude Jr., 616–28. Louisville: Westminster John Knox, 2003.

Martin, Lee Roy. *Toward a Pentecostal Theology of Preaching.* Cleveland, TN: CPT, 2015.

Muir, David. "Theological Education and Training among British Pentecostals and Charismatics." Paper presented for Churches Together in England (CTE), London, February 2015.

Mullings, L. J. "Reading Black: Language and Biblical Interpretation in a Black British Context." In *Text and Community: Essays in Member of Bruce M. Metzge*, edited by J. Harold Ellens, 79–102. Vol 1. Sheffield: Sheffield Phoenix, 2007.

———. "Teaching Black Biblical Studies in the UK: Special Issues for Consideration and Suggested Hermeneutical Approaches." *Discourse: Learning and Teaching in Philosophical and Religious Studies* 8.2 (2010) 81–126.

Newton, Willie, Jr. "The Implications of Harry Emerson Fosdick's Life-Situation Preaching for African-American Preachers." DMin thesis, Divinity School of Duke University, 2016.

Rampton, Anthony. *West Indian Children in Our Schools: Interim Report of the Committee of Inquiry into the Education of Children from Ethnic Minority Groups.* London: HMSO, 1981.

Reddie, Anthony. *Black Theology.* London: SCM, 2014.

Rhamie, Jasmine. *Eagles Who Soar: How Black Learners Find the Path to Success*. Stoke-on-Trent: Trentham, 2007.

Rollock, Nicole. "The Black Middle Class: A Contradiction in Terms?" Seminar for "Race" and Education: Identities and Attitudes: British Education Research Association (BERA), University of Warwick, September 1–4, 2010.

Rollock, Nicole, et al. *The Color of Class: The Educational Strategies of the Black Middle Class*. Abingdon, Oxon: Routledge, 2015.

Stewart, Paul. "Preparing the Black Church for the Twenty-First Century." Paper presented at the Black Theological Forum for Queen's Theological Foundation, Birmingham, June 25, 2015.

Sturge, Mark. *Look What the Lord Has Done! An Exploration of Black Christian Faith in Britain*. Queensway, Bletchley, UK: Scripture Union, 2006.

Taylor, Patrick, ed. *Nation Dance: Religion, Identity, and Cultural Difference in the Caribbean*. Bloomington: Indiana University Press, 2001.

Thomas, Frank A. *Introduction to the Practice of African American Preaching*. Nashville, TN: Abingdon, 2016.

Thomas, Samuel. "The Lectionary." *The Preachers: The College of Preachers* (April 2014) 3–4.

Toulis, Nicole R. *Believing Identity: Pentecostalism and the Mediation of Jamaican Ethnicity and Gender in England*. Oxford: Berg, 1997.

Ukpong, Justin S. "Inculturation Hermeneutics: An African Approach to Biblical Interpretation." In *The Bible in a Word Context: An Experiment in Contextual Hermeneutics*, edited by D. Waters and L. Ulrich, 17–32. Grand Rapids: Eerdmans, 2002.

Trinidad & Tobago Preaching
The Gospel According to Calypso

Catherine E. Williams

EIGHT STUDENTS OF HOMILETICS listened as I shared with them the initial findings of my explorations into the world of calypso at a regional Bible College in Trinidad and Tobago. They were mildly impressed by my topic: "The Gospel According to Calypso." They were taught that the world of calypso was not a place where Trinidadian and Tobagonian Christians did *any* sort of exploration. Gospel and Calypso in the same phrase was tantamount to sacrilege.

I began to identify some of the features of calypso that support its claim as a homegrown rhetorical product: the bold, imaginative, narrative delivery; rustic humor through hyperbole, word play, and picong;[1] pragmatic themes treated concretely using earthy imagery; candor and blunt speech using vernacular and colloquial idioms; communal engagement through call and response; open resistance to an oppressive status quo; and a hermeneutic of experience from the perspective of marginalized people.

As I discussed these elements of the calypso, slipping in and out of local parlance, I noticed a gradual change in their expressions, from polite indifference to disorienting understanding. Much that may truly be called preaching is integral to this local art form of calypso, and the students had been socialized to dismiss this musical public speech as homiletically worthless. I believe such dismissal inhibits these young preachers' discovery of an authentically Trinbagonian[2] pulpit idiom. Such nonacceptance also

---

1. From the French *piquant*, meaning to "cut" or "sting" (Baptiste, *Trini Talk*, 132).
2. Trinbago is a locally-coined, commonly-used name for the twin island Republic

predisposes them to continued, wholesale esteem for and use of imported, ill-fitting homiletical patterns. I believe that somewhere in the pile of post-missionary, post-colonial, Trinbagonian rubble, there *is* a homiletical gem that is the gospel according to calypso.

Early in my religious formation, I had been exposed, like these students, to the same homiletical bias in favor of conventional, formal ways of preaching. However, once I experienced these "classic" forms of preaching in their natural habitat of White congregations in North America, I began to understand just how foreign they were to the Trinbagonian context—particularly in rural or urban areas where a tertiary education is not presumed. Listening to homegrown preachers in those Trinbagonian social locations taught me the value and effectiveness of a homiletic that eschewed mainstream, Euro-centric, literacy-driven methods in favor of a more earthy, pragmatic style where the values of orality infiltrate everyday life.[3] This essay highlights a series of conclusions drawn from ethnographic study of Trinbagonian calypso and grassroots preaching. These are two modes of communication with strong parallels that categorize both of them as "local" to the Republic of Trinidad and Tobago. In the end, there are implications for this type of preaching in a more global setting, particularly in North American classrooms, where homiletical hegemony is presumed.

Trinidad and Tobago

The two islands have distinct colonial histories. What they share in common is their pre-colonial population of native Amerindian peoples. They also share a history of being "discovered" by Christopher Columbus during his political expedition of 1492. Both islands were initially claimed as territories of Spain, but their histories diverged early on. Trinidad continued to fly the Spanish flag for the next three hundred years. Tobago, on the other hand, became an embattled pawn that saw flags hoisted and lowered by Spain, France, Britain, Holland, Courland, and even buccaneers, "operating on a commission issued by the governor of Jamaica."[4]

Ultimately, the British took control of both islands; and it was under British rule that, in 1889, the two islands—just shy of two thousand square miles in total—were brought under unified rule for economic reasons.

---

of Trinidad and Tobago.

3. I use the term mainstream to indicate preaching characterized in part by conventional, North American/European rhetorical theories, and use of identifiable forms associated with key homiletical patterns: expository, inductive, narrative, etc.

4. Williams, *History of the People of Trinidad and Tobago*, 51.

British rule formally ended on August 31, 1962, when the Trinidad & Tobago flag replaced the Union Jack, declaring the country's independence. 1962 thus marks the year Trinbago entered formally into the postcolonial era of its history. Each island has its own historical, sociological, and even cultural distinctions. Although my ethnographic focus is on Trinidad, and the Afro-Trinidadian Christians in particular, the hybridized terms Trinbago and Trinbagonians respect the reality that this is a twin-island republic flying one flag.

Cultural Diversity

Visitors are often surprised by the rich ethnic and cultural diversity of the population. "Trinidadians count among their number the descendants of people from West Africa, India, Europe, China, the Middle East, and those native to the Americas."[5] Each of these groups has added their flavor and ingredient to the callaloo[6] of Trinbagonian citizenry. The population estimate in 2016 stood at 1,220,479. The ethnic breakdown of that total is "East Indian, 35.4 percent; African, 34.2 percent; mixed-other, 15.3 percent; mixed African/East Indian, 7.7 percent; other, 1.3 percent; unspecified, 6.2 percent."[7] The two predominant ethnic groups are Indo-Trinbagonians and Afro-Trinbagonians.

Religious Diversity

Trinbagonian religious affiliations are varied: "Protestant, 32.1 percent; Pentecostal/Evangelical/Full Gospel, 12 percent; Baptist, 6.9 percent; Anglican, 5.7 percent; Seventh-Day Adventist, 4.1 percent; Presbyterian/Congregational, 2.5 percent; other Protestant, 0.9 percent; Roman Catholic, 21.6 percent; Hindu, 18.2 percent; Muslim, 5 percent; Jehovah's Witness, 1.5 percent; other, 8.4 percent; none, 2.2 percent; unspecified, 11.1 percent."[8] Religious influences in Trinidad and Tobago are directly linked to periods of colonization. Trinbagonians owe the Roman Catholic presence to Spanish and French colonization. They owe the Anglican presence to the British. Other Protestant influences are due to the work of Methodist, Moravian, and Baptist missionaries, among others, dispatched to the Caribbean from

---

5. Yelvington, "Introduction," 1.
6. A blended Trinidadian stew, comprised of a spinach base and multiple ingredients.
7. "Trinidad and Tobago."
8. "Trinidad and Tobago."

England, Canada, and the United States. The Muslim faith was introduced both by African slaves and Indian indentured laborers. Most of the Indians who came under the indentured system, however, were of Hindu faith.

Fifteen to twenty years ago, historians reported Roman Catholicism as the dominant expression of Christian faith. It is no longer so. Religious trends have shifted along the lines being reported by today's researchers, who have their eye on the world's southern hemisphere.[9] Now it is the Pentecostal/Evangelical/Full Gospel expression of Christianity that is most rapidly growing. In the context of Trinbago, any of these denominational monikers—Pentecostal, Evangelical, or Full Gospel—may be used synonymously to reflect an expression of Christianity with a high view of Scripture, openness to the charismatic gifts of the Spirit, and conservative theological beliefs, particularly around doctrines of heaven, hell, and personal salvation.

This growing Pentecostal/Evangelical/Full Gospel Protestant demographic is the focus of this essay. The Bible college where I spoke with the students mentioned at the beginning is the West Indies School of Theology (WIST), a school for theological training established in 1946 by missionaries of the Pentecostal Assemblies of Canada. The churches established by this denomination in Trinidad and several other Caribbean islands, were eventually turned over into the hands of local clergy leaders. This transition gave birth to a regional denomination—the Pentecostal Assemblies of the West Indies (PAWI)—in 1964.

Bringing together the preaching of Pentecostals and the artistic genre of the calypso is a bold move for anyone who understands the historical, missionary-generated antipathy most Pentecostal Trinbagonians hold towards Carnival and Calypso. However, looking through the rhetorical lens of the calypso, one can discern a way of proclaiming the good news of Jesus Christ that is faithful to the gospel, even as it is fitting to portions of the country's demographic, which may be called the grassroots. These are people who live and work at the most basic level of society; some might refer to them as the working class or the underclass. Trinidad and Tobago, like many other countries formerly colonized by the British, is an inherently classist society. The persons and communities who find themselves at the bottom of the country's class structure are there primarily because of limited formal education, unemployment or underemployment, and political disenfranchisement. Synonyms such as local, folk, homespun, or indigenous indicate the rootedness of this homiletical approach in the cultural identity of those who self-identify as Afro-Trinbagonians.[10]

---

9. See Jenkins, *Next Christendom*; Pew Research Center, "Global Christianity."

10. Historically both Afro- and Indo-Trinbagonians share a cultural history of

THEOLOGICAL AND BIBLICAL WARRANTS

The dominant homiletical practices taught in Trinbagonian theological institutions were left by a missionary theological legacy that stems from Euro-North American practices in both Evangelical and mainstream, mainline churches. While some of these inherited models of preaching and biblical interpretation are fitting for some Trinbagonian audiences, there are communities that are not well served by these dominant models on account of the rural isolation of such communities from the urbane strata of society. This rural isolation lends itself to an unsophisticated manner of being in the world. Such communities would be considered, in the words of Jesus, "the least of these my brothers and sisters." (Matt 25:40). It was to these "least" that the liberating message of the earthly Jesus was most immediately appealing. The kind of power reversals of which Jesus spoke as he taught about the Reign of God offered light and life-giving hope to the perennially disenfranchised. For "the least," therefore, both the claim of the Gospel and its modes of delivery stand to be critically deconstructed and reconstructed according to a liberating hermeneutic and homiletic that will faithfully and fittingly declare God's good news.[11]

Justo and Catherine González represent a segment of constructive theologians who posit that most of the Bible was written from the perspective of the marginalized. They observe that in the Old Testament it is the weak and relatively powerless nation of Israel that features in divine reversals of a political nature. It is the obscure, politically disenfranchised prophets who issue the oracles of God to the nation's leaders. González sees the same paradigm in the New Testament writings. "Those who hear the gospel gladly are by and large not the powerful within the society of Israel. Rather, they are the fisherfolk, the women, the poor, and those who are marginalized because of their occupations: the tax collectors and the harlots."[12] This perspective justifies every effort preachers make to cultivate

---

being either forcefully or disingenuously transported to the colonies to provide coerced plantation labor. As such, both majority groups are to be found at the grassroots of society. Nonetheless classic calypso is performed predominantly by Afro-Trinbagonians, partly on account of the form's rootedness in slave rebellions and the cultural process of creolization, mostly absent from Indo-Trinbagonian cultural history. The grassroots preaching that mirrors the calypso, however, is more likely to be practiced, with marked effect, in both of the country's majority groups. This study, although it includes broadly the preaching of Indo-Trinbagonians, has limited its analytical scope to Afro-Trinbagonian grassroots preaching.

11. This terminology of "faithful and fitting" is found in the work of Leonora Tubbs Tisdale, particularly in Tisdale, *Preaching as Local Theology and Folk Art*.

12. González and González, *Liberating Pulpit*, 20.

and honor patterns of preaching that issue Christ's call to discipleship in the heart language of society's poor and oppressed.

The compelling variety of biblical genres, the examples of the Hebrew prophets, and the theology of Hebrews 1:1 all give witness to the plurality of ways in which God speaks to God's people. If it is so that God is willing to use modes of communication fitting to the hearers in order to announce God's good news, then we, as proclaimers, are offered a divine model that does not preclude anyone hearing the gospel. I believe it is not enough to simply acknowledge that such a broad-ranging scope of preaching is needful. Homileticians and teachers of preaching do well to afford the preaching of marginalized communities the careful kind of reflection we give to more urbane and mainstream approaches. We do this with humble awareness of God's methodology of paradox, where wise words can be made to seem foolish, while lowly, foolish words can be made to confound the wise (see 1 Cor 1:26–28)

The ultimate theological warrant for this study is Christological; it takes into account the incarnation of the Word. Latina theologian Loida Martell-Otero frames this perspective in her compelling, contextualized understanding of Chalcedonian theology.

> A US Latina/o Christology seeks to be a balanced theology that takes seriously the Chalcedonian claim of Jesus' two natures. As such, it is an incarnational Christology that does not consider Jesus' historical particularity incidental to the good news of salvation. . . . Jesus was killed because he was a *sato* (literally a "mutt") who disturbed the status quo and brought a word of hope to those at the periphery. More importantly, in him, God demonstrated God's steadfast love for those who are in the most peripheral places of society.[13]

It is this irrepressible, incarnate expression of God's love for—and identification with—the least among us that is both a motivating force and a theological warrant. Through such expression and identification, the incarnate Word shines the light of affirmation and hope. It calls out of the shadows a decolonial homiletic that would frame the task of Christian proclamation.[14]

---

13. Martell-Otero, "Who Do You Say I Am?"

14. The concept of decoloniality in this essay is informed by the work of Walter Mignolo. It carries the sense of delinking from oppressive colonial theories, practices, and norms, while claiming the right to employ homiletical methods, and embrace a form and style of public speech, native to the community. Delinking and divesting are important terms to Mignolo.

Calypso and Preaching

Studies of calypso have covered a range of perspectives, including historical (Liverpool, Rohlehr), socio-political (Regis, Phillips), performative (Patton), and rhetorical (Browne, Greaves). The perspective of this essay is uniquely homiletical.[15] As a formally trained musician and practical theologian, I occupy this musico-homiletical vantage point naturally and with great interest. Ostensibly, calypsonians are folk entertainers, yet with rhetorical and theological sensibilities, one could hear and see the proclamatory dynamic of the interplay between singer, musicians, chorus, and audience.

In addition to watching these calypsonians perform, I took the opportunity of speaking with a few of them regarding the spiritual dimension of their work. Without fail, each one acknowledged that their faith and their music could not be bifurcated. They see themselves as messengers, communicating not only to their immediate patrons in live hearing distance but also to a wider audience—those with political and economic hegemony. They see themselves representing a grassroots community whose voices are systematically silenced. As calypsonians, they have mastered an art form that lends itself to extended discourse. Each of these musical orations, as performed on stage, typically lasts six to eight minutes, with four or five verses and a refrain that together encapsulate a succinct, pointed message in metered rhyme. Calypso differs from its musical derivatives, such as Soca, on account of its commitment to story telling. This orientation predisposes the classic calypso toward a slower tempo that facilitates the delivery and understanding of the message proclaimed.

It is this format of crafted, succinct delivery, and this purpose of informing, warning, encouraging, or exposing wrongs that creates, in my mind, a defensible link between calypso and preaching. Many formally trained Trinbagonian preachers may not endorse this connection. Their homiletical formation has been for the most part through seminaries and Bible colleges, in whose syllabi European and North American standard bearers are the dominant voices. These institutions of homiletical learning eschew much of what the calypso's form and content have been associated with, namely the bacchanalian atmosphere of Trinbagonian carnival. Furthermore, calypsonians are typically untrained in the formal art of communication or public speaking; they would hardly be deemed homiletical models by trained communicators. Yet the God of the Bible has a reputation for choosing the foolish things of this world to confound the wise. This same God has chosen to speak to God's people in a variety of ways in

---

15. George Mulrain briefly explores the calypso as a non-traditional yet meaningful hermeneutical lens in Mulrain, "Is There a Calypso Exegesis?"

order to communicate the Divine message as clearly as is needful for Love to be incarnate. Thus if there are elements of Trinbagonian society who may more readily understand and receive the calypso-esque proclamation of the gospel, then the methodology of calypso deserves a place at the homiletical table and merits critical study.

Calypso as Local Music

The Calypso Monarch competition is a highly-charged cultural event, staged each year on Dimanche Gras, the Sunday prior to Ash Wednesday. Dimanche Gras is also the name given to the overall event, which features several displays of prize-winning carnival costumes and award-winning steel bands in addition to the Calypso Monarch competition, in which one winner is selected each year (along with three runners-up). Traditionally, the venue is the Queen's Park Savannah, often simply called "The Savannah," in Trinidad's capital city, Port of Spain. The staging area, where the singers perform, is wide and deep; this accommodates the many skits, props, and signs that are a contemporary feature of the Calypso Monarch competition.

Once the new annual crop of calypsos begins to appear, sometime around November of the year prior to Carnival, the public expects calypsonians will cover the typical range of topics: news-making events, social gossip and commentary, politics, nation-building, and other prime themes. My focus is on the political calypso, with its decolonial thrust. One example that illustrates distinctive features of this genre is the 2015 award-winning rendition of Karene Asche, "Every Knee Shall Bow." Among the striking elements this calypso showcases are (1) candid, concrete treatment of pragmatic content, (2) communal engagement, and (3) a hermeneutic of the socially marginalized.

> I look to the hills from whence my solace comes; aint wielding no sword, my shield is the Lord;
> But some here on earth march to a different drum, yes they live to fight—feel that might is right.
> For those hoping to build their own statues, on pedestals high themselves they perch;
> Humility is the greatest virtue, let them brag and boast, the last shall be first.
>
> **Refrain**
> For all who feel they're almighty, oh so big and powerful, calling themselves 'Majesty'—
> Every knee shall bow.

> *God alone is almighty, he alone is powerful, the one and only majesty,*
> *To him alone I bow.*
> *So whether you are ruler, pharaoh, khalifa, or Lord, some way . . . somehow . . .*
> *Every knee shall bow.*
>
> *And there are those who prey on the weak all day, prefer when you're meek, turn the other cheek;*
> *Only the almighty dollar they obey, see them sell their soul for silver and gold.*
> *Their fortune keeps mounting like a tower, they don't know the meaning of enough;*
> *They like to equate money with power, but things material rust, crumble into dust.*
>
> *For I await the rolling thunder, to hear cymbals clash and trumpets blow!*
> *I believe wrongdoers will go under, like so long ago, back in Jericho*
>
> *I wonder how our leaders sleep at night. Do they ever dream while poor people scream?*
> *The same ones who say they will put the wrong things right,*
> *Once they reach on top become more corrupt.*
> *To the grassroots cries become unconscious, while family and friends they patronize;*
> *And then they wash their hands like Pontius;*
> *Because they in charge, feel they larger than large, warn them. . .*
>
> *[Refrain follows]*
>
> *I call on him in this valley of dry bone; through this veil of death I don't fear no threat.*
> *For all who feel they are the cornerstone, arrogant and proud, head stuck in the cloud—*
> *I remember Nimrod in the Bible, the king who dared to challenge God;*
> *Built his masterpiece the tower of Babel,*
> *Thought he built it well, still it collapsed and fell. Tell them . . .*
>
> *[Refrain follows]*

The calypsonian makes her message repeatedly clear—*it doesn't matter where you are in the social strata or how much fame or wealth you possess, there is coming a time when every person will acknowledge and be humbled before the ultimate sovereignty of God.* The candor of this warning is potent. Unsparing forthrightness is intrinsic to interpersonal Trinbagonian communication and even some public discourse. Candid calypso lyrics reflect the local attitude of Trinis, who, in their most relaxed and natural conversations, do not "put water in their mouth"[16] when expressing their thoughts and feelings. Asche speaks candidly to the wealthy and powerful ones who perch themselves atop the fortunes they have amassed. She declares these rich and powerful have sold their souls for silver and gold, and their god is the almighty dollar. Such bold public speech is concretely grounded in the socio-economic reality of poor citizens, who are expected to meekly turn the other cheek when dealt blows of economic injustice. Asche brings into painful, palpable focus the screams of poor people, rendered sleepless by the terror of starvation, while the corrupt rich sleep and dream. Her pragmatism names the nepotism within the country's political system, calling out politicians who make promises to the poor while canvassing for elections but "once they reach on top, become more corrupt."

Community engagement is intrinsic to this genre. Asche is a powerful representative of her community. Calypsonians often emerge from the grassroots communities at the bottom of the social hierarchy. Asche herself hails from Laventille, one of the country's most drug-infested neighborhoods, where the trifecta of violence, poverty, and crime play out sordidly in daily life. She is a fitting representative of her community when she uses terms like "valley of dry bones" and "veil of death." At this level of social identification, the calypsonian is engaging her listeners who feel the burden of economic oppression described in her song. Community engagement also happens through the call and response arrangement of her song. The title is essentially the "hook" of the piece; whenever it occurs in live performance, the singer pauses and points the microphone to the crowd, which, like a mass back-up choir, joins in lustily, "Every knee shall bow!"

The interpretive lens used by the calypsonian has the perspective from the bottom, looking up, as opposed to the top, looking down. This is critical in understanding the apocalyptic nuances of this calypso and the hermeneutic of so many political calypsos. The calypsonian sings as one representing the community, empowered to speak on their behalf. One calypsonian speaks of the local people as "the ones who send my message forth. They are the ones that will put me in the spotlight to deliver their message."[17] Asche's understanding of the many biblical allusions in her calypso illustrate this perspective. She insists that the day of reckoning is coming where the "last shall be first," when "things material rust, crumble into dust." Rolling thunder will herald this day of reckoning, and images of Jericho's crumbling

---

16. A Trinbagonian expression that indicates frank, blunt speech

17. Brian London, interview with the author, Trinidad and Tobago, January 20, 2015.

walls and the collapsing tower of Babel are both a warning to the proud and encouragement to the oppressed.

These three features—candid, concrete treatment of pragmatic content, communal engagement, and a hermeneutic of the socially marginalized—show up consistently in grassroots public discourse, whether in song or in preaching.

GRASSROOTS PREACHING

The students in the homiletics classroom I referenced at the beginning of this chapter most likely had not analyzed their native music rhetorically, as I had. However, they recognized the characteristics I listed for them: bold and imaginative narrative; rustic humor through hyperbole, satire, word play and picong; pragmatic themes treated concretely and unpretentiously; candor and blunt speech; use of earthy localized imagery; use of vernacular and colloquial idioms; open resistance to and defiance of the status quo; and a hermeneutic that represents the socially marginalized. It was as though I had held up a mirror in which they did not see anything reflected that had been characterized as effective preaching in their course textbooks. What they saw instead was a reflection of themselves and their culture, hence the disoriented, thoughtful looks that came over their faces.

Trinbagonian grassroots preaching has not had the benefit of close reflection or "objective" standards of evaluation against which individual sermons may be adjudicated. As a homiletical practice on the ground, its complexities and nuances often reflect the degree of exposure the preacher has had to foreign influences, and the selective adaptations he or she has made for any number of reasons. However, by and large, I suggest five specific characteristics that stand in contrast to a preaching that has greater ties to a colonial homiletical legacy. These traits are: (1) Pragmatic Content, (2) Hermeneutic of Experience, (3) Sermon as Communal, (4) Use of Vernacular, and (5) Robust Affect and Embodiment. I use two sermons by Trinbagonian preachers to illustrate some of these features: "How to Make the Best out of Your Life," by Evangelist Darryl Edwards, and "Loose the Donkey," by Apostle Sandra Francis.

The content of grassroots preaching is embedded in the logic of pragmatism rather than intellectualism. The issues that shape the sermon are related directly to the existential needs and questions of the audience and their world. Caribbeanist N. Sam Murrell argues for this kind of flatfooted homiletic when he charges Caribbean preachers to make their preaching unapologetically contextual:

> Put flesh and bones, arms and legs, hands and feet to the biblical texts when saying, "Thus saith the Lord," to the people. The Lord himself lives in the people's pantry in Grenada, drops in on their job interviews in Trinidad, sits at the bargaining table of labor union negotiations for just wages in Barbados, and hears their plea for better medical care and land ownership in Jamaica and Guyana. Like the mythical Santa Claus, the God of the Bible knows when our naughty and decrepit Caribbean politicians are stashing away millions of much-needed, hard-earned taxpayers' dollars in their personal Swiss bank accounts while turning a deaf ear to the starving children and helpless people of our land.[18]

It is on this existential and visceral level that sermonic engagement happens first and foremost; theological abstractions and concepts are less consequential in grassroots pulpit speech.

Experience is the primary hermeneutical driver of the folk sermon. Scripture is refracted and interpreted through life in the home and the village in order to help listeners understand the Good News and the God of the Bible. Doctrine and systematic theology emerge from experience. Evangelist Darryl shares with his audience his belief in tithing, and it is not from a doctrinal standpoint. In fact, he finds the prevailing theological arguments and bookish interpretations around tithing confusing and polemical. Frankly, he gives a tithe to God because before he came to faith, he gave his financial "first fruits" to alcohol and cigarette manufacturers, and their products were killing him. Now, as a Christian, he owes it to the One who gives him life to give his tithe. His theology is firmly grounded in his experience.[19]

In Apostle Sandra's sermon, she makes an interpretive move from the bound condition of the donkey in Mark 11:4 to the experience of social repression in her audience.[20] As she moves through the biblical passage verse by verse, she reads herself and her congregation into the story. Such reading is meant to provide an alternative to negative self-talk; it empowers them to deflect verbal abuses and put-downs based on the assurance that Jesus has come to liberate them as he did the donkey. It is the experiences of the preacher and her people that upstage the more theoretical interpretative findings of her commentaries, with which she tentatively begins her sermon, "Loose the Donkey." In this regard, Apostle Sandra preaches in resonance with Liberation theologians and interpreters who have this

---

18. Murrell, "Dangerous Memories, Underdevelopment, and the Bible," 22.
19. Edwards, "How to Make the Best out of Your Life."
20. Francis, "Loose the Donkey."

approach to theology and the Scriptures in common—experience matters first and foremost!

Community matters! As it is all throughout the African diaspora, the mutual value of the local community to the individual is foundational to Caribbean social identity. The colonial homiletical legacy may treat the pulpit as a symbol of the authority of the Word, a symbol that may signify distance and even differentiation between clergy and laity. But for the grassroots preacher, the Word is alive and resides in the entire community, enlivened by the Spirit that moves in all of us. Word and Spirit, as Mark Lewis Taylor eloquently suggests, are not simply an internal, mystical, immaterial dynamic in worship. "The Caribbean mode takes the binariness of 'Word and Spirit' and intensifies it through communal performance—heats it up as it were, to the point that it is transcended in rhythmic repetition that creates polymorphic complexities that defy mere binary rhythms."[21] While binary rhythms, such as walking and marching, may equate with colonial preferences for order and structure in preaching and worship, the polymorphic, syncopated complexities of worship, to which Taylor refers, are more indicative of what goes on in a grassroots sermon. These sermons are often dynamic events where the locus of authority is not a pulpit, but the Spirit who is moving at will in and through preacher and listener, orchestrating the zestful creation and syncopated performance of the Word.

When, throughout the sermon, the preacher calls out randomly to someone in the congregation, when a listener jumps to her feet or gleefully claps or waves her hands in response to something said by the preacher or by her pew neighbor, when someone in the audience shouts the word the preacher is searching for, when call and response rhythms are sustained for minutes at a time between preacher and audience, when the preacher spontaneously begins a song and the audience joins by the end of the first measure, when the audience becomes so effusive and celebratory, it sounds to an outsider like bedlam in the service—these and other indicators of polymorphic preaching are normal—and some would say essential—in grassroots preaching. The critical nature of the communal spirit in every aspect of Trinbagonian life cannot be overemphasized. If the preaching is not communally inspired, community engaging, and ultimately produced by and in community, it will not resonate with or communicate effectively to folk audiences.

Vernacular is probably the most easily discerned marker of an authentically local Trinbagonian homiletic. The use of Trinbagonian dialect, with its colorful colloquialisms culled from several linguistic sources over the

---

21. Taylor, "Polyrhythm in Worship," 120.

centuries, may attract derision from middle and upper class social strata, but when one simply *has* to make a point in local communication there is often no substitute for the well-chosen "Trini" term or vocable. It bears restating that if the Word of God truly became enfleshed so that this Word could reveal what God was like, this Incarnate Word validates the use of a people's mother tongue in preaching.

Standard English, more often than not, is ineffective. In the case of the grassroots preachers referenced earlier, both began their sermons by referring to their outlines or notes in Standard English. During these introductory moments, their congregations appeared distant, unaffected, and disengaged. Once the preachers shifted into vernacular, the shift in engagement and participation by the congregation was simultaneous and marked. This language of the heart viscerally appeals to Caribbean peoples across academic lines. One Caribbean scholar reveals the frustration of theological students who, at their seminary, were constantly exposed to chapel sermons that sounded more literary than oral/aural. "Many students at worship were 'turned off' by this. No more of this academic stuff please! We've had our fill of that throughout the past week in lectures! Rather, talk to us, talk to our hearts!"[22] In Trinbagonian towns, villages, and the rural areas populated by the local working or farming class, oral communication is almost exclusively in vernacular, whether Creole or some localized iteration of Standard English. Decolonial preaching in grassroots communities breaks free from the constraining, often bland, and relatively meaningless confines of linguistic propriety.

It may be argued that vernacular preaching is subversive preaching, particularly since there is often the kind of code switching that happens when the preacher makes a point in Standard English and then elucidates it in vernacular. Citing missiologist Lamin Sanneh, Princeton ethicist, Peter J. Paris surmises that in using translation as a primary instrument of evangelism, Christian missionaries "unwittingly provided indigenous African peoples with some basic tools with which to effect their own liberation from colonial domination. . . . Once the message is translated into the mother tongue of the indigenous peoples, the latter receive a tool of immense interpretive and psychological advantage."[23] Thus affirmed, a people's mother tongue or heart language—vernacular—can undermine a strictly colonialist sense of propriety and its efforts at control. For example, in using the term "ass" rather than donkey repeatedly in her sermon, Apostle Francis was in effect de-linking from colonialized norms of linguistic propriety in

---

22. Mulrain, "Calypso Exegesis," 46.
23. Paris, "Linguistic Inculturation of the Gospel," 78.

the pulpit. Simultaneously, she was lifting from their pit and untying from their bondage people whose self-image needed to be decolonized, scrubbed clean of self-hate. Her interpretation of the biblical donkey stories turned the notion of Western European linguistic superiority and sophistication on its head.

The fifth characteristic of indigenous Trinbagonian preaching has to do with affect—a robust affect, free of the constraints of colonial propriety. Such constraints are frequently taught, modeled, and rewarded in homiletics classes where colonial preferences dominate. Within this category of affect lies the degree to which the sermon is embodied; the percussive, polyrhythmic music that intensifies the sermon's effect—before, during, and after the sermon; preaching gestures and body language; and audience participation. Grassroots sermons are moving, spirited, and impassioned—there are really no affective limits since all of this energy may lead into some form of communal ecstasy by the time the sermon is over. This demonstrates the importance of the sermon being a holistic experience for the listener rather than simply a cognitive event. This embrace and celebration of affect is distinctly anti-colonial.

Activist theologian Mark Lewis Taylor commends this affective freedom to all Christians as a means of helping us lean into the liberative mode of the reign of God: "Worshipers who stand still within the lines of straight pew rows are not rehearsing themselves well for a Christian practice of liberation and resistance, which often requires 'pushing the edges' and 'crossing the lines' that oppressive powers like to set."[24] Indeed, poise and decorum have their place in worship, but acquiescence to such colonialist norms is out of place in worshipping communities yearning to break free of yokes worn during centuries of oppression.

When Evangelist Darryl runs back and forth, moving between pulpit and pew, dramatizing his personal testimony with vigor, this is a moment of robust affect. When Apostle Sandra comes from behind the pulpit to put her ample body on display as she demonstrates the importance of loving yourself regardless, this is a moment of high affect. This is natural in oral traditions where bodies and body language speak as eloquently and expressively as words can. Homiletician Sally A. Brown has observed the paralyzing reluctance of some of her North American students who believe bodies are a distraction from the holy rather than the Spirit's habitation. She admits these are culturally embedded values, yet she reassures her students—and us—we can learn from one another and be guided by God's Spirit: "We can

---

24. Taylor, "Polyrhythm in Worship," 125.

breathe deeply, tell our critical selves to take a break, and let the Spirit move or settle us in new ways."[25]

What are the implications of these new ways, these unconventional ways of preaching? As a homiletics professor, I propose three pedagogical considerations. First, local theological institutions in formerly colonized countries play a vital role in endorsing and advancing a decolonial homiletic. The manner in which theology is taught in these postcolonial spaces—both in theory and practice—often illustrates the stronghold of neocolonialism well into the twenty-first century. As independent nations, their "presently unfulfilled and paradoxical independence"[26] is due in large part to deeply embedded, colonially-bequeathed vestiges of self-hate and self-effacement, an internalized kind of oppression. An important step away from this legacy would be for institutionally trained preachers and homileticians to recognize and value conventional patterns of preaching for what they are—imported and, at best, needing to be adapted. It is just as important to recognize and value local patterns of preaching for what they are—effective and indispensible for a marginalized segment of Trinbagonian citizenry, among whom God desires to be known.

The syllabi of local theological institutions can recognize and analyze local preaching patterns as one valid homiletical option among many. One Trinbagonian professor of preaching acknowledged that his syllabus is designed for the benefit of foreign accrediting institutions, which expect syllabi to reflect what these power-holding boards consider standardized patterns of "excellence" in preaching. According to this informant, what actually happens in the classroom is much more closely related to the experiences of the students. Consequently, they discuss preaching to grassroots audiences, street preaching, deliverance sermons, and Bible Study or Prayer Meeting exhortations—none of which are deemed academically credible topics of study—at length. Academic recognition would mean giving the unnamed paradigm a name and devoting time to examining areas of mutual enrichment between grassroots and conventional preaching.

The second pedagogical implication reaches across the Atlantic waters to the seminaries and congregations of North America. North American religious life often suffers from a silo effect, where denominational, ideological, cultural, and other boundaries keep the people of God from the rich cross-pollination that can fertilize and multiply our efforts at spreading God's good news. Yet the current growth of Christianity in North America has direct links to increasing numbers of immigrant congregations where

---

25. Brown and Powery, *Ways of the Word*, 186.
26. Serrequeberhan, *Hermeneutics of African Philosophy*, 5.

effective grassroots preaching happens regularly, often two, three, four, or more times weekly. This effectiveness is neither measured nor measurable by traditional homiletical standards. Such preaching is marked by cultural differences that tend to be marginalized and discounted as naively pre-critical practices or else sidelined in preaching textbooks and guild discourses. In its macro-view and its broadest reach, this essay validates and brings to light the value of minoritized religious practices that can enrich mainstream Protestantism in North America.

The standard pedagogies of preaching in US seminaries tend to rest upon the assumptions of dominant North American or European theories and practices. Seminary students of color—particularly those spiritually formed in faith communities whose effective (and affective) homiletical practices are often not reflected in classroom instruction—are thus prone to dismiss their own preaching traditions as inconsequential. This is compounded by the lack of critical reflection on preaching common in many faith communities of color, for whom, honestly speaking, homiletics is a non-issue. These communities, whose preference is for orality, would rather preach than *think about or analyze* their preaching. Thus few writings or texts are available to "compete" with the prolific output of the dominant paradigms. The end result is often that students of color in homiletics classrooms are likely to jettison or, at best, hide their preaching traditions in favor of the paradigms privileged in seminary texts. Consequently I have seen students become conflicted and confused about their preaching identity. This impoverishes not just the underrepresented students but also their colleagues whose traditions are privileged in preaching classes. Both dominant and minoritized groups stand to be enriched by traditions outside their homiletical orbit.

The third pedagogical consideration endorses the value of experiential learning, based on Paolo Freire's pedagogical theory of dialogue, which facilitates comparison and contrast of differing preaching paradigms. While we would grant that for two students from different backgrounds to understand each other they must share information about themselves and their communities, Freire's theory has much more in mind than simply hearing one another out. Words and work come together in Freire's dialogue. More than just being signifiers, words do the work of naming realities, thus allowing speakers to achieve the human significance that comes with naming and thus transforming their world. Additionally, this dialogue moves beyond exchange of information towards critical thinking committed to and connected with action. This dialogue, which involves critical thinking and reflective action, is what Freire conceives of as praxis.²⁷ Such praxis is essential to the work of identifying, analyzing, and comparing paradigms of preaching embedded in racial/ethnic communities.

Critical pedagogical strategies in North American seminaries would include: expanding the range of textual material, concretizing principles of justice, establishing liturgical rhythms, and intentionally engaging dialogue as praxis, all of which are attuned to the values and needs of our preaching students of color.²⁸

Students of color approaching the discipline of homiletics, both in their local contexts as practitioners and in the classroom as students, have a larger homiletical toolbox than they sometimes know. The Trinbagonian students whose conversation began this chapter were enlightened and affirmed when they began to think about their local style of preaching in this way—as one viable option among many. In his introduction to *Reading From This Place*, Fernando Segovia, Vanderbilt University Professor of New Testament, summarizes what he hopes would be the intercultural benefit of his edited volume:

> "Speaking in other tongues" within the United States . . . characterizes the most recent development in biblical criticism and reflects the postmodernist turn at large: a world in which readers become as important as texts and in which models and reconstructions are regarded as constructions; a world in which there is no master narrative but many narratives . . . a world in which the fundamental problem lies not in the translation and dissemination of a centralized and hegemonic message into other tongues but rather in having different tongues engage in critical dialogue with one another. Such a world I would submit, is the direct and inevitable result of any process of liberation and decolonization . . . a world where conversation becomes both exciting and fragile, imperative and hard to achieve, understanding and critical—in short a world of "speaking in other tongues."²⁹

When we dare break free of our homiletical silos we discover we have much to learn from one another. This is not under the guise of homiletical tourism, as is the case in many textbooks where some mild allusion is made to practices that depart from the norm. This breaking free calls for homiletical dislocation and relocation. It calls for listening and thinking in

---

27. Freire, *Pedagogy of the Oppressed*, 87–93.
28. Lee, "Teaching Disruptively," 147–66.
29. Segovia, "And They Began to Speak in Other Tongues," 32.

a language that is not ours but which the Spirit of God empowers us to understand as we fully lean into the seeming chaos of the Pentecost experience. The ultimate implication of this paradigm is the proclamation of the Reign of God, where there is room for everyone, where we are all valued and accepted, and where the center is reserved for the Holy One, whose kaleidoscopic image we reflect as we surround the throne, *a great multitude that no one could count, from every nation, from all tribes and peoples and languages . . .*[30]

Bibliography

Baptiste, Rhona. *Trini Talk: A Dictionary of Words and Proverbs of Trinidad & Tobago.* Trinidad & Tobago: Douens, 2011.

Brown, Sally A., and Luke A. Powery. *Ways of the Word: Learning to Preach for Your Time and Place.* Minneapolis: Fortress, 2016.

Edwards, Darryl. "How to Make the Best out of Your Life." Sermon. 14 August 2016.

Francis, Sandra. "Loose the Donkey." Sermon. 20 March 2016.

Freire, Paulo. *Pedagogy of the Oppressed.* London: Continuum, 2006.

González, Justo, and Catherine González. *The Liberating Pulpit.* Eugene, OR: Wipf & Stock, 2003.

Jenkins, Philip. *The Next Christendom: The Coming of Global Christianity.* Oxford: Oxford University Press, 2002.

Lee, Boyung. "Teaching Disruptively: Pedagogical Strategies to Teach Cultural Diversity and Race." In *Teaching for a Culturally Diverse and Racially Just World*, edited by Eleazar S. Fernandez, 147–66. Eugene, OR: Cascade, 2014.

Martell-Otero, Loida. "Who Do You Say I Am?: A Constructive Christological Analysis." Lecture in Systematic Theology course. Palmer Theological Seminary, Wynnewood, PA. 5 February 2008.

Mignolo, Walter. *The Darker Side of Western Modernity: Global Futures, Decolonial Options.* Durham, NC: Duke University Press, 2011.

Mulrain, George. "Is There a Calypso Exegesis?" In *Voices From the Margin: Interpreting the Bible in the Third World*, edited by R. S. Sugirtharajah, 37–47. New ed. Maryknoll, NY: Orbis, 1995.

Murrell, Nathaniel Samuel. "Dangerous Memories, Underdevelopment, and the Bible in Colonial Caribbean Experience." In *Religion, Culture, and Tradition in the Caribbean*, edited by Hemchand Gossai and Nathaniel Samuel Murrell, 9–35. New York: St. Martin's, 2000.

Paris, Peter J. "The Linguistic Inculturation of the Gospel: The Word of God in the Words of the People." In *Making Room at the Table: An Invitation to Multicultural Worship*, edited by Brian K. Blount and Leonora Tubbs Tisdale, 78–95. Louisville: Westminster John Knox, 2001.

Pew Research Center. "Global Christianity: A Report on the Size and Distribution of the World's Christian Population." *Pew Research Center*, December 19, 2011. Online. http://www.pewforum.org/2011/12/19/global-christianity-exec.

---

30. Rev 7:9, NRSV.

Segovia, Fernando F. "And They Began to Speak in Other Tongues: Competing Modes of Discourse in Contemporary Biblical Criticism." In *Social Location and Biblical Interpretation in the United States*, edited by Fernando Segovia and Mary Ann Tolbert, 1–32. Vol. 1 of *Reading From This Place*. Minneapolis: Fortress, 1995.

Serrequeberhan, Tsenay. *The Hermeneutics of African Philosophy*. New York: Routledge, 1994.

Taylor, Mark. "Polyrhythm in Worship: Caribbean Keys to an Effective Word of God." In *Making Room at the Table: An Invitation to Multicultural Worship*, edited by Brian K. Blount and Leonora Tubbs Tisdale, 108–128. Louisville: Westminster John Knox, 2001.

Tisdale, Leonora Tubbs. *Preaching as Local Theology and Folk Art*. Minneapolis: Fortress, 1997.

"Trinidad and Tobago Demographics Profile 2018." *Index Mundi*, January 20, 2018. Online. http://www.indexmundi.com/trinidad_and_tobago/demographics_profile.html.

Williams, Eric. *History of the People of Trinidad and Tobago*. New York: Eworld, 2010.

Yelvington, Kevin A. "Introduction: Trinidad Ethnicity." In *Trinidad Ethnicity*, edited by Kevin Yelvington, 1–32. London: Macmillan, 1993

Singapore: Preaching in the Power of the Pneuma

Johnson Lim

> God's Word to the Church today is the restoration of the Spirit to his rightful place in the church, and in your life, is, by all means, the most important that could possibly take place.... The truth is, God never thought of his church apart from the Holy Spirit. We were born of the Spirit. We were baptized into the body of Christ by the Spirit. We are anointed with the Spirit. We are led of the Spirit. We are taught of the Spirit, and the Spirit is the medium, the divine solution, in which God holds the Church.
>
> —A. W. Tozer[1]

> The Bible summons all Christians to accept the Spirit's empowerment for the various tasks he has assigned us and for evangelizing the world. Woe to us if in a world like today's we try to do his work without him.
>
> —Craig S. Keener[2]

> Without the anointing of the Spirit there can be no authority in living or preaching the Word.
>
> —Stephen F. Olford[3]

---

1. Snyder, *Tozer*, 37–38.
2. Keener, *Three Crucial Questions*, 183.
3. Phillips, *Life and Legacy of Stephen Olford*, 249.

> All preaching must be done in the power of the Holy Spirit. No one can effectively proclaim the Lord Jesus in his own strength. The saving power is in the message and not the messenger.
>
> —Steven J. Lawson[4]

WHEN IT COMES TO preaching, we have myriads of resources to help us become excellent preachers. We have a plethora of books on preaching mechanics. Preaching conferences and seminars are regularly conducted locally, regionally, and internationally. We even have Google to access illustrations and websites dedicated to helping us preach better. Moreover, there are communication theories to help us impact the congregation, powerful computer software to help us exegete and prepare good sermons, and PowerPoint to make our presentations visually stunning and stimulating. In other words, we have at our disposal the tools, technologies, and techniques we need as preachers.

Notwithstanding all these good things, why does preaching appear to have little or no effect on the congregation? Information is conveyed each Sunday, but why is the resulting transformation lagging behind?[5] More pointedly, why is there a visible absence of power in contemporary preaching? Is the Holy Spirit MIA (missing in action)?

From a homiletical standpoint, there are four contributing reasons. First is the marginalization of the Holy Spirit in preaching. A kaleidoscope of homileticians, scholars, theologians, historians, and practitioners have argued cogently that corroborative textual evidence from Scripture and concrete examples from Church history have unequivocally shown that it has everything to do with the marginalization and misplacement of the Transformer, God, the Holy Spirit, in our preaching. Is the neglect and marginalization of the Third Person of the Trinity the result of a biblically, theologically, and historically inadequate and flawed understanding of Pneumatology?[6]

---

4. Lawson, *Kind of Preaching God Blesses*, 119.

5. See Lim, "What's Wrong with Contemporary Preaching?"; "How Then Shall We Preach?"

6. The theme of the 2016 "EPPI Conference" held in Singapore was "Expound, Express, Explode: Making an Impact with your Message." The workshops covered a spectrum of helpful topics on preaching but ironically left the most important one out—the Holy Spirit in preaching. How is it possible to talk about explosive and impactful preaching without bringing in the One whose task it is to make it so? Surprisingly, in a book that seeks to be a helpful resource for preachers, there is no chapter, section, brief discussion, or any reference to the Holy Spirit and preaching! See Day et al., *Reader on Preaching*.

Second is unbalanced priority. Much emphasis has been placed on tools, techniques, and technologies[7] instead of the Transformer. Granted, we are living in a digital world where technology plays an important part in our lives. However, preaching becomes ineffective when we attend exclusively to its mechanics and sparingly on its dynamics.

Third is the failure to take the Holy Spirit seriously. The need to be Spirit-filled is a clear teaching in the New Testament—it is a command, not a suggestion! It is to be daily and continuous rather than once and for all or a one-time experience according to its grammatical construction in the Greek language. Harold Hoehner observes correctly:

> The present imperative indicates that this is not an automatic bestowment at the time of salvation but an injunction for every believer to follow continually. The filling by the Spirit is more than the Spirit's indwelling—it is his activities realized in and through us. . . . With the indwelling, each Christian has all of the Spirit, but the command to be filled by the Spirit enables the Spirit to have all of the believer.[8]

To be Spirit-filled also means to be Spirit-led. Correspondingly, to be a Spirit-filled individual or community (Eph 5:18) likewise means that proclaimers of the Word be pneumatic preachers.[9]

Fourth, priority is not given to the people but rather to the preacher. In homiletics classes in seminaries and Bible colleges, instead of asking, "How do people listen to sermons in today's world," we ask, "How do I prepare sermons?" This is as good as "putting the homiletical cart before the homiletical horse."

Chris Ellis said when the church gathers for worship, they gather to hear God's Word, speak God's word, and meet God in his Word.[10] Indeed, "if preaching is to be effective, i.e., redemptive and life-changing, its

---

7. This is a gadget-oriented culture where technology is a mixed blessing. For the hazards and effects of technology on our spiritual lives, and the role technology plays in helping and hampering our Christian practice and witness, see Kallenberg, *God and Gadgets*. In a media saturated world, the danger of electronic media displacing the spoken word instead of supporting it is as real as ever. Cf. Richard Lisher, who says, "When the brain is asked to multi-task by listening and watching at the same time, it always quits listening" (Lisher, *End of Words*, 25).

8. Hoehner, *Ephesians*, 705.

9. Cf. "The Spirit-filled life is not a special edition of Christianity. It is part and parcel of the total plan for his people" (Tozer, *How to Be Filled*, 18).

10. See Ellis, "Gathering around the Word".

characterization must demonstrate the interaction of God's Word and the Holy Spirit."[11]

> In all Christian work, there are three elements absolutely indispensable: the Spirit of God as the power, the Word of God as the message, and the man of God as the instrument. The Spirit of God uses the message by means of the man.[12]

The thesis of this essay is simple: Preaching (i.e., biblical, theological, and practical)[13] that has a lingering effect or inspires, impacts, and influences the listeners is pneumatic preaching. Pneumatic preaching is a biblically balanced preaching, governed by and grounded in Scripture and guided and goaded by the Spirit. Scripture is to be elevated in all true preaching because it is "the throne of the Word of God" (Charles Spurgeon).[14] It was Karl Barth who said, "Preaching should be an explanation of Scripture; the preacher does not have to speak 'on' but 'from' (*ex*), drawing from the Scriptures whatever he says. . . . God alone must speak."[15]

Introduction

The Gospel of Mark declares, "Jesus went into Galilee, where he preached God's Good News" (Mark 1:14) and ends with, "Go into all the world and preach the Good News to everyone" (16:15).[16] The priority of preaching is emphasized throughout the New Testament (cf. Luke 4:18–19; 43–44; Matt 4:17, 23; 10:7–20; 11:1).

Paul came to a settled conviction on the centrality of preaching. Preaching was his main ministry rather than baptizing (1 Cor 1:17; 1 Tim 2:7). He and his team proclaimed the gospel (Acts 13:43–49; 17:1–4, 10–13, 22–34;

11. Yim, "Preaching God's Word," 73.

12. Thomas Griffith quoted in Zuck, *Holy Spirit in Your Teaching*, 19.

13. David M. Brown makes a good point when he asserts that there is a difference between preaching and teaching. The former is proclamation, while the latter is explanation. Teaching seeks to explain. Preaching seeks to bring the listener to the point of *conviction*. While preaching and teaching involve information sharing, the question to ask is: What is the purpose? Is it to disseminate information/insights? Then it is preaching. If it is to persuade or motivate listeners for a change in attitude or belief, then it is preaching. See Brown, *Transformational Preaching*, 41–42. I might add that teaching seeks to instruct/inform while preaching seeks to inspire/transform. One is transactional the other transformational. Both ministries are needed in the church.

14. Holmes, "Power behind Every Great Preacher's Throne," 54–56.

15. Barth, *Preaching of the Gospel*, 15.

16. Modern scholarship is in agreement that this was the first Gospel to be written, which carries important implications for Synoptic studies.

20:18–31).¹⁷ God chose Paul to be a "preacher, an apostle, and a teacher of this Good News" (2 Tim 1:11). His mission was to preach to the Gentiles when the Jews rejected the message (Acts 13:46–47; 18:6; Rom 11:13).

In Church history, preaching was given priority and primacy in the life of a church.¹⁸ Indeed, "preaching is distinctively Christian in its origin and practice.... The preaching act is *sui generis*, a function of the church established by Jesus Christ."¹⁹ Preaching was also the hallmark of the Protestant Reformation. Hence, preaching matters and is still as relevant as before.²⁰ "With preaching Christianity stands or falls, because it is the declaration of the gospel."²¹

> Preaching is an event in which the congregation hears God's Word, meets their Savior, and is transformed through the power of the Holy Spirit to be the kind of community God intends. Preaching is an event, an action; something happens in the lives of the hearers by way of a divine encounter.²²

Chris Ellis argues that the main purpose of preaching is to "enable an encounter with the living Christ.... The hearers need to be transformed by an encounter with God and not simply with the intellect of the preacher."²³

To write about "transforming preaching,"²⁴ "preaching that comes alive,"²⁵ "preaching that moves people,"²⁶ and "making the Word come alive"²⁷ without mentioning, emphasizing, or relating to the Holy Spirit is as futile as talking about blasting a quarry without the need for dynamite!²⁸ Preaching without the empowerment of the Spirit may convince and convict intellectually but will not lead to change and conversion. "The awakening to

---

17. For a discussion on Pauline preaching, consult Litfin, *Paul's Theology of Preaching*; Gericke, *Prince of Preachers*; Knowles, *We Preach Not Ourselves*; Gross, *If You Cannot Preach Like Paul*; Beeaudean Jr., *Paul's Theology of Preaching*; Thompson, *Preaching Like Paul*; Bailey, *Paul the Preacher*; Stout, *Preach the Word*. Sadly missing, however, is a discussion on the Holy Spirit and preaching.

18. See Edwards Jr., *History of Preaching*; Osborn, *Folly of God*.

19. Moehler, "Theology of Preaching," 13–20.

20. See Lim, "Is Preaching Still Relevant Today?"

21. Forsyth, *Positive Preaching and the Modern Mind*, 5.

22. Wilson, *Practice of Preaching*, 5.

23. Ellis, "Gathering around the Word," 117–18.

24. E.g., Heywood, *Transforming Preaching*; Hooke, *Transforming Preaching*.

25. E.g., Low, *Preaching that Comes Alive*.

26. E.g., Arrington, *Preaching that Moves People*.

27. E.g., Wright, *Alive to the Word*.

28. Wright, *Alive to the Word*. See also note 15.

sin, the realization of judgment, the discovery of Christ, the assurance of salvation, are all the work of the Holy Spirit of God."[29] In other words, the Holy Spirit makes people see that *not* to believe in Christ is a sin (e.g., Acts 2:27; 16:31).

> I am convinced that the main trouble with most of us and with the church in general is that we seem to have forgotten the presence of the Spirit and the power of the Spirit. We have become so formal with everything so set, so organized, all in control of man—and have forgotten this other evidence, the power and the glory of the Spirit and the sanctity and the holiness. I am convinced that the greatest need of the church is to realize again the activity of the Holy Spirit. . . . When the Spirit comes, his evidence is unmistakable and the results are amazing and astounding.[30]

The Holy Spirit has been referred to as the "Forgotten God"[31] and "Cinderella of Theology."[32] Unlike Jesus Christ, the "Holy Spirit has not been integrated in an organic way into the whole theological process."[33]

> Christians talk a lot about Jesus, often address the Father/Creator in prayer, but become vague when it comes to the Holy Spirit. Given that the Holy Spirit is the Third Person of the Trinity and is at the heart of Christian spiritual life, it is hard to imagine the Holy Spirit as invisible, upstaged, silent, or neglected.[34]

Theologically speaking, the renaissance of Pneumatology has partly been ignited due to renewed interest in the Trinity. In the past, the Holy Spirit has been eclipsed by the Father and Son in Christian theology. This renewed interest is like a fresh wind blowing into theological corridors.

Homiletically speaking, however, the Holy Spirit has been given a short shift. Pneumatology has taken a back seat. The Holy Spirit lacks prominence in contemporary homiletics even though it is recognized that the goal of preaching is transformation, which happens to be the Spirit's department. Preaching deals with the "transformation of the listeners"

---

29. Barclay, *Promise of the Spirit*, 45.

30. Lloyd-Jones, *Joy Unspeakable*, 129.

31. Because he "is tragically neglected and for all practical purposes forgotten" (Chan, *Forgotten God*, 15).

32. For an excellent study on the Holy Spirit, see Turner, *Holy Spirit and Spiritual Gifts*; Burke and Warrington, *Biblical Theology of the Holy Spirit*; Thiselton, *Holy Spirit in Biblical Teaching*; Brunner, *Theology of the Holy Spirit*.

33. McDonnell, "Spirit and Experience in Bernard Clairvaux."

34. Dryer, *Holy Power, Holy Presence*, 1.

(encounter paradigm) and not merely "transmission of knowledge" (educational paradigm).[35]

Homiletics has failed to catch up in spite of the fact that Scripture is clear concerning the role of the Holy Spirit in preaching.[36] More surprisingly, a number of well-known books on preaching in the past and even the present have somehow sidelined and undervalued the Holy Spirit (perhaps unintentionally). Lamentably, books on preaching can be classified into three categories: books that ignore or neglect the person and work of the Holy Spirit,[37] books that make indirect or passing reference to the Holy Spirit,[38] and books that emphasize the vital and pivotal role of the Holy Spirit in biblical preaching.[39]

The nut and bolt of homiletics is that without the power of the Pneuma (i.e., as "unction" or "anointing") in preaching, there can be no transformation of lives. To put it in another way, where there is no unction in the pulpit, there can be no action in the pews. Hence, this essay seeks to offer a corrective balance by asking and answering three questions: (1) Why is the work of the Holy Spirit important in preaching? (2) What is unction in preaching? (3) How does one obtain unction in preaching?

Why Is the Work of the Holy Spirit Important in Preaching?

The Holy Spirit is involved in every aspect of the life of a believer—in salvation, supplication, sanctification, and service.[40] From victorious Christian living to vibrant Christian ministry, the Third Person of the Trinity plays a vital role.[41] In terms of preaching ministry, "one's message will still be empty without the Holy Spirit's ministry. . . . The Holy Spirit must anoint and fill

---

35. Stevenson, *Preaching*, 6–7.

36. Our understanding of the Trinity must be situated within the tapestry of the Trinity (God the Father-Sustainer, God the Son-Savior, and God the Spirit-Sanctifier) to make homiletical sense.

37. House and Garland, *Faithful Preaching*.

38. Fabarez, *Preaching that Changes*.

39. Olford, *Anointed Expository Preaching*. Others include Azurdia, *Spirit Empowered Preaching*; Forbes, *Holy Spirit and Preaching*.

40. For a study on the different aspects on the work of the Holy Spirit, consult Lim, *Holy Spirit: Unfinished Agenda*; *Empowering Spirit and Christian Living*; *Holy Spirit: Spokesperson, Scripture, Sermon*.

41. For the relationship between wind, breath, and the Holy Spirit, see Averback, "Breath, Wind, Spirit and the Holy Spirit."

the preacher if he is to turn people to God."[42] Karl Barth reminds us, "It should not be forgotten that true preaching is learned from the Holy Spirit, theological training being subordinated to him."[43]

> Our greatest need as preachers is to be "clothed with power from on high" (Luke 24:49), so that like the apostles, we may "preach the gospel . . . by the Holy Spirit sent down from heaven" (1 Pet 1:12), and the gospel may come to the people through our preaching "not only in word, but also in power and in the Holy Spirit and with full conviction" (1 Thess 1:5).[44]

In the Old Testament, the Lord showed Ezekiel a plain covered with dry bones (Ezek 37:1–14). When the Lord asked Ezekiel whether the bones could live, he replied, "Only you, Lord God, know that" (v. 3). The Lord told Ezekiel to prophesy over the dry bones that God was going to put breath into them and they shall come to life again. God would also put flesh and muscle on them and cover them with skin so that they would know that he is God (vv. 4–6). As Ezekiel began to prophesy, he heard a rattling sound and saw all the bones fit themselves together. Then, as he watched, he saw the dry bones clothed with muscles and flesh, but there was no life. Only when the wind entered their bodies did they begin to breathe and come to life (v. 9). What an instructive message! There are some Sundays (if not many) when we feel we are preaching to a sea of dry bones. But things change when the Wind (Spirit) of God quickens them from the dead.

Experts in the field of communication have long asserted that logos (evidence and logic of message), ethos (credibility of the persuader), and pathos (reason, psychological needs of listeners) are necessary elements for persuasion.[45] I would like to argue that, at best, such communication can convince (i.e., intellectual agreement) but not change/actuate (i.e., to do something about it) a person. Without the Pneuma, there can be no real change that leads to action. "No amount of truth—no matter how well-delivered, no matter how well intended—that is delivered absent the power of the Holy Spirit can transform lives and turn around a nation run amok."[46]

In the New Testament, Jesus did not begin his ministry till he was embued with the power of the Holy Spirit (cf. Luke 4:1, 36; Acts 10:38). If it was necessary for the Master, surely it is also for the messenger. "We have with

---

42. Yim, "Preaching God's Word," 73.
43. Barth, *Preaching of the Gospel*, 35.
44. Stott, *I Believe in Preaching*, 329.
45. Murphy et al., *Effective Business Communication*, 373.
46. Holmes, "Power behind Every Great Preacher's Throne," 56.

us the one whom he had with him."[47] The early disciples had to be "clothed with power from on high" (Luke 24:49, NIV) to do kingdom work.

In Acts, it was the Holy Spirit who orchestrated the ministry, choreographed the mission of the apostles and early converts, and disrupted their normal life. The Holy Spirit was the Disruptor because he "led the first Christians to do unexplainable things, to live lives that didn't make sense to the culture around them, and ultimately to spread the story of God's grace around the world."[48] It is the nature of the Holy Spirit to shake up the church, particularly when the church becomes self-satisfied and content with status quo.[49]

Peter the Coward became Peter the Courageous on the day of Pentecost when he was empowered by the Holy Spirit to preach, resulting in the conversion of 3,000 people (Acts 2:41).[50]

Paul, with the help of the Holy Spirit, planted churches and nourished them across the Roman Empire. The Holy Spirit shocked them by bringing the Word to non-Jews. Paul did not understand the Spirit simply as an abstract power, but as a personal presence intimately connected to God's redemptive work in Christ.[51]

Paul relied on the power of the Holy Spirit to convince, convict, and convert the listeners. He allowed the Holy Spirit to use him and not the other way around.

> I came to you in weakness—timid and trembling. And my message and my preaching were very plain. Rather than using clever and persuasive speeches, I relied only on the power of the Holy Spirit. I did this so you would trust not in human wisdom but in the power of God. (1 Cor 2:3–5)[52]

> For when we brought you the Good News, it was not only with words but also with power, for the Holy Spirit gave you full assurance that what we said was true. And you know of our concern for you from the way we lived when we were with you. (1 Thess 1:5)

---

47. Smith, *Enduement for Power*, 91.

48. Chan, *Forgotten God*, 16.

49. Hauerwas and Willimon, *Holy Spirit*, 55.

50. "In Acts the Spirit is presented as an almost tangible force, visible if not in itself, certainly in its effect" (Dunn, *Christ and the Spirit*, 2:10). See also Haya-Prats, *Empowered Believers*.

51. Shults and Hollingsworth, *Holy Spirit*, 7.

52. Unless otherwise indicated, all biblical quotes are from the New Living Translation.

Paul's letters also point to ways in which the transforming experience of the Spirit can feel both disturbing and disorienting as well as comforting and reorienting in the concrete life of the community.[53] "For the Kingdom of God is not just a lot of talk; it is living by God's power" (1 Cor 4:20). In Acts, Paul is the paradigmatic agent who exemplifies how the Word explodes throughout the world.[54] James Dunn observes that "Paul experienced the centrifugal as well as the centripetal force of the Holy Spirit" (Rom 15:16–19; 1 Cor 2:4–5; 14:24–25; 2 Cor 34–6; Eph 6:17; 1 Thess 1:5).[55]

Pneumatologically, the Holy Spirit is a member of the Trinity who carries the fullness of God the Father and God the Son. The three persons of the Godhead work together in harmony and unity. They are one in substance, one in operation. Their office is distinguishable. In the doctrine of the Trinity, the Holy Spirit is not a junior but a senior partner.

Homiletically, we preachers want our sermons to make a difference and lead to visible changes in the lives of the listeners. The three areas where our preaching can make a difference are attitudinal change (feelings of like and dislike), beliefs (reason we hold those attitudes), and values (deep-seated principles that direct behaviors). For this to happen, the supernatural operation of the Holy Spirit is required. Without the empowering Spirit, sermons fizzle instead of sizzle. When empowered, human activities become divine assignments and motion becomes momentum. Without the Spirit's empowerment, preaching is dry, mundane, and even monotonous. Remove the Holy Spirit and we have a script but not a sermon, a manuscript but not a message. With the power of the Holy Spirit, the early believers "turned the world upside down" (Acts 17:6, KJV)

> Sermons need to ignite the heart.... Such preaching sparks connections in the hearers, who weave from these connections the sermon they need to hear in the given moment. Such preaching is utterly dependent on the Spirit of God brooding over the chaos and vulnerability of the preparation process, bringing to birth a new thing in the event of the sermon.[56]

Anthropologically, the disobedience of the first couple caused a historic fall that not only resulted in the corruption of human nature but a universal catastrophe.[57] To think that by merely using rhetorical strategies,

---

53. Shults and Hollingsworth, *Holy Spirit*, 7.
54. Shults and Hollingsworth, *Holy Spirit*, 53.
55. Dunn, *Christ and the Spirit*, 2:10.
56. Bruce, *Igniting the Heart*, 164.
57. For a detailed treatment of the fall, see Lim, "What's the Big Fuss Over an Apple?"

technological tools, and eloquent words we can change human nature, without the inner working of the Holy Spirit, would be homiletically gullible. "Preaching is not redemptive unless it is incarnational. It cannot be incarnational without the Holy Spirit overshadowing it."[58]

What Is Unction in Preaching?

In the history of preaching, different words have been used to describe the power that is needed to preach effectively and with impact. They include: unction, anointing, power from on high, afflatus of the Spirit, thunder and lightning, pulpit power, Spirit-filled or Spirit-empowered preaching, baptism of the Holy Spirit, and access to power. However, the two most popular words used are *unction* and *anointing*.[59]

What is unction?[60] Unction is a spiritual power that comes from the Holy Spirit which enables preachers to preach effectively with power, authority, and liberty, leading to the conviction of the conscience and conversion of the listeners and resulting in life's transformation. It is something we cannot manufacture or fake.

It is the X-factor (umph!) in preaching that spells the difference between preaching that is full of vim, verve, and vitality and preaching that is dull, boring, and lifeless. According to Martyn Lloyd-Jones, it is "an access to power" or "God giving power and enabling through the Spirit to the preacher in order that he may do the work in a manner that lifts it up beyond the efforts and endeavors of man and becomes a channel through whom the Spirit works."[61]

With unction, the ordinary becomes extraordinary and the preacher becomes a spiritual dynamo. Ordinary preaching becomes extraordinary. Preaching is accompanied by boldness and freedom, presence and power, authority and assurance, freedom instead of fear, courage and conviction. In such preaching, there is freshness like the morning dew.

When preaching is accompanied by unction, lives are touched and changed. Carnality transforms to spirituality. When the congregation departs, it will not be, "Pastor, what a great sermon," but, "What a great God!" There is an unusual sense of the manifest presence and power of God and

---

58. Johnson, "Preaching the Word," 12.

59. The broad outline for this section is from *Preach the Word Protocol* (June 8, 2017) held at Fort Caning Lodge, Singapore, organized by the Singapore Baptist Convention.

60. My preference is the word *unction*, which was used by the Puritans. The word *anointing* is used more commonly in the charismatic circles.

61. Lloyd-Jones, *Preaching and Preachers*, 305.

immediate awareness of the glory of God. The congregation senses it too, and there is awe. At the end of the preaching, the listeners will be touched in one way or another. It may even lead to a renewed personal encounter with God accompanied by repentance of sins and tears of remorse. One thing for sure, as the preacher, you know by its presence at the time of preaching, whether you have it or not, while the congregation knows by its absence.

> Without unction, we are like the disciples toiling but catching nothing (cf. Luke 5:5). Without unction, we become ineffectual. Without unction, our preaching will be like throwing a stone into the stream creating ripples but without any lasting impression. Without unction, our preaching is like the waves splashing against the rock without making any deep impression. Preaching without unction kills instead of giving life. The unctionless preacher is a savor unto death. The Word does not live unless the unction is upon the preacher.[62]

When Elijah confronted the prophets of Baal on Mount Carmel, he told the people the way to differentiate between a true God and a false one: "The god who answers by fire, he is God" (1 Kgs 18:24).[63] When the fire fell the people recognized it as the work of God (1 Kgs 18:36, 39). To preach with unction is to preach with fire. Just as fire burns, kindles, and glows, so preachers who are aflame accomplish great things for God. Fire that is kindled in us by the Holy Spirit achieves awesome results.

With unction, you feel the power of God during preaching. "Power is the anointing of God's Spirit upon the preacher through his Word."[64] Unction propels the preacher along. You are gliding on eagle's wings. It makes the act of preaching special. Words are yours. But there is freedom. Preaching has a mysterious element in it.[65] How does one know the unction of the Spirit?

> It gives clarity of thought, clarity of speech, ease of utterance, a great sense of authority and confidence as you are preaching,

---

62. Ravenhill, *Why Revival Tarries*, 18.

63. Moreover, on the day of Pentecost, "there appeared to them flames like tongues distributed among them flames like tongues of fire distributed among them and coming to rest on each one" (Acts 2:3). Hebrews states, "Our God is a devouring fire" (12:29). John the Baptist said, "I baptize you with water, for repentance . . . he will baptize you with the Holy Spirit and fire" (Matt. 3:11).

64. Wilton, "Preaching of Billy Graham," 11.

65. For better understanding of anointing, see Olford, *Anointed Expository Preaching*, 214–28. See also Duewel, *Ablaze For God*, 251–94; Sargent, *Sacred Anointing*; Heisler, *Spirit-Led Preaching*, 126–53; Eclov, "How Does Unction Function?," 81–84, 541–47, 550–55.

an awareness not your own thrilling through the whole of your being, and an indelible sense of joy. You are a man "possessed," you are taken hold of, and taken up.[66]

The need and necessity for unction has been noted by preachers, scholars, and theologians. Many pointed and pregnant reasons can be given, such as the hardness of human heart, lostness of humanity, we are not wrestling with flesh and blood (Eph 6:12), opposition to truth (2 Tim 3:8), and the kind of society we live in (the work of the enemy; 1 Pet 5:8). The dynamite of divine unction can only break the hardness of human hearts. "Not to have the anointing is the most helpless experience of loneliness and abject defeat in the pulpit, but when the anointing is upon you there is authority that comes through that nobody can resist."[67]

> Spirit-anointed preaching does something to both preacher and people. The anointing keeps the preacher aware of a power not his own. In the best sense of the word, he is "possessed"—caught up in the message by the power of the Spirit. He becomes the channel used by the Holy Spirit. At the same time the people are gripped, moved, convicted. When the Holy Spirit takes over in the preaching event, something miraculous happens.[68]

How Does One Obtain Unction in Preaching?

Divine unction is freely given by God. It cannot be learned, earned, or manufactured but only given through yearning. There are two sides to it: human and divine. Divine unction for preaching is available to all. It is not reserved for some chosen people. There is some truth to the statement that whom God appoints, he anoints. But we still need to ask for it. The impoverishment of preaching is not due to the lack of skillful preachers but rather the lack of unction.

Those who have experienced Spirit-empowered preaching say that unction is connected to prayer.[69] Indeed, unction has *something* to do with

---

66. Lloyd-Jones, *Preaching and Preachers*, 324.
67. Johnson, "Preaching the Word," 9.
68. Vines and Shaddix, *Power in the Pulpit*, 66.
69. Vines and Shaddix, *Power in the Pulpit*, 68–69. It was reported that three days before Jonathan Edwards preached his famous sermon, "Sinners in the Hand of an Angry God," he prayed fervently for three days and three nights. As he paced up and down the room, he cried, "Give me New England. Give me New England." On the following day, he read his sermon and the Spirit of God came mightily to the congregation. A revival broke out. Men and women were deeply convicted of their sins and clung to the

prayer but *everything* to do with God. Much of contemporary preaching is *powerless* because the preacher is *prayerless*. Like Jacob, we must "wrestle with God" and say, "I will not let you go unless you bless me" (Gen 32:26). We need to travail in prayer till God prevails. As preachers, we yearn to have the power of the early apostles of Christ. To have apostolic power, however, we need to engage in the apostolic practice of ardent prayers; only then will we experience apostolic possibilities. We must pray till we prevail. To prevail with God, we need to travail. We need to be "shut up" to God. To obtain unction, we need to spend more time agonizing than organizing ("sue it out with God," to use Thomas Goodwin's phrase).

> Seek Him! Seek Him! What can we do without Him? Seek Him! Seek Him! Seek Him always. But go beyond seeking Him; expect Him. . . . Seek this power, expect this power, yearn for this power, and when the power comes, yield to Him . . . nothing but a return of this power of the Spirit on our preaching is going to avail us anything. This makes true preaching, and it is the greatest need of all today—never more so. Nothing can substitute for this . . . this "unction," this "anointing," is the supreme thing. Seek it until you have it; be content with nothing less. Go on until you can say, "And my speech and my preaching was not with enticing words of man's wisdom, but in demonstration of the Spirit and power." He is still able to do "exceeding abundantly above all that we can ask or think."[70]

Therefore, a preacher needs to surrender himself to God daily. When we believe in the empowering of the Holy Spirit, it deepens our dependence on God. Unless we spend hours alone with God, we will never know the unction of the Holy Spirit (see Acts 1:14; 2:2, 4; 4:31; 8:14–17). Unction is dependent on the sovereignty of the Spirit. There is no neat formula. As Sargent says,

> To receive unction the preacher must be open and expectant as he moves into the pulpit. . . . Dependent on the Holy Spirit, he should enter the pulpit open to the Word. He should endeavor to unfurl the sails of his mind to the wind of the Spirit and proceed along the course, which the Holy Spirit directs.[71]

---

seats and pillars in the hall for fear they would be swallowed in hell. It spread from the church throughout New England and is called in Church history as the Great Awakening. That's what prayer can do.

70. Lloyd-Jones, *Preaching and Preachers*, 339–41.

71. Sargent, *Sacred Anointing*, 36.

There is something mysterious about unction. Many times, unction is dependent on prayers, and at other times (rare occasions), it may not appear to be. Nonetheless, it is fair to say that most of the time, prayer is the gateway to receiving unction. The old adage still rings true: "Pray as though everything depended on God and preach as though everything depended on you."

Another thing about unction is that it seems to come and go like the tides. The message you preach that is accompanied by unction in one particular place achieves certain results, but it does not guarantee the same results elsewhere. In other words, unction cannot be taken for granted. It is not easy to get a handle on the concept of unction. What if we have done everything we know how and there is no unction? We should continue to do and give our best. Who knows, perhaps God will surprise us.

> You and I cannot force him to move. Not even our obedience guarantees that the Spirit will do what we have hoped and prayed that he will do. We cannot compel the presence of the Spirit.... The Holy Spirit wants to be *pursued* but refuses to be *pushed*.[72]

Ultimately, we need to recognize that the secret of obtaining unction is a mystery and is dependent on God's sovereignty. Nonetheless, we need to work hard in fulfilling the conditions of obtaining unction, yet at the same time pray hard and trust him to pour his blessings on our preaching. Our preaching has no warmth, no life, no fire because we neglect the person of the Holy Spirit. John Stott was right when he said that "our sermons will never catch fire unless the fire of the Holy Spirit burns in our hearts and we ourselves 'aglow with the Spirit'" (Rom 12:11).[73]

It doesn't matter how polished our sermon is and how eloquent our delivery is. If our preaching does not have the power to touch and transform lives, it means nothing. Perhaps nothing is more tragic in the life of a preacher than when he/she fails to realize that the power of the Spirit is gone. One of the saddest statements recorded in the Bible concerning Samson is, "He did not know that the lord had left him" (Judg 16:20; cf. 1 Sam 16:14; 18:12).

When all is said and done, we need unction in our preaching. Therefore, in all our getting, get the unction that comes from above. If we want to effect change in the listeners' lives, we need unction. Without unction our preaching will fail.

---

72. Storms, *Practicing the Power*, 35.
73. Stott, *I Believe in Preaching*, 285.

Christians today must rediscover not just the God in whom we believe, not just the God who was one of us, but the God whom we experience, God the Holy Spirit.[74] At the same time, preachers need to rediscover the invisible Spirit's visible presence and power in preaching and in the life of a believer. Without the Holy Spirit's empowerment (unction factor), all that is done in the name of preaching on Sundays is simply "rearranging the deck chairs on the Titanic." We don't lack resources as we have many (in fact, we are spoiled for choices). But what is lacking is the power which can only come from the Holy Spirit. What A. J. Gordon said years ago is still applicable today:

> Our generation is rapidly losing its grip upon the supernatural; and as a consequence, the pulpit is rapidly dropping to the level of the platform. And this decline is due, more than anything else, to ignoring the Holy Spirit as the supreme inspirer of preaching. We would rather see a great orator in the pulpit, forgetting that the least expounder of the Word, when filled with the Spirit, is greater than he.[75]

Conclusion

To write books on homiletics, to teach homiletics, and to have a homiletical discourse without factoring the person and the role of the Holy Spirit is a serious omission. To speak about preaching transformation without the Transformer or change without the Game-Changer is like "taking matter out of physics, heat out of fire, fragrance out of flowers, and numbers out of mathematics." To do so is to create an artificial homiletical gulf between the triumvirate—the spokesperson for the Sovereign, the Scripture, and the Spirit that is characterized by a tripartite partnership. It is my conviction that when we divorce preaching from the Pneuma, we are guilty of "splitting apart what God has joined together."

The dire need for today is preachers on fire—preachers with burning hearts and flaming tongues. We need powerful and faithful preaching to send people away renewed, refreshed, and ready to serve. Instead of unction-*less* ministers, let us be unction-*full* ministers. If we are devoid of fire, nothing else matters. If we possess the fire, everything matters. "It were

---

74. Keener, *Three Crucial Questions*, 61.
75. Heisler, *Spirit-Led Preaching*, 7.

better to speak six words in the power of the Holy Spirit than to preach seventy years of sermons without the Spirit."[76]

We can ignore this homiletical injunction at our own risk. Without fire, there is no overpowering sense of urgency. Without fire, scholarship and style will replace passion and power. Without fire, how can we preach with passion and conviction? Without fire, how can we set the hearts of people aflame? There can be no convincing, convicting, change, or conversion. There can be no genuine transformation but only transfer of information (getting out, not through).

> The gospel is preached in the ears of all; it only comes with power to some. The power that is in the gospel does not lie in the eloquence of the preacher; otherwise, men would be converters of souls. Nor does it lie in the preacher's learning; otherwise, it would consist in the wisdom of men. We might preach till our tongues rotted, till we should exhaust our lungs and die, but never a soul would be converted unless there were mysterious power going with it—the Holy Ghost changing the will of men. O Sirs! We might as well preach to stone walls as preach to humanity unless the Holy Ghost be with the word, to give it power to convert the soul.[77]

Since theology breeds methodology, we need to get our theology of pneumatology right in homiletics. If our theology of pneumatology is defective, distorted, and diverged from the biblical track, our homiletical and hermeneutical trains will be heading for derailment and wreckage. From the vantage point of homiletics and hermeneutics, any preaching that fails to factor in the Game Changer is exegetically iffy, biblically inadequate, theologically defective, homiletically ineffective, and historically untenable.

Through the work of the Holy Spirit, the Living Word became Flesh and tabernacled among us. In the same way, the Written Word that was given to us cannot become Fresh in this postmodern world without the Holy Spirit. "In this new time we need preaching that is bold and urgent, honest and humble, daring and provocative,"[78] which is only made possible when we factor in the Holy Spirit and preach in the power of the Pneuma.

The Church still has a theology of the Holy Spirit, but it has no living consciousness of his presence and power. Theology without experience is like faith without works and is therefore dead.[79]

---

76. Spurgeon, *Sermons 1877–1937*, 733.
77. Charles H. Spurgeon quoted in Stott, *I Believe in Preaching*, 335.
78. Robinson and Wall, *Called to Be Church*, 69.
79. Chadwick, *Way to Pentecost*, 13.

Relatedly, any preaching done within the ambit of a Trinitarian tapestry gives homiletical legitimacy to pneumatic preaching. Pneumatic preaching produces powerful, persuasive, pertinent preaching that creates impact and effect changes in listeners' lives. Consequently, a script becomes a sermon and a manuscript becomes a message when it is delivered in the power of the Pneuma. Such preaching is not dependent on tools, techniques, or technology but rather the Transformer, the Third Person of the Trinity, the Holy Spirit.

When we persuasively proclaim God's Word in the power of the Holy Spirit, then we can expect the Spirit to work in the hearts and lives of those who hear the Word. As people hear the Word preached persuasively by the Spirit's power, then those people must be encouraged to respond to God's Word.[80]

The Triune God's email to those who proclaim the Unchanging Word in a digitally changing world is the same yesterday, today, and forever— "No Unction in the Pulpit, No Action in the Pews." Only Spirit-fuelled and Spirit-filled preaching can inspire people to action, see transformational fruits, and produce tangible results with maximum impact and lingering effect. The good news is that unction is available to all preachers who desire to preach in the power of the Pneuma.

It is important to note that an emphasis on preaching in the power of the Holy Spirit does not in any way minimize the need for developing the discipline of diligent sermon preparation[81] or the necessity of accurate exegesis of the biblical text.[82] When we misread the text, we misrepresent God and mislead the listeners.[83]

> I believe in the primacy of preaching the Word and the efficacy of preaching with unction. In our preaching there must be truth and eloquence, reason and passion, light and fire. Truth and eloquence, reason and passion, light and fire should never be divorced. When combined, they become irresistible in their power namely theology on fire, passionate truth, eloquent reason.[84]

---

80. Overstreet, *Persuasive Preaching*, 192.

81. Because of his sovereignty, it is possible for the Holy Spirit, at the moment of preaching, to lead the preacher to preach a different sermon or text than the one prepared. Such occasion, however, would be the exception rather than the norm.

82. Lim, "Hermeneutical Rules for Reading Biblical Texts"; "How Then Shall We Read?"; "Art of Reading Scripture"; "Theological Hermeneutics."

83. For a detailed treatment, see Lim, *Strategy for Reading Biblical Texts*.

84. Stott, *I Believe in Preaching*, 286. See also Congar, *Word and the Spirit*; Kendall et al., *Word Spirit Power*; Choy, *Powerlines*.

In the Chinese language there is a famous idiom that says, "*Wànshì jù bèi, zh☒ qiàn dōngfēng*" (Everything is ready, only lacking is a strong wind).[85] Let us pray for the wind (pneuma).

> Preacher, make it your pledge that you never again will enter your pulpit alone. Determine that you will, regardless of the cost or consequences, be God's servant on fire. With God's Spirit you will shine the light of your ministry on God's only begotten Son.[86]

As proclaimers of the Word, we have been to Calvary for pardon. But have we been to Pentecost for power? May the words of the prophet Micah be reflected in our preaching ministry. "But as for me, I am filled with power—with the Spirit of the LORD" (Mic 3:8).

Bibliography

Arrington, Yancey. *Preaching that Moves People*. League City, TX: Clear Creek Resources, 2018.

Averback, Richard E. "Breath, Wind, Spirit, and the Holy Spirit." In *Presence, Power, and Promise: The Role of the Spirit of God in the Old Testament*, edited by David G. Firth and Paul D. Wegner, 25–37. Downers Grove, IL: IVP Academic, 2011.

Azurdia, Arturo G. *Spirit Empowered Preaching*. Rosshire, UK: Christian Focus, 1998.

Bailey, Raymond. *Paul the Preacher*. Nashville: Broadman, 1991.

Barclay, William. *The Promise of the Spirit*. Louisville: Westminster John Knox, 1960.

Barth, Karl. *The Preaching of the Gospel*. Translated by B. E. Hooke. Philadelphia: Westminster, 1963.

Beeaudean, John William, Jr. *Paul's Theology of Preaching*. Macon, GA: Mercer University Press, 1988.

Brown, David M. *Transformational Preaching: The Basics*. College Station, TX: Virtual Bookworm, 2010.

Bruce, Kate. *Igniting the Heart*. London: SCM, 2015.

Brunner, Frederick Dale. *A Theology of the Holy Spirit: The Pentecostal Experience and the New Testament Witness*. Eugene, OR: Wipf & Stock, 1970.

Burke, Trevor J., and Keith Warrington. *A Biblical Theology of the Holy Spirit*. London: SPCK, 2014.

Chadwick, Samuel. *The Way to Pentecost*. 1932. Reprint, Dixon, MO: Rare Christian, 2001.

Chan, Francis. *The Forgotten God*. Colorado Springs, CO: David C. Cook, 2009.

Choy, Leona Frances. *Powerlines: What Evangelicals Believed about the Holy Spirit 1850–1930*. Camp Hill, PN: Christian, 1990.

---

85. I want to thank Minister Mentor Daniel Soh who was the former president of Queenstown Baptist Church for sharing this apt idiom at a Church Business meeting about three years ago.

86. Holmes, "Power behind Every Great Preacher's Throne," 56.

Congar, Yves M. J. *The Word and the Spirit*. Translated by David Smith. San Francisco: Harper & Row, 1986.
Day, David, et al., eds. *A Reader on Preaching: Making Connections*. London: Routledge, 2005.
Dryer, Elizabeth A. *Holy Power, Holy Presence*. Mahwah, NJ: Paulist, 2007.
Duewel, Wesley L. *Ablaze For God*. Grand Rapids, MI: Zondervan, 1989.
Dunn, James D. G. *The Christ and the Spirit*. Vol. 2. Grand Rapids, MI: Eerdmans, 1998.
Eclov, Lee. "How Does Unction Function?" In *Art and Craft of Biblical Preaching*, edited by Haddon Robinson and Craig Larson, 81–84. Grand Rapids, MI: Zondervan, 2005.
Edwards, O. C., Jr. *A History of Preaching*. Nashville: Abingdon, 2004.
Ellis, Chris. "Gathering around the Word: Baptists, Scripture and Worship." In *'The Plainly Revealed' Word of God? Baptist Hermeneutics in Theory and Practice*, edited by Helen Dare and Simon Woodman, 101–121. Macon, GA: Mercer University Press, 2011.
Fabarez, Michael. *Preaching that Changes*. Nashville: Thomas Nelson, 2002.
Forbes, James. *The Holy Spirit and Preaching*. Nashville: Abingdon, 1989.
Forsyth, P. T. *Positive Preaching and the Modern Mind*. Grand Rapids, MI: Eerdmans, 1964.
Gericke, Paul. *Prince of Preachers: The Apostle Paul*. New York: University Press of America, 2006.
Gross, Nancy Lammers. *If You Cannot Preach Like Paul*. Grand Rapids, MI: Eerdmans, 2002.
Hauerwas, Stanley, and William H. Willimon. *Holy Spirit*. Nashville: Abingdon, 2015.
Haya-Prats, Gonzalo. *Empowered Believers: The Holy Spirit in the Book of Acts*. Edited by Paul Elbert. Translated by Scott A. Ellington. Eugene, OR: Cascade, 2011.
Heisler, Greg. *Spirit-Led Preaching*. Nashville: Broadman and Holman, 2007.
Heywood, David. *Transforming Preaching*. London: SPCK, 2013.
Hoehner, Harold W. *Ephesians: An Exegetical Commentary*. Grand Rapids, MI: Baker Academic, 2002.
Holmes, Leslie. "The Power Behind Every Great Preacher's Throne." *Preaching* 29.3 (2013) 54–56.
Hooke, Ruthanna B. *Transforming Preaching*. New York: Church, 2010.
House, H. Wayne, and Daniel G. Garland. *Faithful Preaching: Preparing and Delivering Transformational Sermons*. Silverton, OR: Lampion, 2015.
Johnson, Mark A. "Preaching the Word: An Interview with Stephen F. Olford." *Preaching* 13.1 (1997) 8–14.
Kallenberg, Brad J. *God and Gadgets*. Eugene, OR: Cascade, 2011.
Keener, Craig S. *Three Crucial Questions about the Holy Spirit*. Grand Rapids: Baker, 1996.
Kendall, R. T., et al. *Word Spirit Power*. Bloomington, MN: Chosen, 2012.
Knowles, Michael P. *We Preach Not Ourselves: Paul on Proclamation*. Louisville: Westminster John Knox, 2001.
Lawson, Steven J. *The Kind of Preaching God Blesses*. Eugene, OR: Harvest, 2013.
Lim, Johnson T. K. "An Art of Reading Scripture." *Mission Today* 5.3 (2003) 270–76.
———, ed. *Empowering Spirit and Christian Living*. Singapore: Word N Works, 2018.
———. "Hermeneutical Rules for Reading Biblical Texts." *Mission Today* 3.2 (2001) 173–79.

———, ed. *Holy Spirit: Spokesperson, Scripture, Sermon*. Singapore: Word N Works, 2018.

———, ed. *Holy Spirit: Unfinished Agenda*. Singapore: Armour, 2015.

———. "How Then Shall We Preach?" *Church and Society* 6.2 (2003) 55–89.

———. "How Then Shall We Read?" *Church and Society* 5.3 (2002): 85–92.

———. "Is Preaching Still Relevant Today?" *Asian Baptist Journal of Theology* 1.1 (2007) 142–66.

———. *A Strategy for Reading Biblical Texts*. Studies in Biblical Literature Monograph Series 29. Berlin: Peter Lang, 2002.

———. "Theological Hermeneutics: A Reading Strategy." *Asia Journal of Theology* 15.1 (2001) 2–13.

———. "What's the Big Fuss Over an Apple?" In *Take Root Downward, Bear Fruit Upward in A Festschrift Presented to Lien-Hwa Chow on the Occasion of His Eighty-Eighth Birthday*, edited by Johnson T. K. Lim, 171–96. Hong Kong: ABGTS, 2008.

———. "What's Wrong with Contemporary Preaching?" *Church and Society* 4.3 (2001) 115–26.

Lisher, Richard. *The End of Words: The Language of Reconciliation in a Culture of Violence*. Grand Rapids, MI: Eerdmans, 2005.

Litfin, Duane. *Paul's Theology of Preaching*. Rev. ed. Downers Grove, IL: IVP Academic, 2015.

Lloyd-Jones, Martyn. *Joy Unspeakable: Power and Renewal in the Holy Spirit*. Eastbound, England: Shaw, 2000.

———. *Preaching and Preachers*. London: Hodder and Stoughton, 1971.

Low, Maggie. *Preaching that Comes Alive: Delivering a Word from the Lord*. Carlisle, UK: Langham Global Library, 2017.

McDonnell, Kilain. "Spirit and Experience in Bernard Clairvaux." *Theological Studies* 58.1 (1997) 3–18.

Moehler, R. Albert. "A Theology of Preaching." In *Handbook of Contemporary Preaching*, edited by Michael Duduit, 13–20. Nashville: Broadman, 1992.

Murphy, Herta A., et al. *Effective Business Communication*. New York: McGraw Hill Education, 1997.

Olford, Stephen F. *Anointed Expository Preaching*. Nashville: Broadman & Holman, 1998.

Osborn, Ronald E. *Folly of God: The Rise of Christian Preaching*. St. Louis, MO: Chalice, 1999.

Overstreet, R. Larry. *Persuasive Preaching*. Wooster, OH: Weaver, 2014.

Phillips, John. *The Life and Legacy of Stephen Olford*. Jackson, TN: Stephen Olford Ministries, 2006.

Ravenhill, Leonard. *Why Revival Tarries*. Minneapolis, MN: Bethany Fellowship, 1979.

Robinson, Anthony B., and Robert W. Wall. *Called to Be Church: The Book of Acts for a New Day*. Grand Rapids, MI: Eerdmans, 2006.

Sargent, Tony. *The Sacred Anointing*. Wheaton, IL: Crossway, 1994.

Shults, F. LeRon, and Andrea Hollingsworth. *The Holy Spirit*. Grand Rapids, MI: Eerdmans, 2008.

Smith, Oswald J. *The Enduement for Power*. London: Marshall, Morgan & Scott, 1951.

Snyder, James L., ed. *Tozer: Mystery of the Holy Spirit*. Alachua, FL: Bridge-Logos, 2007.

Spurgeon, Charles H. *Sermons 1877–1937*. Vol. 32 of *The Complete Works of C. H. Spurgeon*. Fort Collins, CO: Delmarva, 2013.

Stevenson, Peter K. *Preaching*. London: SCM, 2017.
Storms, Sam. *Practicing the Power*. Grand Rapids, MI: Zondervan, 2017.
Stott, John. *I Believe in Preaching*. London: Hodder and Stoughton, 1982.
Stout, Stephen Oliver. *Preach the Word: A Pauline Theology of Preaching Based on 2 Timothy 4:1–5*. Eugene, OR: Wipf & Stock, 2014.
Thiselton, Anthony C. *The Holy Spirit in Biblical Teaching, Through the Centuries and Today*. Grand Rapids, MI: Eerdmans, 2013.
Thompson, James W. *Preaching Like Paul*. Louisville: Westminster John Knox, 2001.
Tozer, A. W. *How to Be Filled with the Holy Spirit*. 1972. Reprint, Harrisburg, PA: WingSpread, 2008.
Turner, Max. *The Holy Spirit and Spiritual Gifts: In the New Testament and Church Today*. Peabody, MA: Hendrickson, 1996.
Vines, Jerry, and Jim Shaddix. *Power in the Pulpit*. Chicago: Moody, 1999.
Wilson, Paul Scott. *The Practice of Preaching*. Rev. ed. Nashville: Abingdon, 2007.
Wilton, Don. "The Preaching of Billy Graham." *Preaching* 29.3 (2013) 10–13.
Wright, Stephen I. *Alive to the Word*. London: SCM, 2010.
Yim, Howard Robert. "Preaching God's Word 'in Demonstration of the Spirit and of Power.'" In *Essays on Apostolic Themes*, edited by Paul Elbert, 71–81. Peabody, MA: Hendrickson, 1985.
Zuck, Roy B. *The Holy Spirit in Your Teaching: The Relationship that Makes All the Difference*. Wheaton, IL: Victor, 1963.

Preaching to the Javanese People of Indonesia

Sari Saptorini

CALVIN MILLER SAYS THAT a preacher must analyze his audience so that the sermon will not miss the mark. To set the issue straight, he proposes four questions that must be asked: (1) Who's out there?; (2) What do they believe?; (3) What do they know about God?; and (4) How can we help audiences come to terms with who they are.[1] This article focuses on the Javanese people of Indonesia as the audience of the preaching. By taking the Javanese worldview, ethics, customs, and traditions into consideration, an approach in preaching to the Javanese can be developed.

Javanese Ethnic Group

Indonesia has thousands of islands and hundreds of ethnic groups, but Javanese is the largest ethnic group in Indonesia. The majority of Javanese people live in Central Java Province, East Java Province, and Yogyakarta. Besides those three areas, the Javanese people can also be found in Lampung, Banten, Jakarta, and North Sumatra. In West Java, some Javanese people live in Indramayu and Cirebon.[2]

---

1. Miller, *Preaching the Art of Narrative Exposition*, 43–45.
2. Pram, *Suku Bangsa Dunia dan Kebudayaannya*, 47.

Javanese Worldview: Kejawen

The Javanese people's worldview is called "Javanese Philosophy" or "*Kejawen* Philosophy."[3] The Javanese Philosophy was formed by the original Javanese culture (animism and dynamism), a development resulting from the influences of Hinduism, Buddhism, and Islam. The Indian people came to Indonesia bringing Hindu and Buddhist religions. The Muslims also spread Islamic religion and philosophy. The original Javanese culture and the philosophies of Hindu, Buddha and Islam merged into one realm of mind that is now Javanese philosophy.[4] The times certainly affect this Javanese worldview so that it changes and shifts. But history has proven that the changes and shifts that happened did not uproot the Javanese worldview from its roots.[5]

The etymology of the term "Kejawen" or "Kajawen" is from the word "Jawi," which is the cultured form of the word "Jawa." On progress, this term *Kejawen* has been given varied meanings by observers, authors, and even the Javanese people themselves. People often interpret *Kejawen* as "the science of Javanese mysticism." Some give it a broader meaning, that it is the Javanese culture. There are also those who interpret *Kejawen* as the *Javanism* itself. The term Kejawen can also provide a place for what Koentjaraningrat means as "Jawi Religion" or as "Javanese people religion." Niels Mulder interprets it as "the core of Javanese culture." Although it is not a religion in itself, it contains the religious attitude, a worldview that differentiates between the sacred and the worldly.[6]

Javanese philosophy has sailed the vast ocean through the cultural influences of archipelago, Hindu-Buddhist culture, Islamic culture, and modern western culture. Because all of human experience and appreciation cannot be described in words, it has been used figuratively since long ago.[7] The Javanese people like to reveal something with symbols so that those who are not familiar with it can misunderstand in perceiving it.

Mulder views the Javanese way of thinking as a mental act that disciplines symptoms and experiences to become clear. Javanese thought and

---

3. MH, *Falsafah dan Pandangan Hidup Orang Jawa*, 146; Sujamto, *Reorientasi dan Revitalisasi Pandangan Hidup Jawa*, 42–43. According to Sujamto, the term *kejawen* embraces all understanding in the Javanese worldview or Javanese outlook or Javanese Cultural outlook, and it is not different from the term "Javanese Philosophy."

4. Pranowo, *Orang Jawa Jadi Teroris*, 211.

5. MH, *Falsafah dan Pandangan Hidup Orang Jawa*, 148.

6. Mulder, *Mistisisme Jawa*, 39.

7. Ciptoprawiro, *Filsafat Jawa*, 31.

reasons always crave salvation and prosperity.[8] Javanese minds formulate human life in two cosmos (world), i.e., macrocosm and microcosm. The macrocosm in the minds of the Javanese is the attitude and view of the universe containing supernatural powers and other mysterious things. The microcosm is the attitude and view on the real world. The ultimate goal in life is to seek and create harmony and balance between the lives of the microcosm and the macrocosm. Attitudes and views to the real world (microcosm) is reflected in human life with the environment, the human order in society, the order of daily life, and everything that can be seen by eye.[9]

The basic views or concepts of Javanese philosophy include the existence of God, the universe, the origin of humans, Javanese mythology, civilization and cultural practices, and language.[10] There are some general concepts in *Kejawen*. First, the concept of unity, in which human beings and the universe are sparks of divine substance. In Javanese mysticism, that unity is known with the term *Manunggaling Kawula Gusti* (the concept of the Union of God with his creature). Second, the concept of the human being, in which the human being is composed of the outward and inward aspects. Third, the concept of development, in which is the effort to restore the harmonious and consistent unity.[11]

Javanese Worldview on God: *Manunggaling Kawula-Gusti*

In general, Javanese people believe in God. In the pure view of *Kejawen*, God is experienced as the Almighty Substance, which cannot be described in terms of his being and circumstances. In Javanese, the perception of God is illustrated with the words *Tan Kena Kinayangapa* (unspeakable, unimaginable). These are the common names of God in *Kejawen*: *Gusti Allah* (The Lord God), *Gusti Ingkang Maha Asih* (God the Most Merciful), *Gusti Ingkang Maha Agung* (God the Greatest), *Gusti Ingkang Murbeng Dumadi* (The One and Only God, God the Determinant of the fate of all beings), *Gusti Sangkan Paraning Dumadi* (God of the Origin and Purpose of Life), *Gusti Kang Akarya Jagad Saisine* (God the Creator of the Universe), and *Gusti Kang Maha Nikan* (The Almighty God). The perception of God depicted in the phrase *Tan Kena Kinayangapa* recognizes that whenever people try to describe or explain the essence of God, the description or explanation of God must not describe God's nature exactly, properly, or completely. This

---

8. Endraswara, *Falsafah Hidup Jawa*, 46.
9. Dumadi, *Mikul Dhuwur Mendhem Jero*, 31.
10. MH, *Falsafah dan Pandangan Hidup Orang Jawa*, 115.
11. Endraswara, *Falsafah Hidup Jawa*, 46.

can be compared to a blind man who touches an elephant and then describes how he thinks the elephant looks.[12]

Being aware of such a fact, they do not like to debate their stance or beliefs about God. They never assume that their beliefs or convictions are the most correct and that the other is wrong. Why, then, do the Javanese, who think God is unspeakable and unimaginable, believe that God exists? The reason is that many of them, with diligent efforts, can achieve a religious experience, often called *Manunggaling Kawula-Gusti* or *Pamoring Kawula-Gusti* (the union of God with his creatures), *Unio-mystica*, etc.[13]

The term *Manunggaling Kawula-Gusti* is often used in two contexts in Javanese culture, namely: (1) the mystical/religious-spiritual context and (2) the sociocultural context. But in our case, the highlighted part is only its religious-spiritual context, in which *Manunggaling Kawula-Gusti* is regarded as the level of quality, the highest level that can be achieved by human beings in improving their quality.[14] This *Manunggaling Kawula-Gusti* is a form of personal experience.

Javanese Worldview on Human:
Sangkan Paraning Dumadi

The Javanese view of the origin and purpose of life or the beginning and the end of the life of everything that exists in this world, especially the human, is called *Sangkan Paraning Dumadi*. Life in this world, according to the Javanese view, is only a short stop. It is like a brief stop for a drink. Therefore, the transitory world is called the *madya* or *madyapada*, which means it lies in the middle, between the *purwa* (beginning) realm and the *wasana* (end) realm. But the *purwa* realm and *wasana* realm are essentially one.[15] Humans and everything that exist in this universe are the creation, derived from the Supreme Creator, God Almighty. And everything will return to its origin, that is, God the Almighty. Talking about *Sangkan Paraning Dumadi* in Javanese culture usually only revolves around the process of human ontogenic development, with interpretations that tend to be only mystical. The process of phylogenetic development of beings or the evolutionary process are treated as if it were considered "not its business"; instead, this is "the business of the science."[16]

12. Sujamto, *Reorientasi dan Revitalisasi Pandangan Hidup Jawa*, 49.
13. Sujamto, *Reorientasi dan Revitalisasi Pandangan Hidup Jawa*, 50–52.
14. Sujamto, *Reorientasi dan Revitalisasi Pandangan Hidup Jawa*, 68.
15. Sujamto, *Reorientasi dan Revitalisasi Pandangan Hidup Jawa*, 53–54.
16. Sujamto, *Reorientasi dan Revitalisasi Pandangan Hidup Jawa*, 55. Ontogeny is

The view of evolution or *Sangkan Paraning Dumadi* is phylogenetic in Javanese (and in Javanese language), although the source is obviously Indian/Hindu, described in the story of the incarnation of Vishnu up to ten times, where the stages of the Vishnu's evolution process were increasingly moving in a higher direction.[17]

From our exposure to the Javanese worldview on God and human beings so far, we know that the Javanese believe in the unspeakable, unimaginable God. Although the Javanese do not like to debate about their belief in God, they must know what kind of God would be qualified to be the cause of all that we know about the universe. First, God would have to be a God of awesome power. The universe is an effect that demands a very great cause, so God must be supremely powerful. Second, this God must be personal, possessing intelligence and will. Third, God must exist outside of time. Fourth, the God who created would also have the right to bring his creation to an abrupt halt whenever he chooses. God is not only powerful but also moral. The Javanese would agree on that. Here, the Christian God best fits this description.[18] The God-centeredness is basic to the Christian mind. To the Christian mind, wisdom is the fear of God and the pre-eminent virtue is humility.[19]

The Javanese crave union with that God. Preaching to the Javanese should address the concept of *Manunggaling Kawula-Gusti* and *Sangkan Paraning Dumadi*. Preaching about the purpose of life would be very interesting to the Javanese people. Humans often asks about their life's purpose. To know his/her purpose, man cannot start from him/herself. Man must

---

the development or a course of development of an individual organism. While phylogeny is the evolutionary history of a kind of organism, the evolution of a genetically related group of organisms as distinguished from the development of the individual organism.

17. Sujamto, *Reorientasi dan Revitalisasi Pandangan Hidup Jawa*, 64.
The stages of Vishnu's evolution process:
Bathara Wisnu nitis dados mina (Vishnu incarnated into fish)
Bathara Wisnu nitis dados kura (Vishnu incarnated into turtle)
Bathara Wisnu nitis dados garudha (Vishnu incarnated into bird Garudha)
Bathara Wisnu nitis dados landhak (Vishnu incarnated into porcupine)
Bathara Wisnu nitis dados singa barong (Vishnu incarnated into lion barong)
Bathara Wisnu nitis dados cebol (Vishnu incarnated into dwarf)
Bathara Wisnu nitis dados Rama Bargawa (Vishnu incarnated into Rama Bargawa)
Bathara Wisnu nitis dados Harjuna Sasrabahu (Vishnu incarnated into Harjuna Sasrabahu)
Bathara Wisnu nitis dados Rama Wijaya (Vishnu incarnated into Rama Wijaya)
Bathara Wisnu nitis dados Sri Khresna (Vishnu incarnated into Sri Khresna)

18. Lutzer, *Seven Reasons*, 149–50.
19. Stott, *Decisive Issues Facing Christians Today*, 38.

start with his/her Creator, who is God.[20] Only the Creator knows the purpose of his creatures. And to know God, Javanese people need to shift from the concept of *Tan Kena Kinayangapa* to the concept of God who reveals himself.

Through Vishnu's depiction, we can use this as a bridge to introduce the incarnate God in Jesus Christ (Phil 2:6-8), in which the incarnation is not an evolutionary process but rather, once and for all, as the only way for those who believe in him to reach the highest level, namely the *Manunggaling Kawula-Gusti* craved by the Javanese. The holy God was willing to reveal himself, came to the world, and took the form of a servant. Jesus Christ is the only incarnation of God, the Creator and Ruler of the universe, who is different from Vishnu in Kejawen belief. The Incarnation of Jesus Christ is perfect and has the greatest purpose, which is the salvation of humanity.

The concept of *Manunggaling Kawula-Gusti* can be explained as follows: after someone believes and accepts Jesus Christ as his/her Lord and Savior, the Holy Spirit or the Spirit of God will dwell in him/her (Eph 1:13; Rom 8:9; 1 Cor 3:16). The union of God with the person means that God is in us and we are in God (John 17:21; 15:5-7). Whoever believes in Jesus Christ will be in his Kingdom (John 14:2-3). This needs the personal experience of a person. This is the highest level that can be achieved by human beings in improving their quality. A preacher can use the teachings in *Kejawen* as a bridge to preach the truth of God and his Word, but the preacher must also be careful to avoid syncretism.

This syncretism is suspect because the Javanese people have a strong religious spirit. Despite the way the Javanese adhere to religion as pliable, open, and non-fanatical, they are not based on one religion and still adhere to the existing *Kejawen* beliefs. The struggle of the Javanese with their religion, which is pliable and open, has resulted in a number of lifestyles which are all considered spiritual. The Javanese also believe in the calculations of bad and good days and some other superstitions that cannot be understood rationally.[21]

For the Javanese, living everyday life is already a part of religion. Y. B. Mangunwijaya clearly states that everything that Javanese believe, do, and justify in daily life contains values that are full of spiritualism.[22] The Javanese, however, basically have religious tastes, attitudes, and actions.[23] One example of such religious action is that the Javanese argue that human

---

20. Warren, *Kehidupan yang Digerakkan oleh Tujuan*, 18.
21. Mulyana, "Spiritualisme Jawa," 6.
22. Mangunwijaya, *Wastu Citra*, 13.
23. Mulyana, "Spiritualisme Jawa," 6.

beings must endeavor, meaning they must try in all things to *sakadarira* (as possible). The human being is obliged to try, but the provision is in God's hands. Effort in Javanese terms is called *kupiya*, inwardly and outwardly. *Kupiya* implies that life should be lived naturally.[24]

The sermon delivered to the Javanese, therefore, should be applicable to their daily lives. Richard Jackson says, "Biblical preaching brings Scripture alive in the 'now' with application. All that is said about the text must grow out of the text and be a faithful interpretation and application."[25] He also says, "When the text is combined with a simple outline of application, it will remain in the congregation's mind."[26] When the Word of God is applied to their daily lives, then their lives will be changed. Their tastes, attitudes, and actions will be in accordance with the Word of God.

Javanese Ethics, Customs, and Traditions

Regarding Javanese ethics, Magis Suseno says:

> The Javanese society places the individual as a secondary only, whereas the community itself plays a primary role, such that individual actions considered to disturb the general harmony will be deemed unnecessary. The Javanese have a phrase "empan nggawa papan," that means the Javanese must know where the contextual place in the constellation of community life. The difference between a person who acts rightly and acts wrongly is the difference between a person who knows the place and who does not.[27]

The Javanese society is famous for upholding the virtue or value of modesty in social life. For example, in the Javanese culture, there are so-called *andhap ashor* (that is, humility), *tepo sliro* (an attitude to understand other people), and *ewuh pekewuh* (the sense of shame from others that results in behaving more carefully). These three examples of attitude are well known and acknowledged by communities outside Java.

The Javanese have many distinct patterns of behavior. There are many Javanese customs that emphasize decency. This can even be seen at the level of language and speech of the Javanese. The Javanese people are required to always show respect towards others according to their degree,

---

24. Endraswara, *Falsafah Hidup Jawa*, 62.
25. Duduit, *Communicate With Power*, 84.
26. Duduit, *Communicate With Power*, 86.
27. Magis Suseno quoted in Sutrisno, *Sorotan Budaya Jawa dan yang Lainnya*, 19.

position, and social status. The Javanese customs for behaving before elders are: First, in speaking to older persons, we should not turn our backs on or look into their eyes when speaking. In addition, we should use polite words. We should not argue or cut the conversation short. Second, if the younger person will receive or give something to the elder, he or she must use both hands. Third, in shaking hands, the younger person should invite the elder to shake hands first. Fourth, if a younger person walks in front of an older person, he or she has to bow. Fifth, if there is an elder who stands because there are no seats and the younger people are sitting, they should let the older person sit in their place.

Javanese also have etiquette for eating. One should not have too much conversation, not make noise while chewing, leave no food and not let food scatter.

For the Javanese, there is no such thing as an unlucky number. However, due to western influence, some believe that certain numbers are unlucky. Many Javanese also believe in certain holy days, such as Friday *Kliwon*, Tuesday *Kliwon*, and the night before First *Suro* (names of days and month in Javanese Calendar).[28]

Marbangun says the "Javanese cannot escape from their tradition." Something that remains to this day still prevents the Javanese society from being free to think and act.[29] Javanese people are also very concerned about myths and beliefs in life. The Javanese generally still hold to the habits of their ancestors. For example, when a person has something new, such as a car, a house, or something of value, he must perform a ritual salvation first. If not, it is believed that the person will have a disaster or trial. In addition, there is still a custom to avoid marriage in the month of *Muharram*, because Javanese believe that month is a bad month. Such customs have existed since the earlier people, and if such traditions are violated, the people will bear the consequences.[30]

The beginning of Christianity was introduced to the Javanese community by evangelists from the West. However, the growth of believers in Java is most rapidly taking place when the Gospel is delivered by the Javanese laypeople and evangelists themselves. Their evangelism is integrative, encouraging the Javanese to remain part of their culture and society.[31] One of the churches formed by the conflict between Western missionaries and Javanese Christians is the Java Christian Church. The missionaries wanted the

---

28. MH, *Falsafah dan Pandangan Hidup Orang Jawa*, 185.
29. Marbangun quoted in Sutrisno, *Sorotan Budaya Jawa dan yang Lainnya*, 13.
30. Sutrisno, *Sorotan Budaya Jawa dan yang Lainnya*, 186.
31. Partonadi, *Komunitas Sadrach dan Akar Kontekstualnya*, 52.

Javanese who believed in Jesus to let go of their past—all of their attitudes, ways of life, morals, and tendency to address religion as a form of esoteric knowledge. But the Javanese who had become Christians decided they had the right to embrace and develop Christianity according to their own inner feelings and needs.[32]

Preaching to the Javanese people certainly needs to uphold the culture and ethics of Javanese society so that the sermon delivered is not something unfamiliar to the listener. Thus, the preacher must be able to dig up biblical principles and then relate them to daily life. Since the Javanese love the use of figures or symbols, in preaching the sermon, the preacher needs to give an illustration so that it will be easier for the listeners to remember and understand. Addressing the importance of illustration in preaching, Steve Brown says, "If you can't illustrate it, it's not true."[33]

A person who preaches to the Javanese must be able to understand his place in society. He is not only God's spokesperson but also obtains a social status in the Javanese society. The Javanese look upon clergy as someone who deserves to be respected and imitated. If a preacher cannot position himself as he should, it will be difficult for him to be heard when he is preaching. The accuracy of the use of Javanese language in preaching will also affect how the audiences receive the message delivered. Preaching to the Javanese, the preacher also needs to show the attitudes and behaviors that will be appreciated by the Javanese community. Although Javanese society shows respect for preachers who cannot be exemplary, that attitude is more likely to be an *ewuh pekewuh* attitude. The Javanese will not openly denounce their rejection of the preacher, but the rejection can be seen through, for example, the unwillingness to listen to their preaching or avoidance altogether.

There are Javanese people who state that tradition and religion are not contradictory—that in tradition there are also religious values. By practicing traditions, they assume that they have practiced the laws and commandments of the religion.[34] A preacher must be able to understand that the Javanese cannot be separated from their traditions. Therefore, the preacher must be able to convince his audience that the Bible is the ultimate authority in the life of the believer. Traditions or customs that can be given Christian meaning can be maintained. Yet the superstitious beliefs of Kejawen must be released from the life of the Javanese. In this case, the preacher needs to be able to do contextualization.

---

32. "Sinode GKJ."
33. Duduit, *Communicate With Power*, 27.
34. Simanjuntak, *Tradisi*, 156.

Hesselgrave defines contextualization from the Christian perspective as "the attempt to communicate the message of the person, works, Word, and will of God in a way that is faithful to God's revelation, especially as it is put forth in the teaching of Holy Scripture, and that is meaningful to respondents in their respective cultural and existential contexts."[35] In other words, contextualization must have a balance between faithfulness to the Bible and the relevance to the purpose (*meaningfulness to the audiences*).[36] With the guidance of the Holy Spirit, hard work, and appropriate contextualization, the Word of God can be well preached to the Javanese.

Preaching to the Javanese community can also be expressed in the form of art. In the life of Indonesian culture, the value of art is not only fully developed and produces a lot of beautiful artworks, but also—in many ways—the atmosphere and logic of art master the field of other cultures: political life, economic life, social life, and, especially, religious life. Art is one space for the cultural discourse of one society, one nation, or one nation-state, like Indonesia.[37] Based on research data, listeners of religious radio broadcasts are less than listeners of broadcasts concerning Javanese arts. This needs to be taken into consideration, so that preachers might preach through Javanese arts.[38] Some arts that can be used for preaching are *Wayang* (Javanese puppets), *Kethoprak* (Javanese play/drama), *tembang* (Javanese traditional songs), and *carita* (Javanese storytelling).

Conclusion

The Javanese need the truth about God and his Word in their lives. Their desire for the encounter and union with God and their hope for well-being and salvation can only be obtained in Jesus Christ. With the awareness of the brevity of life in this world, they seek to find purpose in life and to be careful in living by being bound to their traditions, customs, and habits that have religious values. The Javanese need to hear biblical, relevant, contextual, and life-changing sermons. A Christian preacher needs to understand the Javanese worldview so that he can preach with an approach that is acceptable to the Javanese. Moreover, because the Javanese also uphold good attitudes, behavior, and speech, then the preacher must also be able to put himself in his place properly. For the Javanese, this attitude speaks more than their words. If they can honor the preacher, they will honor the preaching too.

35. Hesselgrave, *Contextualization*, 115.
36. Hesselgrave, *Contextualization*, 115.
37. Marzali, *Antropologi Indonesia*, 104–5.
38. Simanjuntak, *Tradisi*, 154.

Bibliography

Ciptoprawiro, Abdullah *Filsafat Jawa*. Jakarta: Balai Pustaka, 1986.
Duduit, Michael, ed. *Communicate With Power*. Grand Rapids: Baker, 1996.
Dumadi, Janmo. *Mikul Dhuwur Mendhem Jero:Menyelami Falsafah Kosmologi Jawa*. Yogyakarta: Pura Pustaka, 2011.
Endraswara, Suwardi. *Falsafah Hidup Jawa*. Yogyakarta: Cakrawala, 2010.
Hesselgrave, David. "Contextualization That Is Authentic and Relevant." *International Journal of Frontier Missions* 12.3 (1995) 115–19.
Lutzer, Erwin W. *Seven Reasons Why You Can Trust the Bible*. Chicago: Moody, 1998.
Mangunwijaya, Y. B. *Wastu Citra: Pengantar ke Ilmu Budaya Bentuk Arsitektur Sendi-Sendi Filsafatnya Beserta Contoh-contoh Praktis*. Jakarta: Gramedia Pustaka Utama, 1988.
Marzali, Amri dkk. "Pendidikan Antropologi dan Pembangunan Indonesia." *Antropologi Indonesia, Indonesian Jurnal of Social and Cultural Anthropology* 26.62 (2000) 96–107.
MH, Yana. *Falsafah dan Pandangan Hidup Orang Jawa*. Yogyakarta: Bintang Cemerlang, 2012.
Miller, Calvin. *Preaching The Art of Narrative Exposition*. Grand Rapids: Baker, 2006.
Mulder, Niels. *Mistisisme Jawa: Ideologi di Indonesia*. Yogyakarta: PT LKiS Pelangi Aksara, 2001.
Mulyana. "Spiritualisme Jawa: Meraba Dimensi dan Pergulatan Religiusitas Orang Jawa." *Kejawen Jurnal Kebudayaan Jawa* 1.2 (2006) 1–13.
Partonadi, Soetarman Soediman. *Komunitas Sadrach dan Akar Kontekstualnya*. Jakarta: BPK Gunung Mulia, 2001.
Pram. *Suku Bangsa Dunia dan Kebudayaannya*. Jakarta: Cerdas Interaktif, 2013.
Pranowo, M. Bambang. *Orang Jawa Jadi Teroris*. Tangerang: Pustaka Alvabet, 2011.
Simanjuntak, Bungaran Antonius. *Tradisi, Agama, dan Akseptasi Modernisasi pada Masyarakat Jawa*. Jakarta: Yayasan Pustaka Obor Indonesia, 2016.
"Sinode GKJ." https://www.gkj.or.id/?pilih=halaman&aksi=arsip&id=2.
Stott, John. *Decisive Issues Facing Christians Today*. Grand Rapids: Fleming H. Revell, 1993.
Sujamto. *Reorientasi dan Revitalisasi Pandangan Hidup Jawa*. Semarang: Dhahara Prize, 2000.
Sutrisno, Slamet. *Sorotan Budaya Jawa dan yang Lainnya*. Yogyakarta: Andi Offset, 1985.
Warren, Rick. *Kehidupan yang Digerakkan oleh Tujuan*. Malang: Gandum Mas, 2005.

Embracing an Ocean Homiletic
Fiji's 'New Exodus' and the Sermons of Tuikilakila Waqairatu and Tevita Nawadra Banivanua

JERUSHA MATSEN NEAL

Introduction:

ON FEBRUARY 11, 2014, the Rev. Dr. Tuikilakila Waqairatu, President of the Methodist Church in Fiji, passed away. It was a critical year for Fiji and for the Methodist church. Elections were being held again for the first time since the military coup of 2006 and the church was celebrating 50 years of denominational autonomy, its "Jubilee Year." The church itself was going through a sea change. The years since the 2006 coup had not been easy for the Methodist church. After seizing power, the Fijian military leader, Voreqe Bainamarama, had systematically dismantled the church's funding structures, cancelling the church's Annual Conference and national choir festival.[1] He had jailed church leaders and restricted criticism of the current government from the pulpit. Waqairatu himself had spent several nights in jail for his opposition.[2] The Methodist Church in Fiji, used to acting as a power broker in a nation where the vast majority of the indigenous population identified as Methodist, was coming to terms with its politically diminished reality. It was also facing its demons. Bainamarama's coup was

---

1. Crampton, "Fiji Government."
2. Sekek, "Police Again Detain Church Leaders."

not the first coup in recent memory. Since 1987, the country of Fiji had endured a string of coups fueled by ethno-nationalist rhetoric and tribal fears of a growing Indo-Fijian populace. The church leadership, of mostly indigenous (*iTaukei*) ethnicity, was complicit in these government take-overs.[3] Waqairatu and his successor, Tevita Nawadra Banivanua, were faced with the difficult task of steering the church away from its past abuses of power while asserting the importance of the church's role and voice in an increasingly secular landscape.

In response, the two leaders employed a bold—some might say risky—rhetorical strategy. They co-opted a potent, biblical metaphor that had been previously used by the ethno-nationalist wing of the church and reframed it through traditional imagery and a new hermeneutical lens. Preaching was the primary tool in this effort. In the 1987 coup, the biblical narratives of exodus and exile were used to stoke indigenous fears of land-loss and victimization. They were metaphors used to justify the violent removal of Indo-Fijians from tribally-owned regions, regions that comprised over 80 percent of the Fijian landscape.[4] But for indigenous Fijians, the significance of these scriptural narratives predated the 1987 coup. The stories had enduring emotional resonance for tribes that identified with the biblical Israelites. More than this, the narratives evoked the losses of those who had seen their land occupied, polluted, and silenced by colonial power and rapid globalization.[5] Waqairatu and Banivanua wanted to embrace these latter resonances while rejecting the narratives' former ethno-nationalist function. To do this, they developed the language of "The New Exodus" (*Na Lako Yani Vou*) to describe the church's present season of transition. Echoing a burgeoning pan-Pacific interest in the significance of the ocean (*moana*) for South Pacific theology and recognizing the church's need for renewal, Waqairatu and Banivanua shifted the metaphor of "exodus" away from its previous preoccupation on land (*vanua*) and toward a communal commitment to migration. Employing the image of the mighty sea-faring *drua*, the metaphor of "New Exodus" became a call for transformation in ecclesial identity while maintaining the relevance of the church in Fiji's political future. The "New Exodus" would become a homiletic trope for both leaders, providing a prophetic call to church and state alike in a volatile political season.

---

3. Matt Tomlinson gives a succinct account of this history in Tomlinson, "Generation of Now," 80–84.

4. Kristoff, "Scores of Indians Injured." John Kelly and Martha Kaplan note the particular religious focus of the 1987 coup, describing the burning of mosques and temples in Kelly and Kaplan, *Represented Communities*, 139.

5. This connection between Israelite and iTaukei continues to have rhetorical, religious and political significance. See Jones, "Mountains of Israel," 271–82.

The development of this imagery in Waqairatu and Banivanua's sermons is significant for several reasons. First, it is a provocative example of how a homiletic metaphor can impact societal change. In her article, "From the Land to the Sea: Christianity, Community, and State in Fiji—and the 2014 Elections," social anthropologist Lynda Newland describes the changing relationship between church and state in Fiji over the past decade, noting the critical role that metaphors have played in envisioning that relationship.[6] She observes a rhetorical shift in the language of Fijian Methodist church leaders and a new emphasis on imagery of the ocean rather than land. What she does not fully credit is the role of preaching and biblical imagination in negotiating and communicating this transformation. This paper will sketch the homiletic development of this shift.

But Waqairatu and Banivanua's sermons do more than reveal the holistic significance of preaching in the Fijian context. They describe a specific approach to political theology. Waqairatu and Banivanua handle the "New Exodus" metaphor with deliberation and care, providing an example of rhetoric that honors particularity, attends to relationship, and claims the relevance of a living God within the body politic. It is not only the content of the metaphor that matters. The metaphorical form is itself significant in mitigating the danger and mining the promise of religious participation in political discourse.

Finally, Wagairatu and Banivanua's sermons provide a snapshot of how Fijian church leaders are using contextual biblical hermeneutics on the ground. Speaking from a Tongan perspective, Winston Halapua's influential book, *Waves of God's Embrace: Sacred Perspectives from the Ocean*, asserts the significance of the ocean in shaping a twenty-first century Oceanic theology. Jione Havea, part of the Tongan diaspora, echoes Halapua's argument for the "interconnectedness of life"[7] in his own discussions of the ocean's impact on the "fluid boundaries" of Oceanic identity.[8] Samoan theologian Upolu Vaii argues for a hermeneutical creativity that "leaves the lagoon" and enters the deep water of "fluidity, movement, restlessness, and unpredictability."[9] These broad affirmations of the ocean in pan-Pacific thought are a recurring contemporary theme. This theme, however, reads differently in Fiji. Fiji's political and ecclesial identity is different than those of its South Pacific neighbors. When the British brought large numbers of Indians to Fiji to work as indentured laborers in sugar-cane plantations, they created a multi-ethnic,

---

6. Newland, "From Land to Sea," 109–134.
7. Halapua, *Waves of God's Embrace*, 46.
8. Havea, "Engaging Scriptures from Oceania," 13–17.
9. Vaai, "Motu ma le Taula," 26–30.

multi-religious nation. The "fluidity" in Fiji's identity is not simply a function of its geography; it is a function of its colonial history. To shift the conversation away from the role of the land in Fijian ecclesiology and toward the role of the ocean is a risky, cruciform decision in this context. It requires the letting go of static certainties and stepping into an unknown future. For Waqairatu and Banivanua, such a risk could not be sustained by the rhetoric of secular democracy or the embrace of fluidity for its own sake. It required a robust theology of Spirit-empowered discernment and a regular reminder of God's resurrection power. In short, it required preaching.

Part One: Mapping the Metaphor of the Lako Yani Vou ("The New Exodus")

When Methodist lay preacher Sitiveni Rabuka described the "disgrace" of Fijian Christians in the time period surrounding his 1987 coup, his rhetorical description of the indigenous population as a "holy people" drew on Fijian folk traditions connecting the *iTaukei* people to the biblical Israelites.[10] The connection evoked the "emotional pull of Exodus [and] a people whose land has been taken away from them."[11] Despite the fact that *iTaukei* land-ownership was protected by the Fijian constitution and the danger of land loss is now considered to be "largely a fiction," growing numbers of elected Indo-Fijians in the government added legitimacy to this threat.[12] Rabuka used not only the exodus from Egypt to make his point but also what biblical scholars describe as the "new Exodus" of Israelite return from Babylonian exile. Preaching from Lamentations 5, Rabuka states, "Remember, oh Lord, what has happened to us. Our property is in the hands of strangers. Foreigners are living in our homes. . . . Driven hard like donkeys or camels we are tired but are allowed no rest."[13] Significantly, Rabuka is not referencing British colonizers in these complaints but rather descendants of the Indo-Fijian indentured laborers who had been farming leased *iTaukei* land for generations.

During the years leading up to Rabuka's coup, Tuikilakila Waqairatu was acquiring his MTh at Melbourne College of Divinity with a specialty in

---

10. The popular Kaunitoni migration story is often used to justify claims that Fijians are a lost tribe of Israel. First published in 1892, the story tells of a Fijian migration from Thebes to Tanganyika and then to Fiji. See France, "Kaunitoni Migration," 107–113; Thompson, "Kalou-Vu," 340–59.

11. Newland, "Lost Tribes of Israel," 257.

12. Newland, "Lost Tribes of Israel," 257.

13. Newland, "From Land to Sea," 112.

Hebrew Bible. His Master's thesis explored the book of Exodus in particular. The work of his life would be to translate this academic work into an affirmation and a transformation of the Fijian Methodist Church.

Waqairatu has been a difficult figure for historians to categorize. Born to a chiefly family and serving as principal of the deeply conservative Davuilevu Theological College, Waqairatu has become best known as a reformer, championing the cause of women called into ordained leadership and instigating a theological training program for pastor's wives during his tenure as principal. He stressed the importance of theological education, launching Bachelor of Divinity and Bachelor of Ministry programs at DTC.[14] Perhaps his most provocative stance in relation to the Fijian Methodist church was his call for restraint in the drinking of *yaqona*, a mild narcotic that serves as a staple in Fijian village life.[15] He was also particularly open to ecumenical cooperation between Christian denominations. In 2001, he served as secretary of the newly formed Assembly of Christian Churches in Fiji and returned as Chairman in 2005. At the time of his death, he also chaired of the Fiji Council of Churches. His involvement in the ACCF was significant in that the group provided a link between older, mainline Fijian denominations and newly forming Pentecostal communions. The group was also an outspoken critic of the Bainamarama government. As leader of the ACCF, Waiqairatu would denounce the 2006 coup as a "manifestation of darkness and evil,"[16] and he is widely believed to have co-authored the twenty-point statement, "Here We Stand," which argued that Bainamarama's takeover was a "treasonous act against the state."[17] In response, the military dictator accused the Methodist church of once again getting involved in politics, singling out Waqairatu as trying to "'whip up Fijian emotions,' specifically on the question of land."[18] The claim is not entirely unfair. Like many Methodist Fijians, Waqairatu embraced Christian "Kingdom principles"[19] as the proper foundation for Fiji's future. The church's warning in 2009 that God would curse a land and people that "neglected the true God" built on arguments from the 1990s that Fiji should be declared a Christian state.[20] Indeed, over the course of Waqairatu's leadership, the ACCF was perceived to

14. Methodist Church in Fiji, "Biographical Data of Rev. Dr. Tuikilakila Waqairatu."
15. Rika, "Legacy of Tuikilakila Waqairatu."
16. Newland, "Religion and Politics," 190.
17. Newland, "Religion and Politics," 193.
18. Newland, "Religion and Politics," 195.

19. Tuikilakila Waqairatu, unpublished notes in his personal bible, November 24, 2005. My great thanks to Radini Talatala Joana Waqairatu for access to Rev. Waqairatu's bible and sermon notes.

20. Tomlinson, "Generation of Now," 80–83.

be "the think tank" of Laisenia Qarase, a proponent of a more conservative *iTaukei* agenda, who Bainamarama removed from power.[21]

And yet, by the time of his death, Waqairatu had begun a review of the Methodist Constitution, clarifying the church's non-partisan political posture despite its prophetic witness. He had called the church to reject its complicity in the coups of the past. "We need to . . . ask for forgiveness," he said, "help people come to their senses and to repent." Speaking directly of Indo-Fijians, he continued, "We need to know interfaith relationship and understand them," a significant change in tone from the church's former rhetoric.[22] In addition, Waqairatu had negotiated a careful détente with the Bainamarama government and seen the reinstitution of the Methodist Annual Conference. When he was installed as President, moderate leaders who had stood in opposition to the ethno-nationalists were chosen to lay hands on his head. Waqairatu's six months as MCIF President laid the groundwork for a historic reconciliation service between church factions that took place at the Conference which followed his passing.

Perhaps the most significant contribution of Waqairatu's short presidency was the laying out of "Twelve Pillars" that represented the navigational course for the church's way forward in an uncertain season. Describing this journey as a "New Exodus," the pillars were paired with a new church logo, emphasizing a new inclusivity and a leaving behind of the church's "comfort zone."[23]

The pillars themselves had been officially developed during the years of the Annual Conference's cancellation and were adopted in 2012 at a

21. Newland, "Role of the Assembly," 308.
22. Rasoqosoqo, "Heal Our Land."
23. Methodist Church in Fiji, "Renewed Logo for a Renewed Church."

specially-called leadership retreat. Growing out of the experience of a "suffering church,"[24] the pillars reference the church's necessary liberation through "Christ's exodus in his death and resurrection," and draw on Ephesians 1:10 to define the church's mission as the "uniting and renewing of all . . . things—material and spiritual, in Christ."[25] Though broad, the pillars' themes are significant in emphasizing the spiritual nurture of both clergy and laity, ecumenical and inter-faith relationality, social services to the poor and creation stewardship. "Evangelism" and "salvation" are goals applied to both those who identify as Christian and those who do not, undermining ethnicity as a marker of "God's people."[26]

One might imagine that these pillars of reform grew out of governmental pressure, but Waqairatu's bible tells a different story. On the opening page of the bible presented to him when he became Deputy General Secretary of the church, Waqairatu has carefully copied out the notes of a sermon preached on November 24, 2005, laying out the church's "vision . . . to achieve."[27] There are sixteen points listed rather than the twelve highlighted eight years later, but the resonances between these points and the pillars of the New Exodus are clear. They were not simply reactive; they had been touchstones in Waqairatu's vision for the church prior to Bainamarama's coup.

This is no surprise for anyone who had heard Waqairatu preach. Certainly, the protection of indigenous identity and Christian privilege are themes in in his sermons. Speaking to US church leaders in 2011, Waqairatu uses the term "our New Exodus" to describe the necessity of Fiji's "liberation," implying that oppressive external forces had enslaved the church.[28] But more often, when Waqairatu uses exodus imagery in his sermons, he is discussing the necessary cleansing of the people prior to entering into God's promise (Josh 3:1–17). The oppressive forces are both internal and external to the community.[29]

More importantly, he uses exodus imagery to re-envision the relationship between the promised land of the biblical narrative and the precious *vanua* of the Fijian people. *Vanua,* in its most basic sense, can be translated "land." But it connotes far more. It includes all that the physical earth

24. Methodist Church in Fiji, "Rationale."
25. Methodist Church in Fiji, "Vision"; "Mission."
26. Bhagwan, "New Course for the Church."
27. Waqairatu, unpublished sermon notes, November 24, 2005.
28. Waqairatu, "Farewell to Bishop Warner Brown." The implicit critique of the government in this New Exodus language is never explicitly developed.
29. See, for example, the unpublished sermon notes in Waqairatu, "Na Lotu Ni Mataka"; "Needs of a New Exodus."

sustains, including animals, plant-life, and human communities. Most significantly, it includes the cultures, rituals, and relationships that define those communities. This multi-valent relationality is why iconic Fijian theologian I. S. Tuwere reminds readers that indigenous persons do "not own the land; the land owns [them]."[30] One can imagine, then, the ways that the language of "promised land," or "promised *vanua*," could be co-opted for the purposes of reclaiming a past purity of traditional culture. In his most developed sermon on the relationship between the Exodus narrative and ecclesial life, however, Waqairatu describes the "destiny" of the church not in terms of a *vanua* of the past—or even a reformed *vanua* of the future. Rather, he describes God's promise through the lens of the Lord's Supper. Pairing his Exodus texts with Mark 14:22–25 and 1 Corinthians 11:23–26, Waqairatu reimagines the present-tense ground from which the Fijian Methodist Church's identity grows. He suggests that the "promised land" of God's people is the shared proclamation of Christ's death and resurrection and a participation in a new covenant.[31]

It would require the sermons of Tevita Nawadra Banivanua to give shape and content to this claim. Banivanua and Waqairatu shared deep cultural ties, coming from the same village and tribe.[32] Throughout Waqairatu's leadership, Banivanua played a critical behind-the-scenes role in negotiations with the Bainamarama government, particularly after the imprisonment of MCIF church leaders.[33] Having received his Masters of Arts from Lancaster University's Department of Politics, Philosophy, and Religion in the UK, Banivanua spent over a decade as the General Secretary of the South Pacific Association of Theological Schools (SPATS).[34] An influential voice in shaping of the New Exodus's "Twelve Pillars," Banivanua insisted on the addition of ecumenical/interreligious relationships and the stewardship of creation as key goals.[35] An ecclesial diplomat and a firm believer in the church's ability to serve the common good, Banivanua seemed uniquely qualified to continue the careful balancing act that Waqairatu had left behind. This meant finding common ground with a distrustful government, congregations who remembered that government's abuses with resentment, and those who still desired Fiji's designation as a Christian state—all while

---

30. Tuwere, *Vanua*, 33.

31. Waqairatu, "Na Lako Yani (The Exodus)." For more detail, see Neal, "Exodus or Exile," 22–23.

32. Tevita Banivanua, email correspondence, August 27, 2018.

33. James Bhagwan, email correspondence, August 28, 2018.

34. Bhagwan, "Navigator Turns Captain," 5.

35. James Bhagwan, email correspondence, August 28, 2018.

recasting the Methodist Church's identity within an ethnically diverse populace. Acknowledging the "legally binding" reality of a secular Fijian government, Banivanua continued to affirm the right of the church to speak directly with congregations concerning its stance on political issues.[36] Newland documents his cautious handling of a letter from the Methodist Department of Citizenship and Social Issues critiquing the Bainamarama government's constitution prior to the general elections of 2014. Though he acknowledged the need for a better "internal policy for communication"[37] and denied approving the letter, he maintained the church's role as an advocate for Christian principles in the public domain. This hard-fought nuance in Banivanua's articulation of church/state relations would dissatisfy more polarized voices in church and government but demonstrates the leader's careful articulation of a complex relationality, his respect for proper procedures, and his commitment to the larger mission at stake.

These values would guide his mapping of the "New Exodus." If Waqairatu brought a spiritual muscularity to the "New Exodus" vision, Banivanua brought a specificity and a systematic eye. He recognized that "pillars" need foundations and scaffolding to stand, and his first task was to complete the review of the Methodist Church's Constitution and draft a Code of Conduct for church leaders.[38] Building on Waqairatu's themes of nation-building, Banivanua connects the "New Exodus" vision, not simply with the leaving of the difficult past but also the building of hopeful future—in his words, "a process of birthing."[39] In describing the journey, it is not the crossing of the Red Sea to which Banivanua turns. It is the reception of the law in the time of Moses and the rebuilding of the temple in the time of Nehemiah and Ezra. This institutional work is not sterile and bureaucratic for Banivanua; it is connected to the Fijian understanding of *veiwakani* or proper relationality. In Banivanua's understanding, the spiritual well-being of the church was connected with the restoration of proper relationships with the government, with other denominations, *vanua* leaders, and with the church's non-Christian neighbors.[40] These relationships were not only worked out in individual, spiritual ways; they were also communal, institutional commitments.

36. "New Methodist Leader."

37. Newland, "From Land to Sea," 119.

38. Banivanua, "Mapping the *Lako Yani Vou*." These structural goals of the New Exodus would be named "The Connexional Plan."

39. Banivanua, "Mapping the *Lako Yani Vou*."

40. Banivanua names the "restoration of relations" as the primary challenge of the church in a transitional season.

But such relationships required more than an appropriate meeting of procedural obligation. They required the weaving of a shared history. In his first major address to the church leaders on the direction of the New Exodus, Banivanua begins in a sermonic mode, retelling the story of the prior years through the lens of scripture. He is clear about the struggles that the church has endured, delineating particular abuses of the Bainamarama government. "It was by the grace of God that the Methodist Church stayed intact," he states.[41] But in his description of the Fijian Methodist Church's relationship to their land, he does not tell a simple narrative of loss and restoration any more than the Hebrew scriptures tell that simple story. Walter Brueggeman's classic treatise, *The Land: Place as Gift, Promise, and Challenge,* points to the promise and danger that the land holds for the Israelite people, particularly when that land is "grasped" rather than received as "gift."[42] There is a similar nuance to Banivanua's treatment of the theme. He does not cherry-pick scriptural promises of restoration. He asks the larger systemic question at the heart of the biblical text: "Why did God allow [this loss] to happen?"[43] Similar to the biblical prophets, Banivanua does not shy away from asserting divine "intention" in the difficult events of the previous years and he does not reject the possibility that the struggles of the Methodist Church might be critical to their "people's preparation"[44] for the future. The *Fiji Sun,* a newspaper widely acknowledged as the government's mouthpiece, would seize on Banivanua's statements, using his affirmation of God's sovereignty to assert that the military dictator's rule was an "act of God."[45] Those who heard Banivanua's "New Exodus" vision first hand, however, would know that government legitimization was far from his intent. Instead, the same specificity that shapes Banivanua's mapping of the ecclesial journey shapes his reading of scripture and his church's history. His sermon seems less concerned with rhetorical persuasion and more concerned with teaching his church to read the signs of the times and the narratives of scripture with attentive care.

Like Waqairatu, he is also concerned with a re-reading of the *vanua.* Giving his predecessor's recasting of the *vanua* radical concreteness, Banivanua states, "As Christian Fijians, we need to be inclusive in our understanding of the *vanua* to include all those other ethnic groups that also

---

41. Banivanua, "Mapping the *Lako Yani Vou.*"
42. Brueggemann, *Land,* 157.
43. Banivanua, "Mapping the *Lako Yani Vou.*"
44. Banivanua, "Mapping the *Lako Yani Vou.*"
45. Sovaraki, "Act of God."

live in the *vanua*."[46] There is a cautious mining of double meanings in this assertion, a dialectic between *vanua* as a descriptor of village culture and *vanua* as a descriptor of the land itself. Banivanua uses the diversity within the latter to call for diversity within the former. What Banivanua does with the biblical narrative, he also does for his church's understanding of their land, dislodging the *vanua* from rigid interpretation and opening up new possibilities of faithful, relational understanding.

Part Two: A Multivalent Metaphor: The Function of the Form

There is much at stake in Banivanua's use of "New Exodus" imagery. He is aware that the language draws on deep rhetorical traditions in his church and in the biblical text, as well as the metaphor's history in co-opting the church's witness. In reasserting the metaphor's importance, Banivanua is affirming the relevance of scripture for the Fijian Methodist experience and honoring the metaphor's emotional pull. But in his homiletic interpretation, new meanings emerge. Banivanua broadens the biblical landscape associated with "New Exodus" so that it connotes more than the restoration of promise. It connotes an extended journey, careful discernment of theological questions, and repentance. Sermonically, he accomplishes this in two ways: through careful engagement to extended biblical narratives and a regular return to the metaphor of the *drua* to connote contextually grounded change. Unlike a simple fishing boat, the *drua* was designed to carry whole communities across the ocean to lands that were new. Banivanua and Waqairatu's choice of this image as the visual interpretation of their "New Exodus" theme reclaims migratory movement as part of the indigenous experience alongside its commitment to continuity and place.

In his sermon at the 2016 Annual Conference, following the devastating impact of Cyclone Winston, Banivanau walks through Numbers 9, describing the harmonies in the biblical text between the structures of law and ritual and the people's readiness to follow the cloud of God's presence into newness and change. This is neither a simple call to liberation nor a simple call to build pillars of institutional stability. It is a call that asks the church to lean into the unknown of God's future and "listen to our spiritual instinct . . . following the Cloud and waiting with the Cloud" through "spiritual discernment."[47] Banivanua draws on theological and biblical resources to describe this discernment process, noting the Wesleyan church's

46. Banivanua, "Mapping the *Lako Yani Vou*."
47. Banivanua, "Signposts of the New Exodus."

"constantly reforming" nature.[48] But more than this, he draws on the images of traditional navigational skills—indigenous readings of land, sea, and sky—to argue that this kind of discernment and openness to change is deep *iTaukei* knowledge. "[Indigenous explorers] listened to the ocean and the wind," Banivanua states, "and discerned not only the way to go but [also] when to go."[49] The metaphor of the "New Exodus," in this case becomes more than a descriptor of present circumstances. It describes a process of engaged listening to God and to the world.

If Banivanua's goal is to model faithful discernment in changing circumstances, the use of metaphor itself is a significant strategy. Paul Ricoeur describes metaphor not as a substitute for the object or idea it connotes but rather as a performative "interplay" between the "is" and "is not" of the comparison.[50] Banivanua's sermonic use of "New Exodus" imagery underscores the communal, on-going nature of this interpretative work. In Banivanua's sermons, "New Exodus" is not reducible to a simple set of bullet points or political sound-bites. It describes a journey that, while containing signposts and structures, is ultimately dependent on a Cloud that leads. His sermons resist the flattening of the metaphor before the church's discernment process has taken place. This lack of specificity does not always yield a simple set of blueprints for the future and opens the metaphor to a variety of interpretations. In my years teaching preaching in Fiji, the "New Exodus" was cited in nearly half of the sermons I heard, often indicating very different agendas. The phrase might be used to argue for bible studies one week and working fax machines in district offices the next.[51] What is remarkable, however, is the extent of communal conversation that took place around the metaphor's meaning. Rather than using the language of "New Exodus" as a symbolic marker for a specific set of political and ecclesial goals, Banivanua uses the language to describe a process of contextually and biblically grounded change: a process in which *talanoa*—extended, communal conversation—is at the heart. In describing Pacific epistemology, Jione Havea notes the importance of a community's performance in determining the meaning of rituals and narratives. The goal is faithful, communal praxis rather than a purity of tradition. It is "what we do with and for one another"[52] that forms Pacific identity, Havea asserts, and this brings a brings a certain fluidity

---

48. Banivanua, "Signposts of the New Exodus."
49. Banivanua, "Signposts of the New Exodus."
50. Ricoeur, *Rule of Metaphor*, 248.
51. Neal, "Exodus or Exile," 20.
52. Havea, "Pasifika Secrets," 203–215.

to narratives and practices.[53] As a homiletic metaphor, the "New Exodus" initiates the communal praxis of discernment that it describes in a manner consistent with indigenous Fijian ways of making meaning.

It also leaves room for difference. Banivanua's attention to the biblical text's complexities and his invitation to communal conversation reveal an openness to plurivocal interpretations. This openness to multiplicity in religious conversation is a prophetic posture given the Methodist Church in Fiji's larger questions about faithful witness in a diverse, increasingly secularized context. There are similarities between this posture and Banivanua's insistence on the church's ability to have its voice in a secular world while not silencing the voices of others. In this way, Banivanua's approach to the "New Exodus" metaphor is significant for his political theology. By modeling what it would mean to honor difference and particularity in his sermon rhetoric, Banivanua is teaching what a broader attentiveness to difference and particularity would require. More significantly, he is not teaching "international ideas" in international ways.[54] He is teaching through face-to-face example,[55] drawing on familiar biblical narratives and indigenous tropes to make his point.

It's worth noting that the Fijian Methodist church has not often been characterized as "fluid" or particularly welcoming of difference. Upolu Vaii speaks of an "imperial theology" introduced by colonial missionaries that continues to influence Pacific theological institutions.[56] But Waqairatu and Banivanua's use of metaphor witnesses to contemporary ways that this "imperial hermeneutic" is being subverted in pulpit speech. The "interplay" required in interpreting the metaphor of the "New Exodus" grounds the process of change in indigenous soil.

Part Three: The New Exodus and the Risk of Resurrection

There is an unlikely place where "New Exodus" imagery is referenced in Waqairatu's preaching: at the start of his funeral sermons.[57] Using the lan-

53. Havea notes the Tongan practice of *talanoa fakatatau* that encourages Oceanic storytellers to be "fluid" in "giving a different shape to old stories" (Havea, "Releasing the Story of Esau," 91).

54. Newland, "From the Land to the Sea," 125. Newland notes the tension between a growing Fijian acceptance of "a liberal set of values, most of which originated in so-called Western countries" and a more village-centered *iTaukei* nationalism.

55. Unaisi Nabobo-Baba describes the importance of embodied example in Fijian epistemology and pedagogy in Nabobo-Baba, *Knowing and Learning*, 116–20.

56. Vaii, "*Va'atapalagi*," 42–43.

57. See, for example, Waqairatu, "Sermon for Mrs. Korovou Balelevuka."

guage of exodus and promise to describe the crossing over from death to life is nothing new of course. These comparisons run deep in the liturgy and hymnody of Christian tradition. For Waqairatu and Banivanua, however, the proclamation of resurrection has particular relevance for their larger "New Exodus" project. Finally, for all their talk about pillars and institutional goals, their "New Exodus" sermons are not about human action. They are about the action of God. In particular, they are about the action of God in the face of fear, human inadequacy, and death. For Waqairatu and Banivanua, the "New Exodus" is a witness to resurrection.

This is especially apparent in Banivanua's extended reflection on Revelation at the close of his "Mapping the *Lako Yani Vou*" address. Revelation 1–3 may seem an unlikely biblical "model" for the church's exodus journey.[58] And yet, this is the New Testament text that Banivanua pairs with his reading of the Hebrews' forty-year sojourn. At the heart of his reading of Revelation is the person of Jesus, who reveals himself to the church "in a personal way that tells them that he understands them. He knows what is really going on in their churches"—the good and the bad. After offering a contextually specific "solution" to each of the church's struggles, Christ does one thing more. Four times, he invites the churches to listen to "what the Spirit is saying" (Rev 2:29, 3:6, 13, 22). Similar to the risen Christ's breathing of the Spirit on the disciples after his resurrection (John 20:22), the gift of the Holy Spirit flows from the contextual, contemporary diagnosis of the resurrected Christ. At this point in his sermon, Banivanua shifts course. He states:

> When we were designing the new logo for the Church, we were looking at symbols that would describe who we are, where we are headed, and how we are going to get there. The rough waves [in the logo] symbolize the difficulties we went through and the winds of change facing Fiji. . . . Because of these waves, we needed a stronger boat. . . . The *drua* could do this. The *drua* was led by Jesus Christ, [symbolized by] the cross in the front. But it is the wings of the dove that create the winds that fills the sail of the *drua*. It is the Holy Spirit that leads and guides and energizes this church.[59]

There is an explicit Christological and pneumatological emphasis in Waqairatu and Banivanua's vision. The promise at the heart of their call to a "New Exodus" journey is neither the promise of a particular social and political structure nor are they calling the church to an Oceanic "fluidity" for its

---

58. Banivanua, "Mapping the *Lako Yani Vou*."
59. Banivanua, "Mapping the *Lako Yani Vou*."

own sake. Even when their sermons speak of specifics, like educational and development goals,[60] these plans are finally not the point. The point is the Wesleyan mantra: "Best of all, God is with us."[61]

This may seem an obvious observation: Waqairatu and Banivanua's sermons highlight the agency of a living God. However, Matt Tomlinson's analysis of Fijian homiletics reveal that this has not always been a central feature of Fijian preaching. His seminal work, *In God's Image: The Metaculture of Fijian Christianity*, focuses on village preaching in Kadavu during the years surrounding the 2000 coup. In this very different season of ecclesial life, Tomlinson is struck by the recurring lamentation of a lost "golden age," described through a tarnishing of God's image in Fijian identity. The affirmation of God's image in humankind (Gen 1:26) is understood as something that can be lost and regained through human action. In this way, the verse recurs as a sermonic trope, lamenting the diminished "mana" (spiritual power) of the present and calling the church to future purity and potency.[62] The action of God is implicit as an empowering force for human faithfulness in the sermons Tomlinson describes, but it is not the sermons' primary focus. In his later research, Tomlinson contrasts a Fijian Methodist sermon, which is marked by "formal oratory" and situated in a "calm, tightly coordinated" worship service, with the "raucous" preaching of a Pentecostal crusade in the Fijian capital.[63] Tomlinson notes the similar ways in which the Methodist and Pentecostal preachers use poetry and parallelism, but finds the differences between the preachers "stark."[64] Most striking for Tomlinson is the distinct "performative paths" of each sermon. The Pentecostal preacher includes promissory language and calls for immediate action in his sermon, framed as responses to divine action. The Methodist preacher sticks to "declarative statements that roll in like waves."[65] For Tomlinson, this is indicative of the function of Methodist sermons: "to accurately represent God's relationship to humanity and to encourage people to live up to divine models in their daily lives."[66] In short, Fijian sermons emphasize human faithfulness over time rather than a present encounter with an active God.

---

60. See the *drua* imagery in Banivanua, "Launching of MCIF Decade of Education"; "Sustaining the *Lako Yani Vou*."

61. These words, attributed to John Wesley on his deathbed, appear on the Methodist Fijian logo.

62. Tomlinson, *In God's Image*, 63–67.

63. Tomlinson, "Holy Ghost Is about to Fall," 23.

64. Tomlinson, "Holy Ghost Is about to Fall," 40.

65. Tomlinson, "Holy Ghost Is about to Fall," 40.

66. Tomlinson, "Holy Ghost Is about to Fall," 43.

This description of Fijian Methodist preaching may be an adequate starting place for describing Waqairatu and Banivanua's "New Exodus" sermons. There is nothing "raucous" about their preaching and neither have immediate calls to the altar. Both preachers connect the liberation of Israel with the creation of a "covenant community"[67] and emphasize high "ethical standards" for church leaders.[68] The "New Exodus" is intended to be more than spiritually inspiring. In true Wesleyan fashion, the "New Exodus" is meant to have material, lasting impact on the church's structures and relationships.[69] And yet, something more is going on. Even when concrete calls for human faithfulness and institutional growth are front and center, the "wings of the dove" are clearly foregrounded. Waqairatu and Banivanua's sermons are less about living up to divine models, and more about the presence of the resurrected Christ in the wilderness: the "Incarnation of Jesus . . . that tabernacles with us . . . aboard our *drua*."[70]

It is worth considering the possible reasons behind such a shift. The political struggles of the past decade have left the church with a sense of its own vulnerability, and the rise of a globalizing economy has increased this anxiety. Manfred Ernst notes, in his *Globalization and the Re-shaping of Christianity in the Pacific Islands,* that through a variety of pressures, "cultural values not compatible with the Western world are disappearing."[71] The land itself is under threat. Michael Green notes that "over 60 [Fijian] villages have been identified for relocation" for causes related to climate change.[72] In times like these, calls for increased change, migration, or "fluidity" are cruciform calls that risk an endangered identity. One requires more than the ideals of Western liberalism or a postcolonial celebration of shifting identity to fuel such a journey. One requires faith in a God who can be trusted to lead communities through Jordan rivers—through death to life.

Even as Waquairatu and Banivanua draw on an increasing pan-Pacific interest in the ocean as a hermeneutical lens, their sermons are marked by the particularities of Fijian history. As Tongan and Samoan theologians work to excavate the importance of identity's shifting boundaries in a pre-colonial Pacific, Fijian Methodism grapples with a multi-religious and

---

67. Banivanua, "Staying the Course in Winds of Change."
68. Banivanua, "Priestly and Prophetic Nature."
69. Banivanua would even use the language of the New Exodus to speak about the church's financial decision-making. See Banivanua, "Sustaining the *Lako Yani Vou.*"
70. Banivanua, "Kairos."
71. Ernst, *Globalization and the Reshaping of Christianity*, 4.
72. Green, "Contested Territory," 817–20.

multi-ethnic context, constructed by British colonialism.[73] It cannot be assumed that societal change is an extension of indigenous adaptability. It flows as easily from the "inexorable penetration of western power."[74] In such a context, it is the agency of God—imaged through dove and the person of the risen Christ—that provides the courage necessary for transformation and change. The brilliance of Waqairatu and Banivanua's "New Exodus" imagery is that, even as it draws on contextually-meaningful biblical and indigenous imagery to create a common narrative of hope, it grounds that hope in the theological affirmation of a transcendent God.

Conclusion

In her political analysis of the *drua* imagery in Banivanua's rhetoric as MCIF President, Lynda Newland describes what is at stake in sociological terms. In this move from "land to sea," Newland perceives an attempt to synthesize "indigenous and international ideas"[75] about stability and change, Christian nationalism and secularism, democracy and consensus. For other Pacific thinkers, the ocean hermeneutic is a strategic tool in the wresting of indigenous identity from the false essentialisms of others. Whether the "New Exodus" of the Fijian Methodist Church is invested in these long-term goals continues to be negotiated.[76]

Regardless, Waqairatu and Banivanua's vision reveals the particular importance that both placed on the work of preaching. For both men, preaching is a crucial instrument of leadership, engaging the community in performative discernment, reweaving communal histories, and calling forth courage grounded in faith. As with the Eucharistic table reconceived as the

---

73. The British brought large numbers of Indians to Fiji in the late nineteenth century to work as indentured laborers in sugar-cane plantations. This has resulted in a significant Hindu/Muslim minority (35 percent) in the Fijian populace. For a brief history of this political legacy of colonialism, see, Prasad, "Banished and Excluded."

74. Silverman, "Cannibalizing, Commodifying, and Creating Culture," 342. My thanks to Fijian sociologist and Methodist laywoman, Akanisi Tarabe, for this crucial insight.

75. Newland, "From Land to Sea," 125.

76. The meaning behind the "New Exodus" imagery continues to evolve. New MCIF President, Epineri Vakadewavosa, shaped the 2018 Annual Conference around the theme: "Keeping the *Drua* of the *Lako Yani Vou* Ship-Shape." The MCIF's relationship with its past history is also under negotiation. As of this writing, Sitiveni Rabuka is a candidate in the national 2018 election, insisting that he is now "conciliatory" in his political stance toward those of other faiths. See Radio New Zealand, "Coup Legacy Still Haunts Fiji's Rabuka."

church's promised land,[77] Waqairatu and Banivanua reconceive the pulpit as the *drua's* oar, responding to the winds of a living God.

Bibliography

Banivanua, Tevita Nawadra. "Kairos: God's Plan and Wilderness Formation in the New Exodus." Davuilevu Theological College Graduation Address, Davuilevu Theological College, November 2016.

———. "Launching of MCIF Decade of Education." *Nai Tabe* 7 (2016) 6.

———. "Mapping the *Lako Yani Vou*." *Methodist Fiji* (blog), March 10, 2015. Online. http://methodistfiji.blogspot.com/2015/08/mapping-na-lako-yani-vou.html.

———. "The Priestly and Prophetic Nature of the *Lako Yani Vou* Church." Davuilevu Theological College, November 26, 2015.

———. "Signposts of the New Exodus." *Methodist Fiji* (blog), August 15, 2016. Online. http://methodistfiji.blogspot.com/2016/11/the-signposts-of-new-exodus-presidents.html.

———. "Staying the Course in Winds of Change." Davuilevu Theological College, November 24, 2017.

———. "Sustaining the *Lako Yani Vou*: The Promise of Milke and Honey." Centenary Church, Suva, February 16, 2016.

Bhagwan, James. "Navigator Turns Captain of the Methodist '*Drua*.'" *Nai Tabe* 2 (2014) 5.

———. "New Course for the Church." *Fiji Times*, September 6, 2013. Online. http://methodistfiji.blogspot.com/2013/09/from-fiji-times-new-course-for-church.html.

Brueggemann, Walter. *The Land: Place as Gift, Promise, and Challenge*. 2nd ed. Louisville: Westminster John Knox, 2002.

"Coup Legacy Still Haunts Fiji's Rabuka, Says Academic." *Radio New Zealand*, July 19, 2018. Online. https://www.radionz.co.nz/international/pacific-news/362168/coup-legacy-still-haunts-fiji-s-rabuka-says-academic.

Crampton, David. "Fiji Government Again Cancels Methodist Conference." *Christian Century*, August 25, 2011. Online. https://www.christiancentury.org/article/2011-08/fiji-government-again-cancels-methodist-conference.

Ernst, Manfred. *Globalization and the Reshaping of Christianity in the Pacific Islands*. Suva: Pacific Theological College, 2006.

France, Peter. "The Kaunitoni Migration: Notes on the Genesis of a Fijian tradition." *The Journal of Pacific History* 1.1 (1966) 107–113.

Green, Michael. "Contested Territory." *Nature: Climate Change* 6 (2016) 817–20.

Halapua, Winston. *Waves of God's Embrace: Sacred Perspectives from the Ocean*. Norwich: Canterbury, 2008.

Havea, Jione. "Engaging Scriptures from Oceania." In *Bible, Borders, and Belonging(s): Engaging Readings from Oceania*, edited by Jione Havea, et al., 13–17. Atlanta: SBL, 2014.

———. "Pasifika Secrets." *Studies in World Christianity and Interreligious Relations* 47 (2011) 203–215.

---

77. Waqairatu, "Na Lako Yani (Exodus)."

———. "Releasing the Story of Esau from the Words of Obadiah." In *The Bible and the Hermeneutics of Liberation*, edited by A. Botta and P. Andiñach, 87–104. Atlanta: SBL, 2009.
Jones, Edwin. "'Mountains of Israel': Fijians' Judaic Origins and the Use of the Old Testament in Highland Viti Levu." *Oceania* 85.3 (2015) 271–82.
Kelly, John, and Martha Kaplan. *Represented Communities: Fiji and World Decolonization*. Chicago: University of Chicago Press, 2001.
Kristoff, Nicolas. "Scores of Indians Injured as Riots Sweep Fiji." *New York Times*, May 21, 1987. Online. https://www.nytimes.com/1987/05/21/world/scores-of-indians-are-injured-as-riots-sweep-fiji.html.
Methodist Church Department for Communication. "Biographical Data of Rev. Dr. Tuikilakila Waqairatu." *Methodist Fiji* (blog), February 12, 2014. Online. http://methodistfiji.blogspot.com/2014/02/biographical-data-of-revd-dr.html.
———. "Rationale." *Methodist Fiji* (blog). Online. https://www.methodistfiji.org/uploads/2/3/8/8/23880004/methodist_church_connexional_plan_first_draft.pdf.
———. "A Renewed Logo for a Renewed Church." *Methodist Fiji* (blog), September 3, 2013. Online. http://methodistfiji.blogspot.com/2013/09/renewed-logo-for-renewed-church.html.
Nabobo-Baba, Unaisi. *Knowing and Learning: An Indigenous Fijian Approach*. Suva: University of the South Pacific Press, 2006.
Neal, Jerusha Matsen. "Exodus or Exile: Hermeneutic Shifts in a Shifting Fijian Methodist Church." *International Journal of Homiletics* 2.1 (2017) 22–23.
"New Methodist Leader: Church Must Adapt to Secular State." *CathNews New Zealand*, August, 29, 2014. Online. https://cathnews.co.nz/2014/08/29/new-methodist-leader-church-must-adapt-secular-state.
Newland, Lynda. "From Land to Sea: Christianity, community and state in Fiji—and the 2014 elections." In *The People Have Spoken: The 2014 Elections in Fiji*, edited by Steven Ratuva and Stephanie Lawson, 109–134. Canberra: Australian National University Press, 2016.
———. "The Lost Tribes of Israel—and the Genesis of Christianity in Fiji: Missionary Notions of Fijian Origin from 1835 to Cession and Beyond." *Oceania* 85.3 (2015) 257.
———. "Religion and Politics: The Christian Churches and the 2006 Coup in Fiji." In *The 2006 Military Takeover of Fiji: The Coup to End all Coups?*, edited by Jon Fraenkel, et al., 187–207. Canberra: ANU, 2007.
———. "The Role of the Assembly of Christian Churches in Fiji in the 2006 Elections." In *From Election to Coup in Fiji: The 2006 Campaign and Its Aftermath*, edited by Jon Fraenkel and Stewart Firth, 300–314. Canberra: ANU, 2007.
Prasad, Rajenda. "Banished and Excluded: The Girmit of Fiji." *Himal Southasian*, January 2, 2015. Online. http://himalmag.com/girmit-fiji.
Rasoqosoqo, Losalini. "Heal Our Land." *Fiji Sun*, September 2, 2013.
Ricoeur, Paul. *The Rule of Metaphor: Multi-Disciplinary Studies in the Creation of Meaning in Language*. Translated by Robert Czerny. Toronto: University of Toronto Press, 1977.
Rika, Netani. "The Legacy of Tuikilakila Waqairatu." *Islands Business*, August 15, 2014. Online. https://islandsbusiness.com/about-us/item/1072-the-legacy-of-tuikilakila-waqairatu.

Sekek, Sam. "Police Again Detain Church Leaders." *ABC News,* July 22, 2009. Online. http://www.abc.net.au/news/2009-07-22/police-again-detain-fiji-church-leaders/1363198.

Silverman, Eric. "Cannibalizing, Commodifying, and Creating Culture: Power and Creativity in Sepik River Tourism." In *Globalization and Culture Change in the Pacific Islands,* edited by V. Lockwood, 339–57. Upper Saddle Ridge, NJ: Prentice-Hall, 2004.

Sovaraki, Ana. "Act of God." *Fiji Sun,* March 11, 2015. Online. http://fijisun.com.fj/2015/03/11act-of-god.

Thompson, Basil. "The Kalou-Vu (Ancestor Gods) of the Fijians." *The Journal of the Anthropological Institute of Great Britain and Ireland* 24 (1895) 340–59.

Tomlinson, Matt. *In God's Image: The Metaculture of Fijian Christianity.* Berkeley: University of California Press, 2009.

———. "The Generation of Now: Denominational Politics in Fijian Christianity." In *Christian Politics in Oceania,* edited by Matt Tomlinson and Debra McDougall. New York: Berghahn, 2013.

———. "The Holy Ghost Is about to Fall." In *Ritual Textuality: Pattern and Motion in Performance.* Oxford: Oxford University Press, 2014.

Tuwere, I. S. *Vanua: Toward a Fijian Theology of Place.* Suva: University of the South Pacific Press, 2002.

Vaai, Upolu. "*Motu ma le Taula*: Toward an Island 'Let Be' Hermeneutics." *Pacific Journal of Theology* ss 53 (2015) 26–30.

———. "*Va'atapalagi:* De-heavening Trinitarian Theology in the Islands." In *Colonial Contexts and Postcolonial Theologies: Storyweaving in the Asia-Pacific,* edited by Jione Havea and Mark G. Brett, 41–53. Melbourne: Palgrave, 2014.

Waqairatu, Tuikilakila. "Farewell to Bishop Warner Brown." Unpublished notes. December 9, 2011.

———. "Na Lako Yani (The Exodus)." Unpublished notes. November 4, 2012.

———. "Na Lotu Ni Mataka." Unpublished notes. November 14, 2010.

———. "The Needs of a New Exodus: The Installation of Rev. Iliapi Tuiwai." Unpublished notes. 2013.

———. "Sermon for Mrs. Korovou Balelevuka." Unpublished notes. July 18, 2011.

———. Unpublished notes. November 24, 2005.

India
Homiletics from the Underside

ALFRED STEPHEN

Introduction

GIVEN THE MULTICULTURAL NATURE of the congregation and the increasing complexity and problems because of growing diversity, the church in general—and preaching in particular—can no longer ignore or escape the responsibility of responding to the imperative issue of Homiletics from the underside. If the history of preaching has been the history of the church, and if preaching has been the predominant force behind the growth of the church over many centuries, now again it is preaching which needs to address this burning issue in its functional reality. Homiletics in a multicultural context has been dealt with by many homileticians and theologians. Homiletics from the underside is an emerging field within the overall discipline of homiletics. Not much work has been done exclusively on homiletics from the underside. Therefore I draw on resources from a variety of other subjects—cultural studies, communication studies, historical studies, philosophical studies, anthropology, sociology, hermeneutics, and comparative theological studies—with which homiletics from the underside is also concerned. As it is being developed, a circumspect integration of all these disciplines of studies is required to devise a homiletic paradigm and procedures from the bottom top methodology.

Homiletics includes various stages of preaching, starting from selecting the text for preaching until delivery of the sermon and getting feedback as well. In between these two poles lies a linkage, a rigorous process of preparation through which the preacher has to go in order to reach the other side. This article explores the homiletical methodologies in relations to contextual, to be specific, methodologies of homiletics from the underside. I primarily engage in hermeneutics of this type and in designing the sermon from the standpoint of the oppressed with special reference to the Dalit community in India. While the first section deals with the overall problems faced by the Dalits in India, the second part sets forth an exploration of the intricacies of hermeneutics from the underside.

Contextual Reality of the Dalits: Homiletical Starting Point

The contextual existential reality of the Dalit community in India is not a result of political accident or ideological collapse but rather the continuing and ongoing result of an oppressive religious ideology and discriminative social order, which began centuries ago, and the political system which either encouraged or ignored such social stratification.

Ideology of Purity and Pollution

The caste Hindus also attached a certain amount of purity to castes depending on the work people belonging to each of these castes did. They also related the idea of purity to the ritual assignment they had in the religious milieu. They claim that those who have a religious ceremonial role to play must be pure and clean. In the hierarchical order of the caste, it is undoubtedly the Brahmins who assigned this position, and thus they are considered to be pure. On the basis of this ideology, the upper caste people lived within and at the center of the cities while the Dalits lived on the periphery with lower social conditions. "They had their residence outside the village, and the use of shrouds of corpses as their clothing, broken pots for meals, iron for ornaments, and dogs and donkeys for their wealth. They were to be the hangmen who were prohibited entry into villages and towns during daytime, and they were to have been stamped with some marks and were to serve as the undertakers for the unclaimed corpses."[1] The idea of purity not only relates to the religious sphere but also "relates to persons, place, festivals, time, etc."[2] Claiming to be custodians and the sole authority of accessibility to

---

1. Ghurey, *Caste and Race in India*, 311
2. Dhavamony, *Phenomenology of Religion*, 73–79

god and performers of religious rituals, the Brahmins made themselves indispensable with regard to the religious ceremonies. This ultimately increased their claims on their purity. On the other hand, these claims intensified the idea of pollution and distanced the others even further in the social order. This ideology of purity is the central of idea behind the practice of untouchability.[3] Thus, people belonging to the low caste were called untouchables and discriminated against in all walks of life. Non-accessibility of the Dalits to the temple premises is an implication of other pollution based factors in terms of the impure quality of their vocation, the place of their living, and food that they eat.

The Brahmins assigned the low jobs to the low caste group of people. As Narada, a lawmaker after Manu writes:

> Know that there are two sorts of occupations: pure work and impure work. Impure work is that done by the slaves. Pure work is that done by laborers. Sweeping the gateways, the privy, the road, and the place for rubbish; shampooing the secret parts of the body; gathering and putting away the leftover food; ordure and urine. And lastly, rubbing the master's limbs when desired; this should be regarded as impure work. All other work besides this is pure. In this manner the four classes of servants doing pure work been enumerated. All the others who do dirty works are slaves. . . . Most of the Untouchables are engaged in six occupations which are considered polluting and degrading: skinning and removing the dead animals, cleaning latrines and removing the garbage, tanning and dying leather, washing dirty clothes, tapping toddy, slaughtering animals for food, hunting, fishing, making baskets, brooms weaving, etc.[4]

The low caste people were forced to do such menial jobs. As mentioned above, purity and pollution relate very much to the duty one is assigned. Bodily waste, emissions, and death are always labelled impure and polluting.[5] The low caste people had to carry human and animal waste. In the case of death, they first had to announce the news, then carry the carcasses to the cremation ground and burn them. Because of these vocational assignments forced on them, they were considered untouchable. The Dalits were and are caught up in the cycle of cause and effect of the ideology of purity and pollution. Because they were forced into doing menial jobs, they were

---

3. Prabhakar "Ideology of Oppression."
4. Das, "Dalits and Caste System," 59, 64–65.
5. Srinivas, "Some Reflections," 161.

economically poor. This poverty drove them to eat leftover food and dead animals, which made them all the more impure.

> They had to live outside the society and were not allowed to draw water from the common well; they were not allowed to enter schools; they were not allowed to eat decent wholesome food; they were not allowed to walk on common roads; they were not allowed to put on a decent dress and in some states the men were not allowed to wear loin cloth which went below the knee cap and women had to keep their breasts uncovered; they were not allowed to wear gold or silver ornaments and had to wear clothes made of coarse cotton. Those called to tender evidence had to stand outside the court, lest their breath should pollute the courtroom. They were not allowed to own property or accumulate wealth. In some states women had to be dedicated to the goddess Yellama to serve as "Devadasis" [prostitutes] in the temples and cater to the needs of the pilgrims and priests after having been deflowered by rich landlords. . . . The sweepers had to walk on the roads with a broom tucked underneath the arm and cock's feather in the turban, shouting their presence, "Watch sweeper coming." The leather workers had to carry a dark thread tied round the neck or arm to indicate their caste.[6]

It is not just the discrimination that has to be noted here but also the very fact of the arrogant and inhuman attitude of the caste Hindus, reducing the low caste people to the level of pigs, dogs, and cocks, depriving them of their very humanity, and abusing them to satisfy their physical lust.

Powerlessness of the Dalits

The main social problem of the Dalits in India, besides loss of identity, is their powerlessness. They are numerous but, in reality, powerless. It is a paradox of power and an irony of the majority. They are dependent people, as their power was crumbled by the subtlety of the intelligence of the caste Hindus. "Self-reliance in any sphere of their life, such as economic, political, educational, legal, religio-cultural, is impossible for them. . . . Their problem is living in a framework of meaning, experiencing dependency in all walks of life."[7] The caste Hindus not only discriminated against the Dalits on the basis of their caste but also made them powerless by means of manipulation. They manipulated the religious ideology and rules to affirm and reaffirm

---

6. Das, "Dalits and Caste System," 60–61.
7. Ayrookuzhiel, "Dalit Theology," 251.

their priesthood and high position in the society. As mentioned above, the Brahmins made it possible for their own to occupy the center of the society with all their power and ceremonial responsibility. This, in turn, gave them political power over the society as well, allowing them to rule the others.

Economic Powerlessness

Various factors have contributed to the economic powerlessness of the Dalits. All these factors substantiate the exploitative, oppressive ideologies and systems of the caste Hindus and their powerful tactics of subjugation. The following, then, is a few apparatuses which they employed to subdue the Dalits economically.

Vocational Plight

As has been mentioned above, the caste system allotted specific jobs for the Dalits which did not fetch enough money for them to maintain their families. They also had laws which restricted them from possessing property or accumulating wealth.[8] This ultimately brought them to a very low economic condition. The strategic, systematic subjugation of this group of people caused their economic powerlessness and dependency:

> When they were brought under subjugation, eventually, they were neither incorporated into the main economic activity prevailing at that time, that is agriculture, nor into any other form of production in society. Only unskilled, unproductive, lowly, and menial jobs were assigned to them. Thus, when they were forced to surrender, it was not clemency they received. Instead, they were treated with utter contempt and were segregated as a residual category of people to be employed as and when necessary.[9]

Economic powerlessness and dependency not only caused but also forced them into unwilling vocational compliance. Whether they liked it or not, they had to do jobs which they never would have wanted or thought of doing. The vocation which they had to take up not only fetched them little money but also dehumanized them.

With regard to their economic predicament, not only the work that they do but also the geographical location in which they are placed is

8. Das, "Dalits and Caste System," 61.
9. Mukherjee, *Beyond Four Varnas*, 104.

equally telling. More than 85 percent of the Dalits are placed either by force or without any other option in rural areas and depend on the nature, which mostly fails them, for their livelihood.[10]

They live in the villages and outskirts of the city where they depend on agriculture, forestry, and fishing. This ultimately affects their economic condition. Monsoon failure and droughts effect their very existence and drive them into a state of dependency. The type of occupations they do and the income that they generate is very minimal, barely enough for their survival. When nature fails them, they resort to borrowing from the affluent and rich, which ultimately leads them to being subjected to the powerful. I deal with this factor in the following section under the bonded laborer system. Driven to be economically powerless, their very existence is questioned. Some social scientists have argued that the Dalit problem is not primarily a religious one but rather represents the economic and political realities of power. They are of the opinion that from the standpoint of the untouchables, the political and economic dimensions of the caste system encapsulate the religious ones as the characteristic features of the total Hindu system.[11] However, in this study, I intend to take the overall struggles and plights of the Dalits as well as those various factors which have contributed to their present contextual reality into consideration.

Bonded Labor a Systematic Oppression

Another system which placed the Dalits in a vulnerable situation is the bonded laborer system. They served the high caste people as laborers for decades without any wages, receiving only leftover food. In some cases, the whole family was bonded as laborers. There are various reasons for bringing these people as bonded laborers. Dr. S. Manickam observes that "bonded laborers are often bonded not [only] through debt but also through personal ties with the master, land allotment, social compulsion, brutal force, lack of alternative employment, [or] distress during hard times of drought and famine, which drives the bonded laborer into the hands of the moneylender and the landlord."[12] In such situations, those economically powerful and affluent exploit and indulge in the inhuman practice of arresting them within their power and exploiting them for the rest of their life. Under this system, the high caste people not only get their work done without any wages but also drain the Dalits of their money and blood, leaving behind

10. Kurian, "Overview of the Economic Condition," 94.
11. See Berreman, *Caste and other Inequities*; Beteille, "Pollution and Poverty."
12. Manickam, *Slavery in Tamil Country*, 114.

only poverty and shame. Although the Bonded Laborer Abolition Act is in effect, the practice of either closing the eyes of the authorities with bribes or taking matters through a more subtle form (i.e., employment) is also possible. In Kodaikanal, a hilly place in Tamilnadu (TN), the practice of bonded laborers is still prevalent.[13] The landlords not only own the land but also the poor laborers and cattle along with it. It is conspicuously evident that it is the Dalit community which is victim of this cruel practice.

The result of this cruel system is two-fold: the wealthy, with their exploitative efficiency, manure their land with the blood of the poor and voiceless; on the other hand, the poor are driven to poverty day-by-day and in turn they lose their voice, not only because they do not have strength but also because of their poor economic condition.

Subjective Educational System a Sustained Oppression

Low literacy rates among the Dalits is another factor which has contributed and continues to contribute to their poor economic condition. Of course this problem of Dalits has to be seen in the light of those substandard educational opportunities provided to them, especially at the level of higher education and concerning the rate of dropouts. The problem of the Dalits in relation to education is two fold: (1) the literacy rate among the Dalits is very low and (2) they are "invisible people with no representation in the curriculum."[14] Even though there is a constitutional provision for the education of the Dalits, the literacy rate continues to be very low. There is a drastic dropout rate from schools among the Dalits. Poor economic conditions and demanding pressures in the families to start working early are probably contributing to these massive dropouts, especially after middle or high school education. This leaves them without having access to higher education. This, in turn, also affects their economic condition, as they will not be able to get better jobs to earn more. Dalit parents who are economically poor are unable to send their children for higher education as this requires the paying of a huge sum of money both for admission and subsequently

---

13. My own brother is working among the bonded laborers in Kodaikanal. He is involved in liberating them from the land lords.

14. Ayrookuzhiel, "Dalit Theology," 253. He draws this idea from Krishna Kumar, who presents the reality of the curriculum of Madhya Pradesh. He contends that the curriculum in MP barely talks about the Dalits whereas the majority of the population is from the Tribal community. Even in the few places they are referred to they only represent a slavish identity. I will be dealing with this point later under the topic of Dalit Identity. For detailed study of the curriculum, see Kumar, "Educational Experience of Scheduled Castes and Tribes," 3–10.

for semester fees. In many colleges, students have to pay a large amount to gain admission to study. It is more so with the professional colleges. This unwritten albeit strongly exercised policy of the colleges favors only the affluent and rich and not the poor Dalits. Although there are funds for the Dalits in state-administered colleges for higher education, the requirement to disperse such funds is not enforced. In practice, those seats are given to the higher caste students. The predicament of the Dalit students is that they are either not able to pay their fees or deprived of their chance of entry into the university or colleges altogether.

Another factor worth noting is the government's economic policies. In the advent of the liberalization of economy, the occupations of Dalits were taken away in the name of modernization. When modernization was introduced, works such as tanning and dying leather, which was considered as polluting by high caste people, were converted into big industries. These industries and factories are owned by the rich and affluent although it is the Dalits who attended to the ground work. They continue to earn the same amount of money. However, the difference is that they no longer own these vocations because their handmade goods are not accepted in a market dominated by company-made products. This makes it clear that the liberalization of economy and modernization of industry not only affected the Dalits economically but also hit them hard on their last sources of livelihood.

The Dalits are not only vulnerable but also materially and economically dependent people. The economic system which the caste Hindus have built constantly hinders the Dalits in their economic mobility. Through the allotment of specific jobs to the Dalits, the bonded laborers system and the subjective educational system continues to make the Dalits do menial jobs that involve agriculture. On the other hand, by keeping them ignorant of the land reform policies of the government and the subjugating economic policies, they prevent their economic mobility. Although the government allots land for them, in reality, it is owned by the high caste people, and there is constant increase in landless laborers, especially among the Dalits.

The economic condition of the Dalits makes them dependent people. The bonded laborer system causes young children to grow with a constant fear of vulnerability and low self-image. As they watch the helplessness of their parents, they develop an inferior image of themselves and long for a better life. In this dependence scenario, they are also people who are deceived, exploited, and oppressed. Their property rights are not given to them. Their family bond and social systems are surmounted by the oppressive policies of high caste people. Their family is broken, separated, and illtreated. Their status is made low not only because of their birth identity but also because of their poor, forced economic condition. They seek to establish their family bond and dignity and their own society through liberation from the bondage of high caste people.

Political Subjection and Oppression

The Dalits experienced not only economic powerlessness but also political subjection. They were not given due representation in the political governing bodies and did not have any say in the decision making process. The political power was shared among the economically and socially upper caste people as they held dominant positions in the government. Those who were influential in the administration developed policies which would favor only the upper caste people through their subtle, oppressive administration. In this sense, politics has allowed the situation to be further manipulated and influenced by the power of the caste system instead of being influenced by other systems operating in the society. As a result, on the basis of the caste system, these concentrations of political power prevailed over a more equal distribution of power.

Atrocities on the Dalits

The Dalits are not only powerless in terms of exercising their power over others or achieving what they want, they are also powerless in terms of preventing atrocities on them. They are victims of the atrocious and appalling cruelty of the upper caste people. The ways in which Dalits are tormented are countless. They are murdered and maimed; helpless women are raped; their children are abused and deprived of schooling; they are dispossessed of their property; their houses are torched; they are denied their legitimate rights and their sources of livelihood are destroyed. Following are some more of the examples of such dreadful activities:

- The Dalits were aspiring to possess some land and to achieve this goal they worked hard for many years.
- They were systematically denied ownership of land.
- They were cheated and deceived by the wealthy and by their government.
- They lost their hard-earned money which was their life blood earnings.
- Their development was curtailed.
- They were often accused of lying without any proof of such.

- Their voices were not heard in the courts.
- The police officials and government officers joined hands with the wealthy and powerful to reject the Dalits at every turn.
- The power of the government officials and police was misused to oppress the Dalits.
- They could not exercise their legal right of lodging a complaint.
- Their civil right to possess land continues to be prohibited.
- They continue to be physically assaulted.
- Their human dignity was lost.
- They were reduced to the level of the animals by forcing them to eat human feces.
- They are made to feel that they are fit only for such acts.
- Their humiliation results in a damaged psyche.
- In society, they move around with the stigma of humiliation and often lose their respect.
- Politically they are made to feel powerless and voiceless.
- Religiously they are forced to believe that they are not owners but rather servants, simply by the virtue of their birth
- Their very human identity was put to shame.

It is not just grown up people who are victims of such atrocities. It is in executing atrocities on all age groups of the Dalits that the caste system and the upper caste people operate indiscriminately. Be it grown-up men and women or young boy and girls, they are equally assaulted and made victims. In the year 1999, in Salem, Tamilnadu, a young Dalit girl was beaten up by one of her teachers just because she drank water from a pot which was meant for upper-caste pupils. She suffered devastating blows to her right eye which would in all probability wreck her future. She was beaten up not just for drinking water but also polluting the water and then trying to claim equality with the so-called upper-caste children. This inhuman act left the mark of subjection and subjugation in her young mind. She begins to realize her low status in the society in the early stage of her life. Her psyche is affected and social discrimination has been experienced by her.

Women Victims

In the milieu of implementing power, the vulnerability of the Dalits—especially of Dalit women—should also be noted. Powerless as they are, they succumb to the malicious acts of the upper caste people. The Dalit women are called Dalit of the Dalits, downtrodden among the downtrodden, thrice alienated on the basis of her caste, class, and gender.[15] They are put at the very bottom of the hierarchy. They experience discrimination because of their caste, class, and gender. The leitmotif of their existential reality is nothing but exploitation and discrimination. Dalit women have a culture of their own because of the added discrimination against them on the basis of their gender. Their potentialities, hard work, and contribution to the welfare of the society have not been recognized by any other members of society. They are kept in the society apparently as the possession of men, like cattle and other property. They have to live in utter dependency. Even though they have the potential and, in many cases, are more efficient than men, they are never considered to be their equal. Their life is to be lived for giving pleasure and comfort to their man.

Dalit women are not only victimized by their social structure but in the religious sphere as well. In the name of religion, they were made to devote their life to the service of the god of the upper caste people and offer their bodies to the pleasure of the devotees. Besides this institutionalized sexual abuse, there are incidents of sexual assault on Dalit women by landlords and other powerful people. As discussed above, economic poverty of the Dalits in general leaves them to depend on the rich caste Hindus and other rich people in the society, either by borrowing money or working in their agricultural land or houses. In some cases, they are forced to be bonded laborers. Entangled in the web of poverty, dependence, debt, and cheap labor, they are vulnerable to and victims of sexual assault by the powerful. Although there are traces of development among the Dalit women and signs of them getting organized to resist the atrocities on them, making themselves more powerful, there is a long way to go for them to be fully liberated and assigned equality with others in the paradoxically ideological, patriarchal, and relentlessly discriminating Indian society.

Homiletical Challenges

One of the major challenges any preacher to the vulnerable community needs to face is reflecting the sufferings of these people in preaching.

---

15. See Manorama, "Dalit Women," 164.

Considering the struggles of these people, whose basic life experience is only suffering, and the good news to be proclaimed, can the preachers announce with boldness that there is goodness for them in preaching? While they continue to struggle and face only unjust, ill treatment from their fellow human beings, day in and day out, while their very life is threatened and violence is at their door step, can preachers speak of the protection and justice of God, which flows like a river? Will this message be relevant and acceptable to them? How, then, can the preachers preach good news to this group of people? The mystery of their sufferings and the mystery of God's presence or absence in their suffering need to be explained to them in the process of preaching.

The context of the vulnerable community poses the following homiletical challenges: Can the grace of God be experienced in the suffering of the vulnerable? Is God present in their sufferings? Are we to preach the scandal or the glory of the cross? Is hope a message for the vulnerable? Is reconciliation possible between the victims and the oppressors?

Christian preaching promises the grace of God is to be proclaimed and found in the experience of people in general and those who suffer in particular. Many preachers proclaim the message of hope against hopelessness and promote a theology that justifies the suffering and, indirectly, the oppression. In the pretext of bliss in heaven, suffering is justified by many preachers. However, every community in India and elsewhere knows its own story of grief, pain, death, and hopelessness. News about helpless girls being harassed and sexually assaulted by sexual maniacs, catholic nuns being gang raped, foreign tourists being abducted by deceitful taxi drivers, and young girls in the IT firm being murdered by company cab assistants form the headlines of newspapers and other media. Such news demonstrates to us that our lives are limited and determined by the forces of such atrocities. The system that operates in our society, nation, and the globe seems to have no control over these evils. Listening to the words of hope in the context of nothing but suffering makes the vulnerable community rethink the authenticity of the message being preached. The questions that we must keep asking ourselves in this context are: Can the grace of god be experienced in the suffering of the vulnerable? Is god present in the suffering of the people? Homileticians and preachers are challenged to preach the very absence of God in the suffering of people. "My God, My God, why have you forsaken me?" is the cry of many communities, day and night. Rethinking the suffering cross, which is the worst sign of vulnerability, would lead the preacher to emphasize the cruelty of the human community. Preaching the absence of God in the suffering of people explains the extent of human affliction and suffering and limits of human life. Although the hope of the resurrection, the sacrificial love of God and Jesus which was expressed on the cross, and the eternal hope of life must be the message of the cross, the forces that precede all these are the scandal of the cross and the injustice that took Jesus to the cross. Preachers are called to name the depth of human suffering and pain on the one hand and height of human cruelty on the other. Can there be a message of hope to the vulnerable? The message of hope to the vulnerable is to be realized in the eradication of injustice, oppression, and discrimination. A message of hope can be proclaimed to the vulnerable only through the acknowledgement of their identity as human beings. Likewise, the message of hope can be experienced by the vulnerable only through resisting and fighting against the evil system that oppresses them and makes them vulnerable.

Homiletical Method

Hermeneutics of Resurgence

Hermeneutics of resurgence is a process of interpretation based on the resurgence of the history of the Dalits. It seeks to unearth the realities about these people through a rigorous process of critical analysis of the present and understanding their present status from a historical perspective. Through the process of a critical analysis of their history and their present status, a hermeneutic of resurgence calls for a reversal of history and a journey back into their history. This hermeneutic seeks to address the issues from a historical perspective. This is not to be misunderstood as historical critical hermeneutics. This is revisiting the history of Dalits for a better understanding of their present situation and for a relevant explanation of the scripture in preaching. This revisiting is not placing oneself physically in the past history of the Dalits but rather taking a re-look at the way they have been and how they are now. Therefore, in an intercultural context of preaching, a hermeneutics of resurgence seeks to explain the scripture by understanding the historical reality of its hearers. In this sense, hermeneutics of resurgence clarifies the process of understanding and the factors involved in it. While considering the hermeneutics of resurgence and drawing understanding from and through the historical reality of the Dalits, one cannot miss out on various factors involved in the process of revisiting history.[16] In fact, the

16. A point which needs to be made clear is the subjectivity of the Dalit history. The history of the Dalits in Tamilnadu is very much subjective in terms of its reality. The historiography of the Dalits has been from the affluent classes and hence the reality which has been presented is biased. This does not negate the fact about the history written by the Dalits themselves and others who are committed to the cause of the Dalits.

hermeneutics of resurgence must start from a realization of the pain of segregating one group of people from the other on the basis of a cruelly operated caste system. Resurgence in relation to the subaltern community means having a clear understanding of their history, culture, lives, and experiences. This would also mean revisiting and rereading the history of these people from a new standpoint and with new insights and perspectives within a new situation. This process of resurgence leads to the disclosure of many realities of their original situation. First and foremost, it exposes the facts about the origin of the subaltern community. As has been noted earlier, they are the original inhabitants of the land and they have the identity of being the original Indians. Facts about their origin and their present struggle for their survival in their own land reveal that the people of the soil have been dispelled from the mainland and chased off to the peripheries. This reveals the injustice caused to them. People of the land have been denied a dwelling place because of the concept of the so-called pollution that was forced upon them. This reality of their origin also gives points for a theological understanding.[17] Among those understandings are the injustices caused to these people on the one hand and the sense of separation and segregation which people experience on the other. Not only segregation but also the loss of their own land and the freedom to live in it has led them to lose confidence in themselves and to have a low estimation of their own worth. In preaching, especially in the process of resurgence, these factors are brought to light for reflection in the process of sermon preparation.

A hermeneutics of resurgence not only brings to light the facts related to the origin of the subaltern community but also the way they are put to suffer through the policies introduced on the basis of caste and through the ideology of purity and pollution. The caste system, which the high caste people introduced, has stratified the people of the land and placed the subaltern community at the lowest strand. This has led to the suffering of this community. This again reveals the point for theological understanding and for reflection in preaching, i.e., discrimination. The caste system is evidence of this discrimination which has caused so much suffering. In this context, resurgence and theological understanding reveals that it is the inequality which needs to be challenged against equality. Yet another factor which has caused suffering of the subaltern community is the vocational plight and their poverty. Because they were forced to do menial jobs for which they were not paid very much, they were forced into poverty. Therefore, poverty needs to be addressed against improper assignment of jobs and improper

---

One must be careful in selection of reading materials

17. Buttrick, *Homiletic*, 419.

distribution of resources. The suffering of these people was also caused by denial of access to public places and temples. These factors have caused not only sociological and political sufferings but also psychological sufferings. They have lost their self-respect and the very freedom of worshiping and moving with other fellow human beings. This requires the preacher to challenge the disrespectful attitude and speak for their human rights and dignity.

Caste discrimination has affected the subaltern community not only in the socio-economic spheres but also in the political arena, making them powerless and causing them to suffer. They were denied all of their possible political rights and thus they could not represent themselves and their needs in the political realm. Because they did not have any representation in politics, their needs were not met and they had to continue in their struggles and sufferings. This reveals the injustices inflicted on them that resulted in their powerlessness. This also reveals the denial of their basic rights to be a dignified citizen in their own country, which needs to be challenged in preaching.

In the hermeneutic process of resurgence, two main events take place. First, the issues which need to be addressed are brought to light, enabling the preacher to have a clear theological understanding on the issues and address them in preaching. The preacher is able to put together the events from the existential reality of the hearers with a view of identifying the substance of the problems and cause for their sufferings. In this process, the preacher is also able identify the symbols which are unique to the Dalits. Their cultural context is the result of the forces from outside their own community. In the process of reacting to these forces, they have developed a particular social system and cultural values. These values are exhibited in and through symbols. These symbols carry meanings which are deeply rooted in their existential reality. Identifying the symbols and their meaning demands a deeper relationship with the people and listening to the echoes of their inner feelings. Symbols of their culture and cultural components can be identified towards a deeper and fuller understanding through the process of resurgence. Second, the preacher is able to cross over to the horizons of the hearers, keeping her/himself open to their cultural, social, and religious situations and trying to understand them in their own situation. This would imply willingness on the part of the preacher to accept the reality in which the hearers live

A hermeneutics of resurgence also aims to bring to light some factors regarding the Dalits which have been hidden purposely. Resurgence would reveal the reality of the situation of these people and enhance proper understanding about the way they have been classified. Major problems for the Dalits have been caused by the caste system. The society is stratified and categorized on the basis of this system. Resurgence aims to explain this categorization and aid the interpreter in a proper understanding of the reality of Dalits and their background while ensuring that the superior feelings the "others" have about them are not legitimate. Reality is understood on the basis of historical truths and thus hermeneutics of resurgence critiques the existing social structure of classification and cultural beliefs regarding these social categorizations. This process of critiquing and questioning leads to a revelation of the reality, reality leads to correct understanding of truth regarding the struggles of the Dalits, and this understanding leads to dual actions. On the one hand, this leads to critiquing the illegitimate claims of those who believe themselves to be superior, while on the other hand, it leads to dynamic actions of acceptance. The interpreters are motivated to accept the Dalits through this process of resurgence. In this process, understanding about the hearers emerges, leading to the realization that the hearers are no more strangers but people who need to be considered basically as human beings and then as fellow-beings who are to be treated equally in all respects. It is in the light of this revelation about the reality of the Dalits that the preachers have to study the scripture when they preach to them. This process of resurgence would guide the entire way of interpreting the scripture for them. Therefore, a hermeneutics of resurgence is a dynamic theory of understanding and accepting through a process of critiquing and questioning. The main factor which needs to be borne in mind in the hermeneutics of resurgence is that it critiques the present situation of the hearers in the light of revelation gained through the process of resurgence. It is not just reader based interpretation but critical analysis of the reader's present context and then interpreting the scripture from their original reality. Having identified the issues and the causes of the sufferings of the people with an open mind, the preacher goes on to perceive the suffering with realization and understanding. When this realization is in operation within oneself, then understanding the one whose history is revisited will be dynamic. Dynamic understanding in relation to the Dalits can be explained in the following ways.

Dynamic Understanding

Understandings are conditioned by prejudices and the preconceived notions of the interpreter about a particular historical, cultural, and social reality. In any interpretation, the interpreter tends to use or even overuse her/his own preconception to give the reality a particular meaning which is anticipated. However, the reality of the fact is that these preconceived notions of the interpreter oftentimes leads to partial or incorrect understanding and thus causes misinterpretations. Therefore, the process of understanding calls for a hermeneutics of suspicion of one's own interpretations because they are conditioned by their own background and thus incorrect in terms of the Dalit hearers. This means the interpreters must be willing and able to criticize their own interpretations, taking the historical background of the hearers into consideration. A hermeneutics of suspicion here refers not to the interpretations of the others but rather one's own. The interpreter's historical, socio-political, cultural, and economic realities are critically questioned because they produce an understanding and lead to an interpretation which is not relevant to the Dalits. The interpreters do not give up their own background, however, but they are willing to be open to allowing their understandings to be questioned in the light of the background of their hearers. This is the first factor which needs to be noted in the process of understanding. When it is said that the interpreters or the preachers do not give up their own background, it does not mean that they are prejudiced and arrogant in their attitudes; rather, they try to keep aside their own background and the understandings they have on the basis of this background, willing to see what others have and allowing their own understanding and background to be questioned in the light of their hearer's. Here, the hermeneutic of resurgence leads to or results in dynamic understanding.

When a hermeneutics of suspicion operates by allowing the interpreters to be critical of their own interpretation for a better and deeper understanding, the understanding becomes dynamic. Here, the dynamism of understanding has to be seen in terms of its operational reality. Understanding in this sense is both productive and progressive. Understanding is productive because it creates awareness about reality through a process of interpretation which is conditioned by the background of the interpreter, and it is progressive because it leads to a new understanding and a new awareness. It is in this way dynamic understanding is to be understood. Social categorizing is also explained in the process of resurgence and revisiting. This, in turn, explains the place of these strangers. Resurgence leads to understanding which results in acceptance and willingness to come together. This is a theory of dynamic understanding. It is not a one time understanding but a dynamic one, as each time the process of resurgence takes place, there emerges new understanding. It is because of this reason the hermeneutics of resurgence is progressive and reproductive. Hence it is dynamic. Dynamism refers to action and action qualifies dynamism. When action is more powerful, the dynamism is considered to be on the higher level. However, when action is less powerful, dynamism is not considered to be ineffective. It still has the nature of moving forward. In all cases, dynamism is referred to an action, moving forward, or a happening. Here, the action which is referred to as dynamism is the understanding which takes place.

A hermeneutic of resurgence which leads to dynamic understanding also operates by bringing the person to awareness that one's own self-understanding is not the same as that of the other. Each one understands one's own self and others in a specific pattern which is conditioned by their background. One might esteem her/himself low and the other high, depending on the way one is introduced to life and the level in which one has lived and been respected in the society. The "how" of one's life situation depends on the "how" of the way s/he has been pushed up or down. Hence the self understandings differ from person to person. The hermeneutic of resurgence reveals the level in which one has been kept, treated, and respected, thus revealing the self understanding.

A hermeneutics of resurgence is also concerned with symbols and traditions. Symbols express faith and the reality of the situation. The symbols of the Dalits have been handed down from one generation to the other, enabling them to remember and exercise their beliefs and faith practices and affirm who they are and their position in the society. These symbols are expressions of their very existence and explain their very identity, inner being, and feelings. When they are transmitted and translated into action, they become a tradition which the people consider as a mark of identity. Hermeneutics of resurgence deals with the symbols which express traditions and the past history of the Dalits. Resurgence helps in translating and understanding the present symbols and symbolic expression of the people in terms of their faith and life. Resurgence takes along with it the present symbols and symbolic expressions with a view to understand them in the light of their past. When the symbols are understood in the light of the past through the process of resurgence, then the interpretation of the symbols would be relevant and meaningful to the hearers. In this sense, it is productive and progressive because it brings new awareness and leads to a new understanding.

A hermeneutics of resurgence also aims to reveal, identify, and clarify the "other" in the intercultural encounter. In this case, the interlocutors of the encounter are the preacher and the Dalits. The encounter in preaching and in the process of understanding poses them as strangers to each other because the world view, thought patterns, status, background, identity, and the experiences each have gone through are different. There is suspicion, anxiety, fear, and sometimes even anger in the encounter. Resurgence helps identify the other, their background, and other related factors. When the identification is done accurately in the process of resurgence, there is revelation about the reality of the "other." This identification and revelation about the reality of the "other" clarifies various facts about the "other." This process of identification, revelation, and clarification leads to self-understanding. The preacher is able to understand the power of the oppressed and the affluent.

Hermeneutics of Convergence

In the hermeneutics process of convergence, the main thing that takes place is the movement of the preacher from using the existential reality of human beings as only a preface towards the sermon to the next step of mediating the gospel through the very human experience. In doing so, the preacher revives the reality of the past, not just identifying socio-cultural, political, and economic issues of the people as in resurgence, but analyzing them and searching for possibilities of a new and different living to be proclaimed. The process of reviving the past includes understanding the confused, ignorant, and helpless state in which people had been kept all through. Reviving the history of the subaltern community of the Dalits and perceiving it differently, with a vision of a new prospect of life, creates fresh opportunities for action and response. This would be possible when the reality of their history is re-described by challenging all earlier beliefs about their lives and status. In the case of the Dalits or the subaltern community, their very origin and history has been changed with the intention of subjugating them and oppressing them. When their history is re-described, the presumptions about their present status will have to be reviewed and a new understanding about their present sufferings will emerge. This will not only enable the preacher to challenge the oppressive forces but also to encourage her/him to be in solidarity with them and fight for their rights. Convergence takes place powerfully as the preacher goes back and forth to the reality of the hearers while fabricating the sermon. A hermeneutics of convergence brings into existence yet another factor. When the history is retold with difference, people are exposed to new possibilities of living and they respond positively with hope and aspiration. They not only visualize a hope in their lives but also experience it in reality. This is exactly what the preacher is expected to do through the event of preaching. Effective preaching should bring out new hopes and aspirations and new possibilities of living. When this is achieved, then preaching becomes the Word of God, participating in the purposes of God by giving new hopes and possibilities of living to a hopeless and doomed group of people. Preaching is an endeavor in the realm of divine purpose of God for humans to bring together the gospel message and the existential human situation dialogically, to make sense of both in the light of each other, in order that the purpose of God for humans will be fulfilled. Therefore, rereading the history of the people and re-describing it would have a new perspective and new ending.

In the hermeneutic process of convergence, preachers not only reread the history, analyze the issues, and identify the cultural symbols but also grapple with the relationality of these issues and symbols to the scripture. Resurgence of the history of the Dalits or the subaltern community reveals the problems they have been and are undergoing. The issues identified are discrimination, injustice, powerlessness, denial of human rights and dignity, humiliation, and denial of basic rights to be a dignified citizen. In their socio-cultural life, as identified in the first chapter, the Dalits develop symbols which are unique to them. These symbols explicate their sufferings and inner feelings. While the preacher may not be able to have a direct parallel for these issues in the scripture, it is always possible to reflect on the symbolic expression of these issues theologically and develop a particular theological basis for them. The symbols could be translated in the light of the scripture as deeper meanings and realities underlie each symbol. When translated, these symbols bring out the meanings underlying them and the reality behind the emergence of these symbols. The cultural lives of these people play a major role in the process of theological reflection and preparing a sermon because their cultural symbols are their faith expressions, and these faith expressions are based on their experience of living in shame and suffering, humility and oppression, loneliness and pain. These theological bases, in turn, will find parallels in the scripture. Any problem, when placed against this theological reflection and basis, will reveal the issues to be addressed on the one hand and the scriptural parallel on the other. Theological reflections by the preacher pose yet another problem. Every preacher, like any human person, is born into a particular culture or social system, and they grow in a particular faith tradition which has a strong influence on their thinking patterns. The background of the preacher has a deeper effect on their theological orientation as well. The way one thinks basically results from the influence of this background. In such a case, theological reflection on the problems of the hearers will also be influenced by the same background in which the preacher has grown. It is at this point that the preacher has to detach her/himself from their original background and cross over the horizon into the arena of the hearers, analyzing the problems from their standpoint. It is a dialogical reflection on the human condition or existential reality. In preaching to the Dalits, it is no longer the background of the preacher which controls the thought development but the background or the existential reality of the hearers, which influences the thought process and functions as the basis for its theological formations. In so doing, the preacher does not preach the good news to the suffering community, but listens to the good news they have to share within the spectrum of their existential reality and then interprets the scripture from their standpoint. The preachers are expected to listen to the scripture in the light of the suffering of the Dalits or the subaltern community and identify what good news could be shared with them. When the preacher is able to listen to their stories and understand the good news they want to hear, real convergence takes place. This is a twofold convergence: (1) the backgrounds of the preacher and the hearers and (2) the existential reality of the hearers, preacher, and the scripture. Thus, a hermeneutic of convergence brings the existential reality of the hearers (Dalits), the preachers—with their theological reflections—and the Scripture together. In convergence, the preacher travels between the situation of the hearers and the scripture with his/her theological reflections based on the hearers' situations. It is these theological reflections which are created or formed into a sermon. Most of all, the resurgence process reveals the cultural reality and worldview of the Dalits. By acquiring knowledge about their cultural life and reality, preachers do not engage in the pursuit of identifying similarities between their cultures but rather try to be open to see how dissimilarities are handled.

This raises a question of whether the human situation or the scripture needs to be preached. But it is obvious in the discussion that in preaching, the preacher listens to the echo of the gospel in the existential reality of the subaltern community, reflecting on them theologically, and trying to find a parallel from the scripture. Although it is the fusion of these three parts, it is the scripture which controls the movements of the homiletic plot.

Convergence and Integration

A hermeneutic of convergence also addresses the reality of integration. As mentioned under dynamic understanding, which is progressive and productive, for effective convergence to take place, the preacher has to move out of her/his prejudiced attitude and background. As has been mentioned above (and is true in any hermeneutic process), there is a dominant role of one's own background in interpreting scripture. Whether or not an objective interpretation of scripture is possible is a question which has not been answered with a "yes" so far. There is always a subjective element in any interpretation. So is in the case of homiletics from the underside. The preacher is subject to interpreting the scripture in the light of her/his background. However, the hermeneutics of convergence calls for a radical stepping out of the prejudiced context of the preacher and stepping into the existential reality of the oppressed Dalits. This demands the shedding of all myths about caste, hierarchy, discriminations, and arrogant attitudes. This would mean the preacher emptying her/himself and becoming open to criticisms and learning. Criticisms in relation to the oppressive structure and attitude of which the preacher may be a part and learning in relation to what has been going on and what has to be done from the side of the oppressors. It is this openness to be criticized by the congregation and the scripture that opens the door for convergence. This is an indication of stepping out of the horizon and allowing others to step in. It is through this crossing over that the possibility of being critiqued or criticized emerges. Through such a process, one is able to see the inner side of the other, appreciating the good aspects while criticizing and challenging the bad. This brings to light many realities which thus far have been ignored. This process of realization reveals the attitude of carelessness, avoidance, and discounting. A hermeneutics of convergence at this point calls not for dissection of those realities but rather acceptance of them.

The next step in a hermeneutics of conversion aims to address the issue of a radical pulling of the hearers to the text—and not just pulling the text to the hearers. If the message of the sermon needs to be effective and relevant to the Dalit or subaltern hearers, then it is not the text that needs to be pulled to the context and existential condition of the hearers; it is the hearers, in all their struggles and sufferings. This would mean that the preacher has to return to the scripture with the gained experience of resurgence, crossing over to the horizon of the hearers to see what the scripture says about them and how they would visualize and understand both the scripture and themselves—their life in the light of the scripture. This process is called integration. The process of convergence also integrates: integration of the preacher with the existential reality of the hearers; hearers with the scripture; scripture with the hearers' context; and the preacher with the scripture. This integration leads to understanding, understanding leads to acceptance, and acceptance eventually leads to the formation of a new social order. Therefore, a hermeneutics of convergence aims at the formation of a new social order, where understanding, acceptance, equality, justice, dignity, and respect would be the norm of life.

Hermeneutics of Relevance

As has been noted earlier, the process of convergence opens up new possibilities of living and is focused toward a new ending. These new possibilities and new ending will be materialized in the process of relevance. Relevance is nothing but the application of the developed theological reflections. It has been argued that the preacher is expected to listen to the echo of the gospel in the midst of the existential reality of the subaltern Dalit community. Therefore, when the developed theological reflections are fused both with the situational reality of the people and the scripture, there emerges a need for openness among the hearers, which then calls for new issues to be addressed. While the preacher is willing to cross over to the arena of the subaltern community, they must also be willing to invite and accept her/him in order for a better resurgence, convergence, and relevance to take place. This is in fact a mutual openness on both sides, and it is this openness that the hermeneutics of relevance aims to bring about. This would result in a symbolic transformation of the preacher and the hearers because they enter into a mutual relationship of explaining their reality to each other, allowing for a review and re-description to take place. This is a new ending in the process of preaching. This process of resurgence, convergence, and relevance in preaching the gospel is not oppressive and irrelevant like it used to be—when the preacher was not among the suffering community; instead, the gospel or the good news is heard among those who suffer and the message becomes relevant.

When the suffering Dalits or the subaltern community open up and invite the preacher to their arena, the re-description brings out the inner truth about their situation. This process effects in two ways: on the one hand, it creates new possibilities for better living through challenging the oppressive elements, and on the other, it also retells the community who they are and both encourages as well as challenges them to accept their real identity.[18] New possibilities arise through challenging those forces which were oppressing them and making them suffer. This means, as mentioned under the hermeneutics of resurgence, issues related to justice, discrimination, oppression, inequality, denial of basic human rights, rejection of human dignity and freedom of speech, and living respectfully are to be challenged and addressed in and through preaching. These issues are to be reflected theologically and made relevant for the subaltern or Dalit community. It is through this challenge that the possibilities of a new ending emerges. In these new possibilities, the preacher her/himself is liberated and also the hearers. The hearers are no more aliens and strangers but familiar

---

18. This point is made here only to make a fact clear. There are some Dalits who do not want to accept themselves as Dalits because of their better living conditions and better status in the society. Although in recent Dalit theology the Dalitness is emphasized as an instrument for Dalit liberation still there are people who do not want to identify themselves as Dalits. However, here the emphasis is made on those who are willing to accept their real identity with view of getting recognized identity and liberation.

people; thus, the preacher and the hearers become one as they are mutually liberated. New endings would mean possibilities for the subaltern Dalit community to achieve liberation from such oppressive forces as they are challenged in preaching in equality and in dignity in the society. The evil of discrimination is challenged in and through preaching. This means it is not just the symbolic transformation of the preacher and liberation of the hearers but also the anticipation of social change and a new social order. As Hilkert puts it, "Retelling the story of a suffering people becomes a 'subversive' way of reinterpreting history, criticizing oppressive power, and empowering the impulse toward liberation. This is true because they foster freedom and anticipate a new social order."[19] In the process of resurgence, the preacher gets her/himself rid of the prejudice and wrong presumptions about the subaltern community. In the process of convergence, there is a deeper understanding of their problems which leads to an openness and a willingness to challenge issues which affect the hearers. Therefore, to reflect on the existential reality of the subaltern or Dalit community is to reflect on their sufferings and struggles. Like any other preaching, intercultural preaching also has a particular aim. With regard to the Dalits, the aim of a homiletic from the underside is not just liberating them from all oppressive forces, helping them to regain their self-dignity, freedom of speech, and basic human rights, but also to help them understand God within the context of their existential reality and how the hermeneutic functions as catalyst for living together as a harmonious community. This means that preaching needs to reflect on the dialogical interaction of humans as well.

A hermeneutics of relevance also aims to address the issue of Dalits and others living together as a harmonious community. If resurgence reveals the reality of Dalits and convergence brings the preacher and the Dalits together, then relevance aims to address the harmony and harmonious living of all. The focus here is to create or build up a new community in which love, acceptance, equality, and dignity are norms of life. It is in this process of resurgence, convergence, and relevance that a cultural net is weaved. Each thread of this net represents various cultural elements of different people. These cultural elements are unique to the particular community which holds them high. They are distinct to each cultural background. They do not lose their uniqueness in the process of convergence and relevance; rather, through the process of crossing over in order to understand the other, they form a net of commonness, harmony, and solidarity, liberating both themselves and the others.

---

19. Hilkert, *Mary Catherine*, 97.

Bibliography

Ayrookuzhiel, A. M. A. "Dalit Theology: A Movement of Counter-Culture." In *Indigenous People: Dalits, Dalit Issues in Today's Theological Debate*, edited by James Massey, 251. Noida: Academy, 1994.
Berreman, G. *Caste and Other Inequities: Essays on Inequality*. Meerut: Folkdore Insititute, 1979.
Beteille, A. "Pollution and Poverty." In *The Untouchables in Contemporary India*, edited by Michael Mahar, 4–5. Tucson: University of Arizona Press, 1972.
Buttrick, David. *Homiletic Moves and Structures*. Philadelphia: Fortress, 1987.
Das, Bhagwan. "Dalits and Caste System." In *Indigenous People: Dalits, Dalit Issues in Today's Theological Debate*, edited by James Massey, 59–61. Noida: Academy, 1994.
Dhavamony, M. *Phenomenology of Religion*. Rome: Gregorian University Press, 1973.
Ghurey, G. S. *Caste and Race in India*. Bombay: Popular Prakashan, 1969.
Hilkert, Mary Catherine. *Naming Grace: Preaching and the Sacramental Imagination*. New York: Continuum, 1997.
Kumar, Krishna. "Educational Experience of Scheduled Castes and Tribes." *Economic and Political Weekly*, September 18, 1983. 3–10.
Kurian, C. T. "An Overview of the Economic Condition of Scheduled Castes in India." *Bangalore Theological Forum* 14 (1982) 94.
Manickam, S. *Slavery in Tamil Country: A Historical Overview*. Madras: Christian Literature Society, 1982.
Manorama, Ruth. "Dalit Women: Downtrodden among the Downtrodden." In *Indigenous People: Dalits and Dalit Issues in Today's Theological Debate*, edited by James Massey, 159–76. New Delhi: ISPCK, 1998.
Mukherjee, P. *Beyond Four Varnas: The Untouchable in India*. Shimla: Indian Institute of Advanced Study, 1988.
Prabhakar, M. E. "Ideology of Oppression: Caste and Untouchability." *Religion and Society* 45.4 (1998) 5–50.
Srinivas, M. N. "Some Reflections on the Nature of the Caste Hierarchy." In *Caste in Modern India: And other Essays*, 161. Bombay: Media Promoters, 1994.

Existential Realities and the Preaching Dynamics of Some Nigerian Pentecostal Preachers

BABATUNDE ADEDIBU

The Changing Global Ecclesial landscape

THE HISTORIOGRAPHY OF THE changing global Christian landscape is incomplete without reference to the Southernization of Christianity in the twenty-first century. The redrawing of the political map of World Christianity has led to the emergence of a distinctive indigenous appropriation of the Christian faith across the Global South, a movement away from Western-dominated influences. The obvious implication within the context of this seismic shift in the center of gravity of the Christian faith from the Global North to the Global South has led to varigated expressions of the Christian faith in terms of liturgy, preaching dynamics, creativity and innovations, ritualization, and religious idiosyncrasies and diversities amongst churches—particulalrly the pentecostal stream. Inexplicably linked to the changing face of World Christianity is the rise and proliferation of Pentecostal and Charismatic movements within the Global South. Thus, the twenty-first century might be labelled the "Global South Christian Century" due to the radically changing ecclesial landscape within this context.

The changing ecclesial landscape in the twenty-first century is inexplicably linked to the rise in the proliferation of Pentecostalism and Charismatic movements in the Global South. Although it is imperative to assert that the shift in the center of gravity of the Christian faith, as noted by previous scholarship,[1] is not essential in terms of the quality of the faith or its spirituality but rather a product of diverse, push-and-pull factors, including globalization, mass migration, and technological advancement, leading to deterritorialization and reterritorialization of churches in diverse contexts hinged on the rendition of the gospel to a particular vernacular. However, Katalina Tahafe-Williams posits that the shift in the center of gravity to the Global South does not "necessarily imply a similar shift in the content of pedagogical approaches to theological education and formation."[2]

A number of African biblical scholars have opted for other convenient modes of biblical interpretation, amongst which is "Inculturation hermeneutics," as championed by Justin Ukpong.[3] It designates an approach to biblical interpretation which seeks to make the African context the subject of interpretation; this means that every dimension of the interpretative process is "consciously informed by the worldview of, and the life experience within that culture." Justin Ukpong includes the historical, social, economic, political, and religious as elements of inculturation hermeneutics. These elements, then, make a substantial contribution to the ideo-theological orientation of inculturation hermeneutics. Like other forms of African biblical interpretation, Inculturation hermeneutics takes its cue from life outside the academy. The general experience of African Christians was that African social and cultural concerns were not reflected in missionary and Western academic forms of biblical interpretation. Inculturation hermeneutics arose as a response, paying attention to the African sociocultural context and the question that arises therefrom.

The contemporary Western academic modes of reading the bible, which focus on the history of the text or the text itself, serving western interests and goals, are inadequate for addressing questions and issues from African contexts, hence the development of Inculturation Hermeneutics, using the mediation of African cultural resources for reading the bible in its social-historical context and contemporary contexts. In this way, the reading will be informed by both contexts and the biblical message will be enabled to come alive in the contemporary context.

Moreover, Africa—and particularly Nigeria—is noted to be one of the hot spots for the growth of Christianity, especially for Pentecostal and Charismatic churches not only in Nigeria but also in the Diaspora. Interestingly, despite the declining economic fortunes of Nigeria, the religious

1. Kalu, "African Pentecostalism in Diaspora"; Jenkins, *New Faces of Christianity*; *Next Christendom*.
2. Tahafe-Williams, "Foreword," xix.
3. Ukpong, "Re-Reading the Bible with African Eyes," 4.

sector, particularly the Pentecostal churches, have defied all odds and seem to be the only non-export commodity from Nigeria to the rest of the world as Nigerian Pentecostals are now globalized. The next section of this study examines the trajectories of Nigeria in relation to the geo-social, economic, and religious pluralities. This inevitably will give an overview of the existential realities within which the historiography of the Nigeria Pentecostal movement is weaved, leading to the creativity and innovations of Pentecostal Church leaders in their preaching dynamics.

The Trajectories of Nigeria[4]

Nigeria is perhaps one of the most diverse and multi-ethnic nations in the world. The Nigerian nation, in recent times, has been noted for the wrong reasons in light of the endemic moral and fiscal indiscretion of the political class. This inevitably has given Nigeria a bad image; its citizens are subjected to rigorous scrutiny by various security agencies across the world. Nigerians are stereotyped as criminals, accentuated by the nefarious activities of fraudsters, which has led to the reinvention of Section 419 of the Criminal Code Act as a name tag for fraudsters. Section 419 denotes the offense of obtaining the property of another by false pretenses. In Nigeria, 419 is commonly used to refer to the offense of obtaining the property of another by false pretenses, primarily because Section 419 of the Criminal Code Act is the section that criminalizes the offense in the southern part of Nigeria; the expression "419" has, therefore, gained popularity and acceptance among Nigerians.[5] However, it is pertinent to argue that many Nigerians are hard-working, honest people who are highly aspirational and desire good governance, just as in most developing and developed nations of the world where there is respect for the rule of law, employment opportunities, and economic and infrastructural developments for its citizens.[6]

Nigeria is a very large and diverse country of about 924 kilometers with a teeming population of about 190 million people as estimated in 2017. With such a teeming population, it is not surprising that Nigeria is stated to be the most populous nation in Africa and the seventh most populous nation in the world.[7] The population of Nigeria has been projected to become the "the fifth largest country in the world by 2030 (with a population estimate

---

4. This section is an adaptation of a section in a previous 2019 publication of the author in Adedibu, "This Is Nigeria!," 43–48

5. See Pierce, *Moral Economies of Corruption*, 153–97.

6. Okonjo-Iweala, *Fighting Corruption is Dangerous*, xv.

7. Associated Press, "Nigeria to Pass US."

of 364 million) and third largest by 2050 (estimated population of 410 million). Currently, 63 percent of Nigeria's population is under twenty-five years of age, and, like the rest of Africa, its youthful population can either be harnessed for a demographic dividend—or it can pose a tough employment and outmigration challenge."[8] It is quite intriguing that President Muhammadu Buhari opined that Nigerian youth are lazy.[9] This contradiction in the assessment of the youth has not helped to critically appreciate and harness their prowess and creativity for national development.[10] Nevertheless, such a contraption seems more designed to foster continued class division with the ruling class, masked in democratic overtures that are mainly face saving. Such unfounded criticism of Nigerian youth is an effort to scapegoat Nigeria's young people, owing to a lack of social and economic policies that are not geared towards infrastructural development but rather continued patronage of the privileged class to the detriment of the Nigerian masses. In terms of religious subscriptions, Nigeria is almost split between two religious movements—Christianity and Islam—with the northern part of the country mostly Muslim dominated and important Christian minorities dotting various communities of the Region. Likewise, the Southern parts of Nigeria are significantly Christian dominated whilst Muslims are a minority. In terms of democratic structure, Nigeria has adopted the Presidential system of government, characterized by a very dominant executive president and vice president, but this is seemingly a major drain on the nation's dwindling economic fortunes.

Due to inept political leadership over the years, the Nigerian economy might be described as being in a comatose state. The avalanches of social and economic inadequacies are reflected in systemic failings in governmental policies and social structures that seemingly perpetuate systemic socio-economic and political injustices to some sections of the country.[11] Interestingly, Nigeria was estimated to be Africa's largest economy in 2017, with a gross domestic product (GDP) of $400 billion. The country constitutes 71 percent of West Africa's GDP and 27 percent of the continent's GDP. GDP per capital is $2,123, and Nigeria is classified as a lower middle income nation.[12] Despite being a major oil producing nation, rather than being a blessing to the development of the Nigerian state, this perhaps seems like

8. Okonjo-Iweala, *Fighting Corruption is Dangerous*, xv.

9. Ogundipe, "What I Meant."

10. Chiroma, "Tapping into the Unexplored Power," 167–84.

11. Ukah, *New Paradigm of Pentecostal Power*; Ojo, *End-Time Army*; Cox and Haar, *Religion in Contemporary Africa*; Ajayi, "Prosperity Churches in Nigeria"; Marshall, "Power in the Name of Jesus," 21–37

12. Okonjo-Iweala, *Fighting Corruption is Dangerous*, xvi.

a curse, as the economy is solely dependent on the oil sector, which makes over 90 percent of exports and 70 percent of revenues. Within the global oil producing nations, Nigeria is the "fifteenth-largest oil producer in the world in 2016, it has the world largest oil reserves and ninth largest oil reserves."[13] The United Nations (UN), in a press release in February 2018, stated that, "Nigeria attained the undesired but inevitable position of the Poverty Capital of the world with 64 percent of the total population in poverty, a figure that translates to roughly 80 million people."[14] This depicts the downward spiraling effect of years of economic plundering of the treasury and abuse of the ruling class. Despite the endowment and exportation of petroleum over the years, the mono-commodity export nature of the Nigerian economy and poor leadership with profligacies of its past and present leadership has exposed many Nigerian citizens to a poor standard of living. In 2016, the prevalence of people living below the poverty line in Nigeria ranged between 54 percent to 60 percent, but today, 82 million Nigerians are living below the poverty line of 1.9 dollars a day." Nigeria is number 187 out of 190 countries.[15] This type of development resonated in Van Dijk's assertion that "the new charismatic type of Pentecostalism creates a moral and physical geography whose domain is one of transnational cultural inter-penetration and flow."[16]

The economic plight of Nigeria is seemingly induced by the moral and fiscal corruption of the political class that plundered the nation's treasury in connivance with their cronies. Intriguingly, the declared war on corruption by the Mohammed Buhari-led government seems to be a farce due to the complicity of the members of the political class through "Clientelism, Prebendalism, Patrimonialism, and Neopatrimonialism" over the years.[17]

Interestingly, the religious landscape of Nigeria has been redefined by the proliferation of Pentecostal and Charismatic churches in every nook and cranny of Nigeria. The broad classification of these churches as Pentecostals inevitably does not exclude the heterogeneous nature of these churches in terms of liturgy, leadership model, rituals, and worship. The re-sacralization of urban spaces as religious spaces is now a common feature in urban cities and highbrow areas in Nigeria. A typical example is Lagos; the former capital of Nigeria has all the shades of social and religious diversities as various Pentecostal churches advertising boards adorn the streets.

13. Okonjo-Iweala, *Fighting Corruption is Dangerous*, xvii.
14. Adelowokan, "Tithes."
15. Donli, "Most Nigerians."
16. Van Dijk, "From Camp to Encompassment."
17. Ogundiya, "Political Corruption in Nigeria."

Space contestation, noise pollution, and competition of these churches are evident with a high degree of commercialization and digital advertizing as avenues for recruiting and sustaining their clientele. One of the prominent Nigerian Pentecostal churches is the Redeemed Christian Church of God (RCCG), founded in 1952 by the late Rev. Josiah Olufemi Akindayomi, now led by Pastor E. A. Adeboye, with a transnational network of churches in 197 countries across the globe. In Nigeria, the RCCG has over 44,000 parishes, in the United Kingdom, it has 736 parishes, and in the United States, there are more than 800 parishes.[18] Nigeria also has Deeper Life Christian Ministry, established by W. F. Kumuyi; Church of God Mission, established by late Archbishop Benson Idahosa; and Living Faith International Ministries, also known as Winners' Chapel, founded by Bishop David Oyedepo. Several Pentecostal churches came into being in the 1990s, which included Mountain of Fire and Miracles, established in 1989 by Rev. Dr. Olukoya, and Christ Embassy, led by Pastor Chris Oyakhilome, in 1991, which started off as a Campus fellowship at the Bendel State University (now Ambrose Ali University, Benin, Nigeria). Fountain of Life Church, formed by Pastor Taiwo Odukoya, was established in 1992. House on the Rock, led by Rev. Wale Adefarasin, was set up in 1994, Daystar Christian Center, founded by Pastor Sam Adeyemi, was inaugurated in 1995.[19] The implosion of Pentecostal churches is not limited to Nigeria but also can be found in the Diaspora. Most of the renowned churches have also registered their presence in Europe and North America. Intriguingly, there is a corollary between declining economic fortunes of Nigeria with the implosion of churches in Nigeria. The implosion of Pentecostal churches has led to a gradual rethink with respect to the *modus operandi* of many historic denominations and even amongst some sects of the Islamic faith. The rethink has caused their adherents to reflect on some of the distinctive practices of Pentecostalism, e.g., liturgy, ritual practices, and worship experiences.

The military and political class that governed Nigeria during the 1980s to 1990s led the nation into the grips of the International Monetary Fund through the instrumentality of the Structural Adjustment Programme (SAP), which nearly emasculated the citizens of the nation through hyperinflation and fiscal constraints imposed on the nation. Due to the systemic failings of the social, political, and economic policies of the Nigerian state, Neo-Pentecostal denominations provided a default coping mechanism with respect to providing hope to cope with the economic meltdown, making claims of meeting the existential challenges of Nigerians. Neo-Pentecostal

---

18. Adedibu, "Missional History and Growth," 82.
19. "Daystar Experience."

churches gave many Nigerians hope in the midst of their hopeless economic situations. This development gave rise to a new generation of Pentecostal churches in Nigeria that began to fulfill part of the statutory obligations of the Nigerian state through various social, economic, and educational initiatives. The claims of meeting the existential realities of Nigerian Pentecostal churches is not limited to just social or educational interventions of these churches but also a well-crafted and ingenious preaching dynamic as well as understanding the worldview of Nigerians to address both temporal and celestial matters. This inevitably has led to a major source of recruitment and sustenance of their clientele over time. The next section of this work examines the preaching dynamics of some of Nigeria's popular Pentecostal churches in terms of their major programs in relation to meeting the existential realities of their adherents in Nigeria.

Thematic Overview of Nigerian Pentecostal Church Leaders' Preaching/Teaching Dynamics

Nigerian Pentecostal preachers, like their Global South counterparts, make use of a literal interpretation of the Bible, causing them to be labeled fundamentalist in their reading of the word of God. This is a shift from the Western normative subscription of critical, contextual reading of the Christian Writ. This is predicated on the locus of acceptance of the Christ Writ as divinely inspired and infallible to most Nigerian Pentecostal preachers like their counterparts in other regions of the Global South. There is a deep sense of attraction to texts that have elements of supernaturalism, such as miracles, healings, and deliverance charismata. There is also a belief that the Old Testament is just as authoritative as the New Testament. For instance, a classic example is Pastor E. A. Adeboye preaching on a social media site about tithing. He declared that the Bible makes tithing mandatory. He based his argument on the continuing authority of the Old Testament. Whilst addressing his congregants, he noted that various scriptural references in the Old Testament are appropriated by Christians such as: "[The] Lord is my Shepherd, I shall not want" (Ps 23:1); "The Lord is my strength and my shield; my heart trusts in Him, and I am helped: therefore my heart greatly rejoiceth; and with my song will l praise him" (Ps 28:7; Deut 28:1–12). Adeboye argues that if we are going to quote the Old Testament concerning other matters of faith, we should also quote it and obey it when it comes to tithing. Why, he asks, should Malachi 3:10 be different?[20] Why should tithing not continue

20. Unpublished address delivered by Pastor E. A. Adeboye at Redeemed Christian Church of God, Redemption Camp, Mowe, Nigeria, November 4, 2017.

to be relevant as it was in Old Testament times? This type of literalism is evident in the sermons and teachings of most Pentecostal church leaders in Nigeria (e.g., Bishop David Oyedepo,[21] Rev. Chris Oyakhilome,[22] and Mike Okonkwo[23]) and also in the diaspora (e.g., Pastor Matthew Ashimolowo,[24] the Senior Pastor of Kingsway International Christian Centre in London, and a host of others). This author has observed that Nigerian Pentecostal church leaders, like their counterparts in the Global South, have produced a

> spectrum of theological interpretations, just as churches in the United States do. The North-South difference is rather one of emphasis. Though conservative and literalist approaches are widely known in the global North (which mainstream political discourse and the media are fond of labeling as controversial and reactionary), in the South biblical and theological conservatism clearly represents the Christian mainstream.[25]

Moreover, the "mainstream" of Nigeria Pentecostal churches' literal interpretation has made the Bible come alive as they can see their lived experiences in it, which makes its applicability inevitable. Thus, it is succinct to note that "societies that identify with the biblical world feel at home with the text."[26] In essence, in Africa, Asia, and Latin America, the Bible is used by Pentecostal preachers to address the lived experiences of people in these contexts.

It should be observed that the average Nigerian Pentecostal preachers are themselves products of Nigerian society with its multifarious problems and challenges. They are not immune to the various challenges that confront the average citizen: bad roads, epileptic power supplies, high costs of living, and a widening gap between the rich and the poor. Nigerian Pentecostal preachers find ample scriptural basis to address the existential challenges of their context. The socio-economic, political, and religious challenges in contemporary Nigeria present a herculean task for an average Nigerian to navigate without recourse to a religious subscription. The resonance of such a disposition amongst Nigerian Pentecostal preachers is that

> the new Christianity will push theologians to address matters of faith that center on poverty and social injustice, political

21. Opejobi, "Bishop Oyedepo."
22. Oyakhilome, "Question 4."
23. Opejobi, "Popular Bishop."
24. Ashimolowo, "Power of Your Tithe."
25. Jenkins, "Reading the Bible in the Global South," 68.
26. Kanyoro, "Interpreting Old Testament Polygamy."

violence, corruption, the meltdown of law and order, and the place of the Christian witness amidst religious plurality. They will be dealing with the need for Christian communities to make sense of God's self-revelation to their pre-Christian ancestors.[27]

A cursory observation will note Pentecostal pastors' penchant for the use of the Old Testament in their exegesis. For instance, in Pastor E. A. Adeboye's message to the ministers of his denomination at Jos, during the RCCG Ministers and Workers Conference (May 9, 2015), he noted that he studied the life of Elijah for three years. In retrospect, this formed the basis of his expository teachings on lessons from the life of Elijah that he preached extensively in 1996 and 1997 during the monthly Holy Ghost Services of his denomination. The thrust of this fascination might be in relation to the incredible success of Elijah, but it also points to the congregants' familiarity with the Old Testament world within the African worldview. Scottish Missiologist Andrew Walls was succinct as he observed, "You do not have to interpret Old Testament Christianity to Africans; they live in an Old Testament world."[28]

The description of biblical era famines also resonates in some African countries. Although most Pentecostal churches are situated in the nooks and crannies of urban cities, nevertheless, some preachers, like the generation of Pastors E. A. Adeboye, W. F. Kumuyi, and Prophet J. Abiara, make intermittent references in their sermons to agricultural seasons and the hardships they bring to illustrate certain points. Many of these metaphors and anecdotes might be alien to people in the Global North due to the fact that many of them only see the finished, consumable products and not the process of harvesting—such is not the case in Africa.

Pentecostal preachers also use their own life experiences to encourage the hearts of their listeners. For example, Pastor E. A. Adeboye, noted for his creativity in the use of anecdotes and life experiences, spoke of the time when he bought a second hand car:

> Several years ago, when I just bought my second hand car, it was the first car I ever bought, something strange happened. Somebody among the lecturers shook my hand and greeted me saying, "How is your car doing today?" I realized that this was a new greeting; they had never greeted me like that before. I discovered I had joined the category of a car owner.

---

27. Carpenter, "Christian Scholar."
28. Jenkins, "Reading the Bible in the Global South," 68.

While Adeboye is telling this anecdote, the crowd is listening actively, laughing and participating with affirmative noises. Expectantly, they waited for the punch line of his anecdote: "Tell your neighbor very soon they will ask you not 'how is your car doing today, but how is your JET doing today?!'"

The attendees, who responded by stretching out their hands in an expectant mood as if about to receive a gift, simultaneously shouted a thunderous, "AMEN!!" Adeboye further added:

> To some of you that may sound impossible, but God will surprise you, so shall it be in Jesus' name. Some people say I don't preach about prosperity that I only preach holiness. Well, that is true because, if you live holy, you will prosper automatically.

The importance of the use of anecdote to complement his sermons is due to Adeboye's awareness of the socio-economic challenges of his adherents in a seemingly collapsing economy, bereft of social and economic infrastructures. Thus he offers hope to the seemingly challenged listeners.

Also intriguing is the creative way in which Nigerian Pentecostal preachers use the traditional African worldview to address various existential challenges. The sermons of most Nigerian Pentecostal pastors address issues of malevolent forces, curses, healing, and deliverance. One of the popular Pentecostal preachers is Pastor Kayode Olukoya, who is the General Overseer of Mountain of fire and Miracles Ministries. His monthly program, tagged "Power Must Change Hands," meets on the first Saturday of every month and attracts well over 500,000 adherents to Prayer City, located along the Lagos-Ibadan Expressway. The home page of the MFM website states that "MFM Ministries is a full gospel ministry devoted to the Revival of Apostolic Signs, Holy Ghost fireworks, and the unlimited demonstration of the power of God to deliver to the uttermost."[29] In the Nigerian Christian scape, MFM is noted as "Do It Yourself" (DIY) deliverance ministry par excellence. The website attests to this as it states that "MFM is a do-it-yourself Gospel ministry where your hands are trained to wage war and your fingers to do battle."[30] Afe Adogame observes that this DIY approach "serves as a source of spiritual empowerment to the laity in the acquisition and retention of spiritual power, and plays down the interlocutory role of the clergy as the bridge between members and the spiritual entities."[31]

Various book publications from the stable of *Mountain of Fire and Miracles*, mostly authored by Dr. Daniel Kayode Olukoya, are a reflection of

---

29. Mountain of Fire and Miracles Ministries, "About MFM."
30. Mountain of Fire and Miracles Ministries, "About MFM."
31. Adogame, "Dealing with Local Satanic Technology," 6–7.

his preaching dynamics on malevolent spirits, spiritual wickedness, curses, local satanic altars, deliverance from Captivity, and ancestral or hereditary problems. Rosalind Hackett, in her work on *Discourses in Demonization in Africa*, described the modus operandi of the MFM through the Battle Cry Ministries, a sub group of MFM. Hackett noted that the MFM is committed to "(a) teaching and disseminating information on Christian spiritual warfare, (b) making available life-changing Christian articles and books at affordable prices, and (c) preparing an army of aggressive prayer warriors and intercessors in the end time."[32] The thrust of the prayer against malevolent forces and satanic manipulations are the hallmark of Dr. Olukoya's sermons as members are noted to respond to his literal interpretation of the scriptures as well as utilization of the African Traditional worldview of spirits. The members are taught to pray aggressively, using violent words and gestures such as "fall down and die," "the enemy of my soul must die," and a host of other phrases to deal with "bad foundations," destructive linkages, spirit husbands, family curses, family idols, and much more. Hackett noted that "this is the tone of most of Olukoya's sermons and writings. He wants to offer deliverance from what he calls 'bad foundations,' destructive linkages, and wrong connections."[33] The uniqueness of MFM is reflective of the dominant demonological orientation as well as advocacy of power against power to the experiential challenges of its adherents in Nigeria and diaspora.

An emerging trend in some Nigerian Pentecostal churches is religious transnationalism. For instance, within the RCCG and Mountain of Fire and Miracles Ministries (MFM) is the pliability and uniformity of their belief practices. Adogame, quoting Larm, notes:

> The importation of churches like MFM into Europe involves not just personnel, buildings, or a renewal of Christianity but also additional belief systems that may or may not be familiar to the mainstream[Evangelical] population. These worldviews are often effectively reproduced within the setting through socialization procedures, which occur in the spatial-temporal locus of the church.[34]

The de-territorialization of a familiar interpretative framework of the vicissitudes of life through the lens of MFM is now prevalent in various countries across the globe, particularly in cities that have high numbers of Nigerians, such as London, Baltimore, Manchester, and Edinburgh. The re-enactment

32. Hackett, "Discourses of Demonization in Africa and Beyond," 65.
33. Hackett, "Discourses of Demonization in Africa and Beyond," 65.
34. Jackie Larm cited in Adogame, "Dealing with Local Satanic Technology," 87.

of familiar religious frameworks situated within the African Traditional worldview has been a source of attraction for many migrants from Nigeria in Europe. This might likewise account for the continued "Nigerian cultural captivity" of many Nigerian Pentecostal churches in the West. Paradoxically, Nigerian Pentecostal churches—like MFM, RCCG, and Winners' Chapel—are perhaps the fastest growing churches, as their sermons and writings meet the experiential needs of their followers.

Analyzing the "inglorious" modes of interpretation used by the colonialists, Mark Brett[35] opines that biblical interpretation ought to bring some leverage to the oppressed and downtrodden. With an ethics of reconciliation and restitution in view, Brett brings great insight to his analysis of biblical texts—especially those which have been used by imperial interests to support colonization categories, e.g., "traditional owners," learned in his dialogue with indigenous people. He holds that a genuine and open conversation with the biblical texts is possible. Where he finds them useful, Brett draws on a variety of critical and post-colonial theorists to inform this conversation. He illustrates uses of the Bible in colonization, colonialism, and resistances to such. Recognizing that the production of most biblical texts occurred under the influence of and in response to "the shifting tides of ancient empires," Brett is prompted by the ambiguous status of the Bible in relation to the colonization of Australia to re-read key biblical texts with a view to opening an interpretive space for a "decolonization of God."

When the above submission of Mark Brett is put in line with the mode of preaching by some Pentecostal preachers in Nigeria, it answers the obvious. For instance, the late Archbishop Benson Idahosa was quoted to have said, "My God is not a poor God, so you have got to give him the best of your resources so as to be blessed." He based his assertion on 3 John 2. The prosperity gospel has become a very good ecclesio-theological product, brazenly displayed by some Nigerian Pentecostal preachers with the aim of making themselves, as well as members, financially wealthy. This is what Adekunle Dada[36] referred to as "a millionaire through Jesus." Many poor people in the church want to get rich, live comfortable lives, and contribute their quota to the expansion of the kingdom of God here on earth. This also causes preachers to select passages from the bible to buttress the point that God wants everyone to be rich. As earlier stated, 3 John 2 is usually expounded for this purpose. The word " prosper" is dug out of context and applied to financial wealth.

35. Brett, *Decolonizing God*.
36. Dada, "Millionaire Through Jesus."

Moreover, the understanding of the African ontology and agentive causal principle, which explains the indigenous African belief about matter, is pivotal to the worldview of Africans on witchcraft, which Olukoya has mastered—as is evident in most of his sermons. Due to systemic failings within the socio-economic space, Nigerians construct their social reality on the basis of such religious paradigms, particularly Pentecostal adherents. The African traditional worldview believes the universe is a complex mixture of spiritual and material forces. Within this complex mix of forces, reality unveils itself in terms of points or entities that are dynamic. This means that what we see as matter is active because it is imbued with an internal power or energy. Matter within the African traditional belief is active and living, which is power. It thus implies that the decisive source of causality is power, considered as spiritual force. To a large extent, the underlying epistemological grounds for the Olukoya (and most Nigerian Pentecostal preachers) witchcraft rhetoric in their sermons is reflective of three theories on witchcraft, according to Opoku Onyinah,[37] which are:

> (a) Function as a release of tension within certain types of African social structure, as espoused by Clyde Mitchel, Middleton and Winter and Marwick;[38]
>
> (b) Social instability and an opportunity for the interpretation of various social, economic, and natural phenomena, such as famine, economic distress, and rapid social change, based on assertions by Nadel, Gluckman, and Debrunner;[39] and
>
> (c) Psychological reactions of those suffering from ill-health, misfortunes and inability to control their destinies.

Preaching dynamics of most Nigerian Preachers is the appropriation of contextual knowledge of their communities as what is perceived to be reality within a community is defined by the functional belief system within the community. Gittins observed that:

> Reality is, very largely, what a community agrees to be real. In this sense, reality is socially or religiously constructed. Witchcraft concerns the really real, except by its presumed effects: crop failure, sickness, unexplained events, even death, identification of these effects points incontrovertibly to what underpins them; in essence, personal agency and the abuse of (spiritual power).[40]

---

37. Onyinah, "Deliverance as a Way of Confronting Witchcraft."
38. Gittins, "Witchcraft: Twenty Talking Points," 1.
39. Gittins, "Witchcraft: Twenty Talking Points," 1.
40. Gittins, "Witchcraft: Twenty Talking Points," 3.

To disregard the prevailing worldview and the experiential realities within Nigeria might be a foolhardy task, as most Pentecostal adherents are eager to get rid of their socio-economic and spiritual challenges. The relevance of the preaching of most Nigerian Pentecostal Pastors reflects the understanding of the needs of their congregants and are deeply rooted in the African cosmology. It might be appropriate to argue that Nigerian Pentecostal Churches "play a crucial role in the production of the 'figure witch'"[41] in the Nigerian religious landscape. Worthy of note is the fact that there is presently an increasing consciousness amongst some Pentecostal adherents in Nigeria that failure in life may be a result of laziness/indolence, a lack of networking with other people, or the inability to key into the scheme of things, and not some malevolent outside force. These views seem to resonate among some who, through dint of hard work and perseverance, were able to break the jinx of poverty, thereby setting up a new foundational basis of wealth for posterity. Despite this, many still believe that the problems of life are caused by supra-normal powers. Many "smart preachers" key into this concept, exploring passages from the bible to address the issue. This has led to unbridled uses of imprecatory Psalms to combat spiritual and supposedly physical challenges.[42]

In summary, the Christian landscape in Nigeria has changed significantly through the proliferation of Pentecostal churches. Its impact on the entire religious landscape is profound in the area of theology and worship. The active participation of the laity in the ritual, worship, and preaching ministries of these Pentecostal churches is a complete departure from the historic denominations. However, the happy-clappy dispositions in Pentecostal churches are now replicated in most historic denominations while many Pentecostal songs are no longer utilized only within Pentecostal spaces. Above all, most of the Nigerian Pentecostal denominations are exceptionally creative and innovative in terms of programs specifically tailored to meet diverse needs. The creativity of these churches thus attracts focused preaching themes to address the perceived challenges of the attendees. For instance, the RCCG has over 42,000 parishes[43] in Nigeria. The church leadership have initiated and sustained various special programs. Moreover, such creative dexterity has its origin in the routinization of the charisma of the General Overseer, Pastor E. A. Adeboye. For Instance, Mount Zion Hour is a prayer meeting program of the RCCG held at the Redemption Camp for the members of the church and the entire Christian community.

41. De Boeck and Plissart, *Kinshasa*, 173.
42. Adamo, "Reading Psalm 109."
43. Odesola, "50 Million Free Meals Project."

It is most specifically held for those who are seeking a solution to problems with child bearing. The focus of the preaching at this program centers on claims of the supernatural power of God to eliminate any challenges of childlessness. Scriptures that dominate such sermons include Genesis 1:28; 29; Deuteronomy 7:14; Luke 1:37; and Exodus 23:26. In a society where basic medical facilities are in a deplorable state, health care delivery is uneven, and public hospitals are better described as public slaughter slabs, many Nigerians resign their faith to Pentecostal churches.

In view of the deplorable healthcare delivery situation in Nigeria, some of the adherents of these churches attend maternity classes where they not only receive basic medical care but also congregate to listen to sermons on hope, faith, and fruitfulness. RCCG is a typical example that has translated this model of social care with religious creativity in programs. The denomination has full-fledged medical centers in most of the Provincial headquarters of the church in Nigeria, particularly in the Southern part of Nigeria.

Neo-Pentecostal churches in Nigeria are brazenly described by some scholars as properity churches.[44] This charge belies the fact that prosperity churches do much good for the dispossesed in Nigeria. In fact, some Nigerian Pentecostal churches that, in their founding days, were known to be world-rejecting and characterized by a strong puritan emphasis are now world-accomodating. A typical example is the RCCG and Winners' Chapel of Nigeria, where Pentecostal preachers commonly teach their adherents that Christ became poor so that that they might be rich.[45] For Instance, Bishop David Oyedepo, the presiding Bishop of Winners Temple, stated, "Christ purposely died in poverty, leaving everything behind, so that we might live in spiritual and physical wealth, and the more abundantly."[46] A similar disposition is noted in Sunny Obada, the founding Pastor of Christian Reach Out Church Inc.:

> Preachers of the past had what I call a poverty mentality. . . .
> When Jesus was on earth, I believe He wore clothes [made] by

---

44. One of the most recent critics of the prosperity gospel in Nigeria is Gary Maxey. In his book he highlighted the various challenges of the health wealth gospellers and the American influence on the Nigerian church scene. See Maxey, *Seduction of the Nigerian Church*, 79–121.

45. One of the texts mostly cited by these preachers in the New Testament is 2 Cor 8:9. The literal interpretation of the scripture provides ample basis for Pentecostals to make such an assertion. Others include 1 John 3:1; Ps 34:10; 50:10; Hag 2:8, and a host of other references.

46. Oyedepo, *Breaking Financial Hardship*, 181

the best designers of the time. That was why the soldiers had to cast lots on who will keep his clothes after he was crucified.[47]

This is eisegesis and an outlandish claim, as the cloth in question was merely an article of antiquity and not a priceless garment desired by man. They did not cast lots for its value. This type of exegesis has come under the scrutiny of biblical scholars, as it negates all hermeneutical principles. Nevertheless, in view of the appeal of the prosperity gospel, the quest for material success, cars, vehicles, properties, and clothing in a poverty-driven society heightens the quest for membership in many Nigerian Pentecostal churches.[48]

Obviously, the preaching dynamics of most Nigerian Pentecostal preachers show their total digression from the Reformation preaching form they inherited, which is used generally in evangelical circles, consisting of the exposition of biblical passages[49] into "a chaotic phenomenon with what seems to be all style and little substance."[50] The primary aim of this type of preaching is building faith in the listeners' hearts to meet their existential challenges with the power of spoken words, but it totally negates all hermeneutical principles of biblical interpretations.

Conclusively, the preaching dynamics of most Nigerian Pentecostal preachers are reflective of the existential realities of Nigerians, primarily honed through the traditional African religion lens, which provides a familiar intepretative framework for their teeming adherents. Their hermeutical approach is a literal interpretation of scripture mostly characterized by eisegesis. There is clearly an absence of critical analyses of texts through an examination of contextual issues that warranted the writings of the books that are the hallmarks of a Western hermenutical enterprise, particularly within the evangelical cycle.

Bibliography

Adamo, David T. "Reading Psalm 109." *Old Testament Essay* 21.3 (2008) 575–92.
Adedibu, B. A. "The Missional History and Growth of the Redeemed Christian Church of God in the United Kingdom Till Date (2015)." *Journal of European Pentecostal Theological Association* 36 (2016) 82.
———. "This Is Nigeria! Creativity, Development, and Contemporary Indulgence Amongst Some Pentecostal Churches." *Akungba Journal of Religion and African Culture* 6.1 (2018) 43–48.

47. *Weekend Concord,* May 28, 1994.
48. Dada, "Millionaire Through Jesus," 8.
49. Cruz, "Preaching among Filipino Pentecostals."
50. Johns, "What Can the Mainline Learn?"

Adedigba, Azeezat. "Most Nigerians have slipped into extreme poverty—ActionAid." *Premium Times*, June 9, 2018. Online. https://www.premiumtimesng.com/news/more-news/271752-most-nigerians-have-slipped-into-extreme-poverty-actionaid.html.

Adelowokan, Seun. "Tithes: Pastor Adeboye Is Wrong but That Is Not the Problem." *Pulse.ng*, April 19, 2018. Online. https://www.pulse.ng/religious-gist-tithespastor-adeboye-is-wrong-but-that-is-not-the-problem/h975etk.

Adogame, Afe. "Dealing with Local Satanic Technology: Deliverance Rhetoric in the Mountain of Fire and Miracles Ministries." *The Journal of World Christianity* 5.1 (2012) 87.

Ajayi, S. Ademola. "Prosperity Churches in Nigeria: A New Phenomenon in a Depressed Economic Setting." In *Money Struggles and City Life*, edited by J. I. Guyer, et al., 259–69. Ibadan: Bookbuilders, 2003

Ashimolowo, Mathew. "The Power of Your Tithe." *Youtube* (video), 1:10:14. November 28, 2017. https://www.youtube.com/watch?v=_oMZFOVp59k.

Associated Press. "Nigeria to Pass US as World's Third Most Populous Country by 2050 UN Says." *NBC News*, June 22, 2017. Online. https://www.nbcnews.com/news/world/nigeria-pass-u-s-world-s-3rd-most-populous-country-n775371.

Brett, Mark G. *Decolonizing God: The Bible in the Tides of Empire*. Sheffield: Sheffield Phoenix, 2008.

Carpenter, Joel A. "The Christian Scholar in an Age of Global Christianity." Paper presented at Christianity and the Soul of the University, Baylor University, March 25–27, 2004.

Chiroma, Nathan. "Tapping into the Unexplored Power and Potential of the Youth in the Fight against Corruption." In *Corruption: A New Thinking in the Reverse Order*, edited by Benson O. Igboin, 167–84. Oyo: Ajayi Crowther University Press, 2018.

Cox, James L. "African Identities as the Projection of Western Alterity." In *Uniquely African? African Christian Identity from Cultural and Historical Perspectives*, edited by James L. Cox and Gerrie ter Haar, 25–37. Trenton, NJ: Africa World, 2003.

Cruz, Dela. "Preaching among Filipino Pentecostals and Exposition through Testimonial Hermeneutics: A Positive Contribution of the Pgcag to Evangelicalism in the Philippines." *Asian Journal of Pentecostal Studies* 13.1 (2010) 98–123.

Dada, Adekunle O. "A Millionaire Through Jesus: 2 Corinthians 8:9 from the Perspective of some Nigerian Prosperity Preachers." *African Journal of Biblical Studies* 16.1 (2001) 82–92.

"The Daystar Experience." Online. www.daystar.org.

De Boeck, F., and M. Plissart. *Kinshasa: Tales of the Invisible City*. Ghent: Ludion, 2004.

Gittins, Anthony. "Witchcraft: Twenty Talking Points." Summary of a symposium entitled Christianity or Occult: Emerging Trends in African Diaspora Christianity, City Hall, West Minister, London, UK, May 22, 2006.

Hackett, Rosalind. "Discourses of Demonization in Africa and Beyond." *Diogenes* 50.3 (2003) 61–75.

Jenkins, Philip. *The New Faces of Christianity: Believing the Bible in the Global South*. New York: Oxford University Press, 2006.

———. *The Next Christendom: The Coming of Global Christianity*. New York: Oxford University Press, 2002.

———. "Reading the Bible in the Global South." *International Bulletin of Missionary Research* 30.2 (2006) 67–73.

Johns, C. B. "What Can the Mainline Learn from Pentecostals about Pentecost?" *Journal for Preachers* (1998) 3–7.
Kalu, Ogbu U. "African Pentecostalism in Diaspora." *Penteco Studies* 9.1 (2010) 9–34.
Kanyoro, Musimbi R. A. "Interpreting Old Testament Polygamy through African Eyes." In *The Will to Arise*, edited by Mercy Amba Oduyoye and Musimbi R. A. Kanyoro, 87–100. Maryknoll, NY: Orbis, 1992.
Marshall, Ruth. "Power in the Name of Jesus." *Review of African Political Economy* 18.52 (1991) 21–37.
Maxey, Gary S. *The Seduction of the Nigerian Church*. Lagos: WATS, 2017.
Mountain of Fire and Miracles Ministries. "About MFM." *MFM HQ*, January 19, 2015. Online. https://www.mountainoffire.org/about.
Odesola, Johnson, ed. "50 Million Free Meals Project." *CSR Chronicles* 1.1 (2018) 17.
Ogundipe, Samuel. "What I Meant Describing Nigerian Youth as Lazy—Buhari." *Premium Times*, May 2, 2018. Online. https://www.premiumtimesng.com/news/headlines/266869-what-i-meant-describing-nigerian-youth-as-lazy-buhari.html.
Ogundiya, Ilufoye Sarafa. "Political Corruption in Nigeria: Theoretical Perspectives and Some Explanations." *Anthropologist* 11.4 (2009) 281–92.
Ojo, Matthews A. *The End-Time Army: Charismatic Movements in Modern Nigeria*.
Okonjo-Iweala, Ngozi. *Fighting Corruption Is Dangerous: The Story Behind the Headlines*. Cambridge: MIT Press, 2018.
Onyinah, Opoku. "Deliverance as a Way of Confronting Witchcraft in Modern Africa: Ghana as a Case History." *African Journal of Pentecostal Studies* (2002) 107–132.
Opejobi, Seun. "Bishop Oyedepo Reveals What Will Happen to Those Who Don't Pay Tithe." *Daily Post*, November 24, 2017. Online. http://dailypost.ng/2017/11/24/bishop-oyedepo-reveals-will-happen-dont-pay-tithe.
———. "Popular Bishop Reveals How He Threatened His Members to Pay Tithe." *Daily Post*, March 7, 2018. Online. http://dailypost.ng/2018/03/07/popular-bishop-reveals-threatened-members-pay-tithe-video.
Oyakhilome, Chris. "Question 4 on Tithes, Offerings, and Seeds." *Pastor Chris Online Transcripts* (blog), August 22, 2010. Online. http://pastorchrisonlinetranscript.blogspot.com/2010/08/episode-4-question-4-on-tithes.html.
Oyedepo, David. *Breaking Financial Hardship*. Lagos: Dominion, 1995.
Pierce, Steven. *Moral Economies of Corruption: State Formation and Political Culture in Nigeria*. Durham: Duke University Press, 2016.
Tahafe-Williams, Katalina. "Foreword." In *Encyclopeadia of Christianity in the Global South*, edited by Mark Lamport. MD: Rowan and Littlefield, 2018.
Ukah. *A New Paradigm of Pentecostal Power: A Study of the Redeemed Christian Church of God in Nigeria*. Trenton, NJ: 2008.
Ukpong, Justin S. "Re-Reading the Bible with African Eyes." *Journal of Theology for Southern Africa* 91 (1995) 3–14.
Van Dijk, Rijk. "From Camp to Encompassment: Discourses of Transsubjectivity in the Ghanaian Pentecostal Diaspora." *Journal of Religion in Africa* 27.2 (1997) 136–59.

"To Each Its Own Meaning"
Interpreting the Bible in Nigerian Context

Deborah Doyinsola Adegbite

Abstract

"To Each its own Meaning" is the title given to the 256-page *Introduction to Biblical Criticisms*, edited by Stephen R. Haynes and Steven L. McKenzie. The book is a collection of essays reflecting a comprehensive history of the development of various scholarly views of biblical interpretations. The use of this title has almost nothing to do with this work. It is just to show that Africans—and particularly Nigerians—have their own way of interpreting the Bible in the context of their shared "Africanness." This essay aims at presenting some Nigerian methods in preaching as well as highlighting the cultural values and prevailing socio-economic and political conditions that underlie those preaching methods and interpretative stances. This study, which employs both historical and sociological methods, emphasizes the ways in which the socio-political, economic, and cultural values of the society affect the biblical interpretation and preaching style of Nigerian preachers.

Key Words: Nigeria, Nigerian, Politics, Homiletics, Sermons

Nigeria and the Nigerians

Nigeria is a West African country with Benin in the west, Chad and Cameroon in the east, and Niger in the north. The population is about 200 million across the globe. It is considered the eighth most-populous Black Country in the world and largest in Africa.[1] Interestingly, it is also postulated that one in every four or six Africans is a Nigerian.[2] Nigeria has the total area of 923,768km^2 (910,768km^2 of land and 13,000 km^2 water).[3] This population is one of the reasons why Nigeria is considered the giant of Africa, alongside the fact that they are a hardworking people with an unbridled drive to succeed.[4]

Nigerian People, Culture, and Christianity

Nigerian culture is shaped by various ethnic groups. It is suggested that the number of ethnic tribes in Nigeria is over 250, but there are three notable ethnic groups which are larger than the others—Yoruba, Igbo, and Hausa, which includes the Fulani.[5] Nigeria is a unique country. Each of the ethnic groups are noted for different cultural beliefs and practices. Yoruba tribes, for example, train their children to respect elders by prostrating (if a boy) and kneeling[6] (if a girl) to greet them. But among the Igbo tribe or Hausa, kneeling and prostrating makes no sense at all since they have their own way of doing the same. Generally, it should be understood that Nigerians are hospitable, warm-hearted, and hard-working people (including the youth) who are not deterred by challenges. The different cultures among the Nigerians play an important part in the way they believe, serve, and preach about God. Because the researcher lives in the southwestern part of the country, most of what is described in this paper is from, but not limited to, that context.

---

1. Victor, "Is Nigeria Still the 'Giant of Africa'?"
2. "Why Is Nigeria Called Giant of Africa?"
3. "Geography Statistics Of Nigeria."
4. "Why Is Nigeria Called Giant of Africa?"
5. "Ethnicity in Nigeria."
6. Prostration and kneeling are important values among the Yoruba. The method is used for greeting elders and in-laws. It is used for apologies, and expressing one's appreciation as well.

Greeting is done by prostration and kneeling. Prostration is done by stretching the whole body out and lying face-down on the ground, while the feminine version of showing such respect is kneeling, bowing the two knees on the floor. This is a sign of showing respect to the elders in general and in-laws in particular. It does not necessarily mean worshiping them; it only shows that such a person, especially a child, has manners and moral training. The women brought up in this way are considered better wives than those who ignore the culture in the name of civilization.

Language

The Yoruba tribe values their language and they use it in their daily interactions whenever they are in unofficial gatherings. Some preachers also prefer using the language in preaching so that their messages can carry a particular weight that the English language does not convey to a Yoruba-speaking audience.

---

7. Fatiregun et al., "Epidemiology of Measles in Southwest Nigeria," 37.

Names

Names among the Yoruba speaking tribe of Nigeria are very important, and it is an even more important part of the ministerial lives of preachers in Nigeria. Yoruba sayings that prove this importance are many, e.g., "*Ile la wo ka to somo loruko,*" meaning you have to look back into your family linage before naming your child; "*oruko eni ni ijanu eni,*" meaning one's name is one's brake, implying that if someone is doing something bad or shameful on the assumption that they are not known in the area, they are caught in the act, or their name is called, it will serve as a brake to what they are doing or about to do at that moment. In Yoruba culture, people do not give names to their children like Westerners do.

Names sometimes identify the tribe that people come from with either the beginning or the ending of their names, especially among the Yoruba. For an example, names of people who come from Ile-Ife in the Osun State usually starts with Omi (Omilabu, Omikunle, Omisope, Omisore) or Elu (Eluwole, Elufisan, Elusade, Elusoji). Names of people who come from Ijebu, in the Ogun State, vary. One such example would be the name "Sho" which is a short form of Osho: Shokomaya (wizardry makes me bold), Sholarin (wizard came in between), Sholanke (we care for wizards), Showunmi (I love wizardry), Shodehinde, Shonaike,[8] and so forth. It is possible that the families known by these names belong to a family where wizardry is known to be practiced since *Osho* means wizard. There are other Ijebu names, like Ifenaike, Ogunnaike, Adenaike, Okuribido, Okukenu, Olubogun, Ifebogun, etc. The Ibadan people of Oyo state are known by Bayonle, Aleshinloye, Adelabu, Omilabu, Adedibu, Ibikunle, Akinosun, Gbada, and Akinyele. These names are common among Ibadan people of Oyo State.

Apart from the aforementioned names, there are names that depict the gods worshipped by family members. In most cases, the first phrase of the names tells of the god that the family worships, e.g., Ogunwale, Ogungbemi, Ogunfunmbi, Ogundeyi, Ogunyemi, signifying those whose names start from Ogun or the family of Ogun (god of iron) worshipers. Osuntoun, Osunfunmi, Osungbemi, are worshipers of Osun river goddess.[9] The *eegungun* (masquerade) worshipers are given names such as Eegunjobi (masquerades jointly give birth to this one), Eegunleti (masquerade have ears), etc. Other common names that are not attached to any religion or tribe among the Yoruba are names on the order of Omolewa, Ayotunde, Ayodeji,

---

8. The Ijebu tribe is known for many types of pagan worship and Osho (wizardry) is one of them.

9. Osun Osogbo, the river goddess, is a mermaid in Yoruba land. She is noted for providing children for the childless.

Omotunde, Adedoyin, Doyinsola, Ibilola, Adesola, Adeyinka, Olanrewaju, Omotoye, Omolabake, and Adebimpe. Any of these names can be given in any family, regardless of their tribe or religion, but Yoruba Christians prefer to start the names of their children with *Olu*, a short form of Oluwa. Oftentimes they will change Olusola to Adesola, Oluyinka to Adeyinka, Oludoyin to Adedoyin, Olusegun to Adesegun, and Olugbemi to Ogungbemi.

The Yoruba believe that the name by which a person is called has a lot to do with his or her life. Many Yoruba Christians whose names are rooted in the worship of Ogun, Esu, and Eegun (Masqurade) have changed their names because they reflect their family gods or goddesses. Most Christians have changed their names from Ogunponle (god of iron honors me) to Oluwapomile or Jesuponmile (the Lord or Jesus honours me); Omilabi (we have given birth to water) to Omolabi (we have given birth to a child); Esubiyi (Satan has given birth to this) to Oluwabiyi (the Lord has given birth to this); Osunbunmi (Osun goddess has given me) to Olubunmi (the Lord has given me); Oguntomi (god of iron is enough for me) to Oluwatomi (the Lord is enough for me); and Oguntomisin (god of iron is enough for me to serve) to Oluwatomisin (the Lord is enough for me to serve). It is believed that these gods or goddesses can lay claim to their lives and ministries if they do not change their names. Some go even further to get themselves delivered from the negative effects that the names may have had on them.

The Effect of Education (and Lack of It) on Nigerian Preachers

Education has been defined many ways by educationists, but a general definition of education is the delivery of knowledge, skills, and information as well as the process of receiving the same. From time immemorial, education has never been robbed of its importance to human development. According to Plato, it develops all the beauty and perfection in the body and soul of the pupil that they are capable of. It is also believed that Plato's philosophy of education provides a comprehensive vision to solve the problems of modern education.[10] The importance of education in Nigeria cannot be over emphasized. When Chief Olusegun Obasanjo, a former President of Nigeria, had just finished a PhD program, he was asked why he did the program, and he replied that education should be taken seriously from the cradle to old age. According to Obasanjo, "Once you stop learning, you will begin to die."[11]

---

10. Lee, "Plato's Philosophy of Education," 236.
11. Obasanjo, "Interview."

Some Nigerian preachers are educated, but many are not. The percentage of those who are educated is difficult to pin down. Although it is not gainsaying to assert that for almost all of the twenty-first century, Nigerian preachers had an elementary education, some also achieved a secondary education before claiming to receive their call into pastoral ministry. In some cases, those who dropped out of secondary school blame it on their call into the ministry. They claim that they failed their final examinations because God wanted them in the ministry! On the other hand, many have one degree or more in other fields—such as mathematics, physics, medicine, and so forth—before taking up their pastoral calling. It means that there are both educated and illiterates among Nigerian preachers and their educational status plays a significant role in their lives, personalities, ministries, and preaching styles.

Nigerian Preachers and Theological Education

Nigerians typically believe that any Nigerian preacher who is educated in any secular field but not trained as a preacher in a theological school is still an illiterate.[12] Many Nigerian preachers, especially Pentecostal ministers, do not value theological education. "Religious Education" is also not given its due respect as an academic course in Nigerian universities. Some private universities (even faith based institutions) initially avoided having departments of religious studies because of the fact that such a department will not bring financial profit since very few people enroll in them. Most people see no reasonable grounds for studying theology or sending their wards to do the same. Many of the Pentecostal ministers believe that theology is not necessary for ministerial competence, especially if one can display some spiritual gifts. Such preachers operate under the erroneous slogan, "You shall receive power, not a theological college certificate." This is a misinterpretation of Acts 1:8, where the bible says, "You will receive power when the Holy Spirit has come upon you." They erroneously belittle theological studies, thinking that it is meant for school drop-outs. Some of them are even being misled into believing that, as prophets, they do not need theological training. They believe that the Holy Spirit will tell them everything they need to know. They have forgotten that Jesus himself taught his disciples for about three and a half years before telling them to wait for the power of the

---

12. Since it is not right for a lawyer to use their law degree to work as a medical doctor in the hospital, it is therefore a crime for anyone to cross into pastoral work with degrees in other fields thinking that their doctorate degree is enough to claim competence in the pastoral ministry.

Holy Spirit.[13] It is unfortunate that some of them who are educated up to the PhD level in other disciplines, such as mathematics and physics, assume that that PhD is enough for pastoral ministries. These preachers can be subdivided into several fractions. Examples of each will be given, considering their backgrounds, conversion history, how they got into the ministry, life style, messages, their major contributions to Nigerian Christianity, the place of salvation in their ministries, and what other Christians say or feel about them.

Interpretative Concept of Nigerian Preachers' Spirituality

Discussing spirituality is not out of place at this moment since the spiritual life of preachers cannot be removed from their messages. Spirituality means the process of living a Holy Spirit-filled life. It has also been described as the process of recovering "the image of God" in humankind. Alex Tang opines that spirituality describes the attitudes of beliefs and practices that animate people's lives and helps them to reach out towards the supra-natural realties.[14] For Philip Sheldrake, our relationship with God is often confined to narrow spiritual experience and does not effectively enter our daily lives.[15] Various Preachers are noted for their styles of spiritual practice both in the church and at the street level. Few are mentioned with short explanations below:

> **Authoritarian Spirituality** is a particularly strong form of spirituality that is based on rules. The Preachers known for this type of spirituality believe they possess absolute knowledge of some "doctrinal truths" through revelation and therefore lay claim to authority. Many of the deliverance ministers falls under this category. Most preachers who practice deliverance claim to have some spiritual gifts with a level of faith and special knowledge of demons, their names, specific locations of their blood bank, and other uncanny manifestations. They claim to possess knowledge that is more than ordinary or more than the general knowledge about God, Jesus, Holy Spirit, demons, and the victims to be delivered. All these are somehow parallel to first- and second-century Gnosticism.[16] It is evident that there could be a specific knowl-

---

13. Adegbite, "Supremacy of Religious and Theological Education."
14. Tang, "Christian Spirituality."
15. Sheldrake, *Image of Holiness*.
16. Adegbite, "Theology and Practice of Deliverance."

edge that backs their faith in the process of deliverance ministrations. Many do claim to possess some kind of in-depth knowledge of demons to the extent of knowing their names, office, location of their abodes, places of their meetings, their ranks, and the specific assignment given to them in the spiritual world.[17] The questions that come to mind are: Are these claims rooted in the bible? Can they be supported with any biblical tradition? Can they be judged according to the teachings of apostles such as Paul, Peter, and others?

Intellectual Spirituality focuses on building knowledge and understanding spirituality through analyzing history and spiritual theories. This approach can be found among many of the preachers who think that once they are professors of physics, mathematics, and the like, from the university, it automatically qualifies them to be professors of theology as well. Such preachers use their knowledge in other fields to interpret the Bible out of context.

Service Spirituality is a common form of spirituality in many religious faiths. This type of spirituality is built around serving others as a form of spiritual expression. For the purpose of this paper, this kind of spirituality has nothing to do with a personal relationship with God or commitment to spiritual things. Rather, it is a way of giving back to society out of the abundance of one's wealth. Thus, it is only practiced by some (not all) of the wealthy Nigerian preachers, like Temitope Balogun Joshua of Synagogue of All Nations Church in Lagos or Prophet Jeremiah Omoto Fufeyin of Christ Mercyland Deliverance Ministry in Delta State.

Social Spirituality is often practiced by people who only experience spiritual feeling when they are in the company of other spiritual people. They cannot practice spirituality alone; they need to be with others who can influence them in that way. Notwithstanding, social support is often seen as one of the important aspects of spirituality in general.

Obnoxious Spirituality is an offensive kind of spirituality. It can also be called a malicious or barbaric spirituality because in some cases it is cruel in its approach and borne out of a deliberate wilingess to harm others. This is the kind of spirituality that is practiced in some deliverance ministries, especially where lunatic people or witches are believed to be present.

---

17. Especially in Mountain of Fire and Miracles Ministries and in God Will Do It Ministry.

Contagious Spirituality is the kind of spirituality that can be transmitted from one person to another either by direct or indirect contact with the person. It is a transmittable spirituality and is practiced in the white garment churches.

Divergent Spirituality is a kind of spirituality that becomes increasingly different or separate from the original. It is used for describing the spirituality of those denominations or pastors that drift away from the spirituality of their mother churches or their General Overseers.

Hilarious Spirituality is an extremely funny display of spirituality. It used for the description of the pastors who have turned the pastoral office into an entertainment industry. The church members are made to laugh off their sorrows. The pastors who engage in this type of spirituality sometimes invite professional jesters to perform in church services. In most cases, these jesters make the audience laugh at biblical truths. This is also spirituality but a nonsensical kind because of its meaninglessness to members' spirituality. Although the word "nonsense" is a technical term in logical positivism and linguistic analysis[18] to designate something which (though having grammatical sense) lacks real "meaning."

Inherited Spirituality is a type of spirituality that is passed on from one generation to the next or from parents to their children. It is a kind that is usually caused by an inherited code of spirituality that comes from the parents of a child. Inherited spirituality, whether good or bad, is like hereditary diseases which may not develop in all generations or in all children carrying the genes of such spiritual conduct.

Chameleon Spirituality, just like the chameleon, capable of "blending its skin" with the color of its environment in order to escape being noticed by predators. The chameleon also changes color to communicate with other reptiles, to attract a mate, warn a rival, or to shed its outer layer of skin. This adaptive method is practiced by some people, too. This kind of spirituality reflects the environment in which it is located. They are able to adjust to suit different circumstances or different purposes.

Apart from these, there are also other spiritualities, found at the street level. Such spiritualities are found in the day-to-day lives of market women,

---

18. Adegbite, *Concise Theological & Philosophical Dictionary*, 190–91.

commercial bus drivers,[19] Tipper and lorry drivers,[20] etc., depicting their beliefs about God, humanity, and other things.

Examples of Preachers and Their Messages

In Nigeria, there are various types of preachers: prosperity preachers, deliverance preachers, holiness preachers, faith preachers, and so forth. As I said earlier, the way in which each ministry is treated depends on their backgrounds, the conversion history of their leaders, how they got into the ministry, life styles, messages, their major contributions to Nigerian Christianity, the place of salvation in their ministries, and what other Christians say or feel about them.

The History of Deliverance Preaching in Nigeria

It is possible to say that in Nigeria, the operations of deliverance ministration have their origins in the ministries of some indigenous Christian ministers who led healing and deliverance crusades in the 1920s and 1930s, mainly: Moses Orimolade Tunolase of Cherubim and Seraphim; Joseph Ayo Babalola and Daniel Orekoya of Christ Apostolic Church; Prophet Omotunde of Aramoko-Ekiti; and Prophet Dasofunjo of Ibadan. For example, it was recorded that during the ministry of Joseph Ayo Babalola, many who were possessed by witchcraft spirits were delivered instantly at a place called Oke-Ooye in Ilesha, a town in Osun state of Nigeria. At that time, the ministry of Joseph Ayo Babalola was mainly regarded as one of healing because at that time the term "deliverance" was not a commonly used term like it is now. His ministry was concluded in 1959, when the man of God died suddenly on July 29th. But there is no doubt that his ministry was one of deliverance, which includes healing from various kinds of diseases. He also possessed special knowledge of how to recognize or deal with demons. This knowledge is far above that of his contemporaries, yet he never made any noise about it.

---

19. Examples of such spirituality is found on their stickers, which might read: "Enter and have your seat, God knows the thoughts of your heart"; "I am not afraid of my enemies, I am afraid of my friends, even you!"; and "Ola mummy" meaning, "courtesy of mummy," etc.

20. "Ajani baba Ramo" simply means Ajani the father of Ramo, and "Ibaje eniyan ko da ise Oluwa duro," is bad mouthing of human being cannot stop the works of the Lord, etc.

The practice of deliverance can be traced to the emergence of the Nigerian Pentecostal movements with their backgrounds rooted in evangelical Christianity. Their history is traceable to the Student Christian Movement (SCM) and the Christian Union (CU), which were introduced to Nigeria's educational institutions between 1937 and 1955. The idea of "Prayer Mountain" in connection with deliverance seems to be a later development. Christianity found a fertile ground in which to grow in Nigeria. Initially, the religion was embraced because of its attractive elements like education, orthodox medicine, and opportunities for foreign trade and travels. Later, when Christianity became rooted on Nigerian soil, it prospered much better than it did through foreign missionaries. Deliverance ministry is known to be one of the Pentecostal movements in Nigeria, any number of which are linked with "Prayer Mountains."[21] It remains to be seen whether their individual practices fit into the biblical concept.

In the 1960s, there was scanty record of deliverance ministries, possibly because Nigeria was seriously disturbed with political problems and the changing of governments. However, the ministry of Pastor Odusona, another minister in Christ Apostolic Church, cannot be forgotten. He was regarded as a specialist in ministering deliverance to those possessed with witchcraft spirits to such an extent that he was nicknamed, "Erujeje Oko Aje."[22] In the late 1960s, another minister of God, Evangelist Timothy Iyanda of "Go Ye Evangelistic Ministry,"[23] settled in the Sango area of Ibadan in Oyo state. His evangelism was aggressive, and his ministry was accompanied with the deliverance and healing of many. Another such prophet of deliverance was T. O. Obadare of World Soul-Wining Evangelical Ministry, popularly known as WOSEM. In the 1970s, many miraculous healings and deliverances took place under his ministration in Ibadan (Oyo State), Lagos (Lagos State), Ilesha and Ile-Ife in Osun State, and Akure (Ekiti State) to the extent that some of the places where these revivals took place are still named after him today.[24] Many who were possessed with various demons, including psychiatric patients, were delivered in the revival of Obadare. The fact

---

21. Prayer mountains are where people go for special prayers to battle serious physical and spiritual problems and sometimes to be alone with God. A prayer mountain is not necessarily on a mountain top, although many of them are situated on physical mountains. Generally, such mountains are simply used to avoid distractions in prayers and to aid concentration.

22. Erujeje Oko Aje literally means the fearful husband of the witches, but the term "husband" is not literal; it is better translated as the fearful one who lords over the witches.

23. Popularly known as "Go Ye," also identified as "Go Ye Center."

24. The Ibadan center known as "Elewure" is also called "Sango Obadare," after his miracle crusades on the land.

remains that if any of today's deliverance ministers are not directly related to the ministries of the aforementioned ministers of God, it is still reasonable to say that they are greatly influenced by them, directly or indirectly. However, the deliverance messages of that period are not the same as the method being used today.

Deliverance messages of the twentieth century were mainly for repentance, after which deliverance of the penitent sinner followed naturally. Deliverance ministrations have experienced changes from how it was in the first half of the last century when compared with present day deliverance ministrations.

There is no doubt that healing miracles were mixed with deliverance in the first half of the last century. The reason for this mix is high rates of illiteracy. In that period, the major reason for crusades was simply to heal people of various diseases and to show them that Jesus is the Savior who has the power to heal them. However, no one can deny that much of the deliverance that took place was from witchcraft, wizards, and occultism. For example, it was recorded that almost the whole town of Efon-Alaaye (now in Ekiti State) was delivered from a hosts of demonic forces to the extent that many of the sorcerers surrendered their powers and idols to the god Babalola.[25] In the same decade, Daniel Orekoya was also ministering in a similar way, but none of them tagged the miracles performed as "deliverance." This is not because they were not acts of deliverance but rather the general knowledge of the period was that of healing.

In this twenty-first century, the term "deliverance" is used simply as embellishment that results from educational knowledge because many of those who are now involved in deliverance ministries are the elites. Up to the 1960s, deliverance ministrations had nothing to do with the knowledge of the names, ranks, or operation of demons; that only began at end of the twentieth century, becoming rampant by the twenty-first. The predominant aspect of the last century was faith, and demons were cast out with faith in the name of Jesus. There was no emphasis on names or occupations of demons. In fact, those ministers had no interest in such. All they wanted was for the victim to be freed from demonic possession. In some cases, the demons were not even allowed to speak at all nor was there any talk of asking for their names or what they were appointed to do against the victim.

It should be understood that the opinion of Burgess that Nigerian Pentecostal theologies resonate with the search for spiritual power in traditional piety[26] is an overstatement. Ojo notes that the Pentecostal revival of

---

25. Olori, *Joseph Ayo Babalola*, 12.
26. Burgess, *Nigerian Pentecostal Theology*, 29–63.

the mid-1970s was also a sign of progressive knowledge as it gained strength beyond the University campuses into a wider society.[27] The emphases extend to healing of the socio-economic problems of Nigeria. Ojo gave four major areas of application of healing that could serve as their contributions to Nigerian Christianity: physical healing, healing from demonic or satanic attacks, healing from all failures of life, and healing for the socio-economic and political problems of a country.[28] It is true that healing is dynamic and problem-solving, attracting people with problems such as employment, marriage partners, children, and illness.[29] And since humanity is always in need of healing and deliverance one way or the other, it becomes a necessity that even some leaders of non-Pentecostal churches are becoming specialists in the area of deliverance ministrations in order to keep their members, trying to cater to their spiritual needs.

The late Dr. Pheme Ibeneme, a gynaecologist, was the first known deliverance specialist for those suffering from childlessness without any reasonable medical reasons. He was doing well until his untimely death. He founded the Faith Clinic. After Faith Clinic was God-Will-Do-It-Ministries and The Mountain of Fire and Miracles Ministries, which are the most popular ministries of this kind today.

Deliverance Preachers—Background and Ministry

God-Will-Do-It-Ministries (GWDIM) was founded by Gomba Fortune Oyor who was said to have been called into the ministry on July 28th, 1983, after a miraculous deliverance from insanity in 1979. He was a founding member and President of the Student Christian Movement (SCM) of the Rivers State University of Science and Technology, Port-Harcourt, for five consecutive years, from 1979 to 1984. He was also the National Travelling Secretary of the SCM of Nigeria from 1985 to 1990.

Oyor has no formal theological training apart from a certificate from the Haggai Institute of Advanced Leadership Training in Singapore (a very short course of about six weeks). He holds a BA degree in Secretarial Administration from the Rivers State University of Science and Technology, Port-Harcourt, an MA in Education, and a PhD in Community Development from the University of Ibadan.

According to "Greater Power Convention," one of the ministry's pamphlets, published in 1998, the ministry is documented as an

---

27. Ojo, *Pentecostal Movement in Nigeria Today*, 115–16.
28. Ojo, "Charismatic Movement in Nigeria Today," 115–16.
29. Ojo, "Charismatic Movement in Nigeria Today," 115–16.

interdenominational one. In 1992, it started as a deliverance ministry and was registered in 1995, probably without the aim of starting a Church. But that changed in 1998, when GWDIM metamorphed into a Church. This change caused serious confusion and discomfort to many other churches whose members had an affiliation with them. Questions about trust were raised as a result. When asked why, one of the Church workers alleged that the Church necessarily had to start at that time because there was not enough financial support for the ministry.[30] On the contrary, Pastor Oyor affirms that it was the Holy Spirit who ministered to him in March 1997 that his ministry needed a prayer base. The name of the ministry is taken from Oyor's quarterly teaching paper, "God Will Do It," which he had started writing in 1984 and was mailed to all interested persons free of charge.

Mountain of Fire and Miracles Ministries (MFM) was founded by Daniel Kolawole Olukoya, who is said to have received the call at a very tender age. It seems plausible to say that his present ministry is based on the vision of an eight-year old boy many years ago. The vision he claims to have seen was of a mountain burning with fire, interpreted as a praying church with manifestations of the gifts of the Holy Spirit. This is probably why the Church was named the Mountain of Fire and Miracles Ministries. Olukoya is a graduate of the University of Lagos with a first-class honors degree in Microbiology and a PhD in molecular genetics from the University of Reading in the United Kingdom. He is said to have over seventy scientific publications to his credit. The Mountain of Fire and Miracles Ministries began in 1989 as a prayer fellowship, but it became recognized as a church in November 1991.

The Preaching of Deliverance

In most deliverance messages, the miracles of Jesus or his disciples are usually the starting point, but later, the message can include how the individual preacher had ministered the same or similar healings somewhere in the past that none of the members knew anything about. With encouragement, the same miracle can be repeated in their midst. In most of their messages, holiness is rare because the main emphasis is on deliverance.

In the practice of deliverance in GWDIM, the "Holy Ghost Theatre"[31] plays an important role in the prayer life of the participants. Through prayer, a difficult issue can be solved easily. A particular experience on July 5th,

---

30. Rotimi, interview with the author, June 5, 2005.

31. "Holy Ghost Theater" is just a demarcated part of the prayer ground where individuals are being ministered to or where individuals pray on their own fervently.

2005, was an interesting one because it claimed that every sickness, whether major or minor, is believed to have a particular demonic spirit behind it. Before going to the Holy Ghost theatre, the person to be delivered must have explained his/her problem(s) to one of the deliverance ministers. While narrating the story, the deliverance minister in charge of his/her case will be busy writing down prayer points, which, in most cases, includes mentioning the names of the spirits or demons behind each of the problems. An example is the case of a woman who brought her daughter (a young Yoruba lady) and son-in-law (an older Igbo man) for deliverance from the demon(s) working against their marriage. The couple frequently misunderstood each other and would fight about minor issues.[32] The woman herself decided to use the opportunity to ask for prayer assistance concerning her health problem. She said that she is diabetic and not the first wife of her husband. She informed them that she was from a Muslim background but had been a Christian for the past twenty years. While she was narrating her story, the following prayer points were written for her so that God should break the covenant and nullify the curses of (1) the ancestral spirit; (2) the spirit of inheritance; (3) the spirit of infirmity; (4) the diabetic spirit; (5) the blood pressure spirit; (6) the Islamic spirit; (7) the spirit of Baal; (8) the spirit of Belial; (9) the Luciferian witchcraft spirit; and (10) arrows of infirmity. Prayers were also directed against any possible "spiritual husband." Naturally, one will begin to wonder why all these problems were being written down for a woman who was already a grandmother and had been a Christian for over twenty years just because she needed prayer support for her poor health.

In the Mountain of Fire and Miracle Ministries, the practice is similar, but in addition, the MFM seems to be practically motivating people and teaching them how to pray their way to a breakthrough. This is reflected in all their books and magazines. Similarly, according to the Spiritual War College manual, the ministry is said to be devoted to the revival of Apostolic signs, Holy Ghost fireworks, and miracles.

Doctrinal Emphases and Teaching on Deliverance

In the God-Will-Do-It-Ministries, "deliverance" is the central theme of their teaching, but some traces of religious dualism are also present in the writing

---

32. Without minding their different socio-cultural, ethnic, family, or other backgrounds, which may have been affecting or influencing the couple's misunderstanding, the deliverance minister assumed it was demons working against their marriage. They simply needed to be delivered, as if after this deliverance they would not misunderstand each other again!

of the founder, Dr. D. Oyor. He claims that Satan is fighting with God: "A war has been going on for thousands of years between God and Satan, and Satan, on his part, has sworn to kill, to steal, and to destroy all God's people with sickness, oppression, bondage, and poverty as well as failure in business, education, marriage, and other areas of life."[33] This kind of assertion seems to be an insult to the being and personality of God.[34]

Like the GWDIM, in MFM, deliverance is a means of rescuing people from captivity and the lies of the devil. Pastor Olukoya, the General Overseer, asserts, "It is impossible to enjoy one's life here on earth without going through some form of deliverance."[35] This assertion is not accepted by those who do not belong to deliverance ministries. To the Mountain of Fire and Miracles Ministries, the word "deliverance" can be defined as liberation from anything that will not allow one to enjoy one's Salvation in Christ—which may include cockroaches, wall gecko, dogs, cats, and pigs—because they are capable of being possessed by demons. Despite the similarity in the belief of these ministries, their practices still differ in some ways. Unlike GWDIM, the MFM believe and practice deliverance on anything and great importance is attached to some ethical teachings. They lay emphasis on liberation of Christians from their traditional past. It is believed and taught that one's past is always a stumbling block to living a fulfilled life. For this reason, contrary to the GWDIM, the MFM believe that everyone at least needs deliverance from evil family ties if not from demonic possession. They believe everyone is connected to an evil foundation or ancestral curse, and they see their ministry as deliverance experts in that area, operating like general practitioners, giving the necessary solution to people's problems. They sometimes give people appointments just as it is done in the hospitals, prescribing simple and funny spiritual medications.

Their belief about the etiology of sicknesses affects their practice of deliverance; this is reflected in a majority of Olukoya's writings. In fact, it is believed and practiced (but not accepted theoretically) that anyone attending MFM for the first time must have come as an agent of darkness or with a problem and will be treated like someone who has a problem. This is reflected in the fact that their ministers cannot counsel or talk to anyone who is a first timer after the service on Sunday without the person going through deliverance prayers immediately after the service. It is believed and taught that everyone is under bondage, and to them, whatever bondage it is, it is usually from one's background:

---

33. Oyor, *Complete Deliverance and Healing*, ii.
34. Adegbite, *Concise Theological & Philosophical Dictionary*, 263.
35. MFM, *Spiritual War*, 6

> For an individual to appreciate the level of bondage in his life, that person should cast his mind back to what happened in the lives of his grandparents two hundred years ago. They should ask questions like: "Who were my grandparents? Did they fight inter-tribal wars? Did they get involved with ritual killings?" . . . Were your forefathers' hunters and warriors who sucked human blood? Did they pay homage to powerful gods? . . . It is believed that by the time you obtain sincere answers to these questions, you will have discovered that your ancestry was deeply demonic, bloody, and terrible. No doubt, the conduct of your progenitors would have injected a lot of demonic viruses into your life.[36]

These beliefs always affect the practice of deliverance in the MFM. Some prayer points are good examples of this belief, such as: "Lord, purge my foundations from polygamy, evil dedication, fellowship with local idols, demonic initiations, and so forth. I command all foundational strong men attached to my life to be paralyzed in the name of Jesus; I break and loose myself from every inherited evil covenant."[37]

The MFM has no special place called the "Holy Ghost Theatre," like that of the GWDIM. The person to be delivered must have explained his/her problem(s) to one of the deliverance ministers. While narrating the story, just as described earlier (about the GWDIM), the deliverance minister will be busy writing down prayer points, which, in most cases, include mentioning the names of the spirits or demons behind each of the problems. Everyone who has marital problems is seen as either suffering a spiritual husband, ancestral curses, or implantation of some kind of evil seed. This is seen in most of Olukoya's writings. Some examples of the prayer points he wrote for those with such problems are as follows: "I break myself loose from every covenant of a late or useless marriage"; "I renounce and break all evil curses and bewitchment put upon my marriage"; "I break and release myself from every anti-marriage curse."[38] All the prayer points must be prayed in the name of Jesus and should be prayed aggressively.

Another important part of deliverance ministrations in MFM is counseling, but this is not so important in GWDIM. Anointing oil is very important in all Deliverance Ministries. Both GWDIM and the MFM use oil for deliverance to the extent that it seems deliverance cannot happen without it!

---

36. Olukoya, *Spiritual Warfare*, 7–8
37. Olukoya, *Pray your Way to Breakthroughs*, 88.
38. Olukoya, *Pray Your Way to Breakthroughs*, 88.

Deliverance Schools

Both the GWDIM and MFM have schools where they train their church workers for ministry. God Will Do It Ministries (GWDIM) started the School of Deliverance and Healing (SODAH) in May 1992. Only those who have completed a course in their School of Deliverance and Healing can be granted a leadership position in the church. It was formerly a six-month training course, where participants were taught how to know and cast out demons from themselves and from others. Later, the course was extended to twelve months, and it has now added discipleship and missions to its curriculum.

The Mountain of Fire and Miracle (MFM) started the Spiritual War College (SWC), which aims at broadening the horizon of Christians aspiring to increase their knowledge of members who desire to integrate themselves more fully into Christianity. The SWC is not the usual training seminary. The college is believed to be a place that one must attend before or after the formal Bible College training because it is stressed that one should not attempt to fill the head with knowledge without feeding the spirit. The SWC is considered to be "feeding the spirit," and it is claimed that every graduate of the Spiritual War College becomes a "Giant-Killer."

Some of the Deliverance Prayers

1. Every satanic embargo on my career or marriage die. Die, die, die, in Jesus' name.
2. My Father, my Father, every power in my father's household, every power in my mother's household, that is holding me down, working against my success, die by fire.
3. My Father, my Father, every negotiation with my marital bliss; any power working against the fruits of my womb, let them die by fire.
4. No enchantment against Jacob, no divination against Israel, therefore, every household enemy that is using them against me, all should back-fire by fire

Prosperity Preachers

The term "Prosperity" grammatically means to be successful, especially financially, and the term is not different from how it is used for the "Prosperity Gospel." It is used with the same idea in mind when describing the materialistic Christian doctrine that God will answer all prayers and grant all wishes of his people. This doctrine is actually contrary to fundamental Christian belief and preaching from the early Church. The president of Southern Baptist Theological Seminary rightly noted, "The Prosperity Gospel is neither prosperous nor is it a gospel as defined by scripture."[39] He is correct in his assessment since the proponents of the prosperity gospel are fond of promising their followers the miracles and comfort that Jesus did not promise to them. In most cases, it has led to devastating situations and a bastardized kind of Christianity. It is important for us to explore the root of such a poisonous gospel in Nigeria.

The History of Prosperity Preaching in Nigeria

According to David Jones and Russell Woodbridge, the modern prosperity gospel is traceable to William Kenyon, who is considered to be the father of the modern prosperity gospel movement. He blended this "new thought"[40] with the Bible and repackaged it with new faces, new technology, new venues, and a slightly altered message.[41] Like the modern prosperity preachers' belief that they must be prosperous by force and by fire, Kenyon was noted for saying: "What I confess, I possess." In Nigeria, there are many prosperity preachers, such as Ayo Oritsejafor, the founder of Word of Life Bible Church, Warri; Bishop David Oyedepo, the founder of Living Faith Church, aka, Winners' Chapel; Bishop Francis Wale Oke of Sword of the Spirit Ministries; Chris Oyakhilome, the founder of Believers' Loveworld Incorporated, UK and Christ Embassy, Nigeria, just to mention few. They vary in form; there are both liberal and conservative prosperity preachers, but the history of prosperity messages in Nigeria can be traced back to the arrival of the late Benson Andrew Idahosa from the United States.

Benson Andrew Idahosa—Background and Ministry

Benson Andrew Idahosa was born to poor parents in Benin, Edo state. He had primary and secondary school education, but due to financial problems, he could not attend any higher institution after secondary education. He was the founder of Faith Miracle Center and founding President of the

---

39. New thought, which began around 1895, is not a church or a denomination but rather the teaching of Emmanuel Swedenborg (1688–1772) and Phineas Quimby (1802–1866).

40. Jones and Woodbridge, *Health, Wealth & Happiness*, 22.

41. Jones and Woodbridge, *Health, Wealth & Happiness*, 22.

Pentecostal Fellowship of Nigeria (PFN). According to his biography, in 1952, after his conversion to Christianity at the Assemblies of God Church in Benin, he began to evangelize, and he later became a leader under Pastor Okpo at the very church where he converted. His problem stemmed from the fact that he did not stay long enough the tutelage of Pastor Okpo before deciding to establish his own church. He went to the Nations Institute in Texas, coming back to Nigeria in 1972, all in the name of a zeal devoid of wisdom. It was reported that he asked permission from Gordon Lindsey to go back to Nigeria and permission was granted.[42] It was never ascertained whether he went back to complete his studies, but it was recorded that he earned a Doctorate degree in Divinity and Law.

The Doctrinal Emphases, Teaching, and Characteristics of Prosperity Preachers

It is noted that many of the Nigerian prosperity preachers are influenced by American preachers of the same ilk. That connection is common to them all. They all see salvation as deliverance from poverty and teach material blessings and good health as the believer's right. The second coming of Christ does not appear to be important to them. Some of them combine prosperity teaching with deliverance. Most of them have television ministries.

The prosperity preachers usually teach their members to give generously to them so that they can get whatever they want from God. They call it "sowing the seed of faith." They believe that God is a millionaire and that they should be millionaires as well. They do not teach anything on holy living and they hardly preach the Kingdom of God.

N. C. Rotimi asserts that there are two broad perspectives on the prosperity gospel in Nigeria. The first perspective sees the prosperity gospel as a way through which bourgeois clergymen extort money from their naïve and unwary congregation. Those who oppose the prosperity gospel as enunciated by contemporary Pentecostal preachers argue that one of the fundamental teachings of Christianity is detachment from material possessions in lieu of heavenly realities. This means that the vision of Christian life is living this earthly life in a way that will guarantee admittance into the heavenly kingdom. Though few in number, Nigeria can be proud of the few preachers who have not soiled their garments with the so-called prosperity gospel. These few holiness preachers are found individually in different Pentecostal and Indigenous churches apart from William F. Kumuyi of Deeper Life Bible Church. Faith Tabernacle, also known as Winners' Chapel, led

42. Half back theology.

by David Oyedepo, is called the faith builder; the Apostolic Church (TAC) is identified with prophesy; Christ Apostolic Church (CAC) is known for healing and prayer; Gbile Akani represents discipleship ministers; Sam Adeyemi teaches on leadership; and Temi Joshua teaches on miracles.

There is no doubt that the preaching ministries in Nigeria are closely linked to the backgrounds and religious experiences of their founders. Generally, every Nigerian believes in the existence of demons. A majority believe that every evil is rooted in one demon or the other, even when natural disasters happen, such as flood, careless road accidents, and so forth. These and many more demonic ideologies are part of the Nigerian culture, but the way preachers preach depends on the preacher's interest. In deliverance ministration, virtually everything is demonic and needs deliverance. In prosperity ministration, members must give; if not, cankerworms will eat up members' gains or wealth. It has also been noted that many preachers fail to see the necessity of digging deep into their biblical messages; therefore, they fail faithfulness to the biblical text.

Conclusion

This work began with the introduction of the Nigerian people's understanding of culture, language, and Christianity. The paper also showed the effects of education (and the lack thereof) on Nigerian preachers with different spiritual practices to justify the assertion that everyone preaches biblical messages according to their own individual meaning. The problems discovered are not restricted to heretical doctrines only. They also include the creation of various new spiritual and sociological problems in Christendom since the deliverance ministries put members in the bondage of groundless fears. The church members of prosperity preachers do not understand what holy living entails or even the meaning of the kingdom of God. They are only out to make huge amounts of money because their god is a millionaire, and this thinking leads many of them into dubious behaviors. Furthermore, it should be noted that theological illiteracy is affecting some, while self-centeredness affects others. The sociological situation and poverty of the masses, including economic and political failures, have their own role to play in this theological mess because it seems every one of these Nigerian preachers is trying to bring a solution to members' problems using the methods best known to them. With all their errors, good things still come from them. For example, the Deliverance Ministries help to keep many closer to God—at least by way of continuous prayers for health and healing.

Bibliography

Adegbite, Debbie D. *Concise Theological and Philosophical Dictionary*. Osogbo: BIP, 2015.

———. "The Supremacy of Religious and Theological Education." *Journal of Education and Social Research* 4.7 (2014) 161.

———. "The Theology and Practice of Deliverance in Nigerian Pentecostal and Charismatic Churches." MA thesis, Obafemi Awolowo University, Ile-Ife, Nigeria, 2003.

Burgess, R. "Nigerian Pentecostal Theology in Global Perspective." *PentecoStudies* 7.2 (2008) 29–63.

"Ethnicity in Nigeria." *PBS News Hour*, March 26, 2018. Online. https://www.pbs.org/newshour/arts/africa-jan-june07-ethnic_04-05.

Fatiregun, Akinola A., et al. "Epidemiology of Measles in Southwest Nigeria: An Analysis of Measles Case-Based Surveillance Data from 2007 to 2012." *Transactions of the Royal Society of Tropical Medicine and Hygiene* 108.3 (2014). Online. https://www.researchgate.net/publication/259959977_Epidemiology_of_measles_in_Southwest_Nigeria_An_analysis_of_measles_case-based_surveillance_data_from_2007_to_2012.

"Geography Statistics Of Nigeria." *WorldAtlas*, April 7, 2017. Online. https://www.worldatlas.com/webimage/countrys/africa/nigeria/nglandst.htm.

Innocent, Osuji. *Nigeria the Giant Of Africa* (blog). http://www.osujiinnocent.wordpress.com.

Jones, David W., and Russell S. Woodbridge. *Health, Wealth & Happiness*. Grand Rapids: Kregel, 2011.

Lee, Myungjoon. "Plato's Philosophy of Education: Its Implication for Current Education." PhD diss., Marquette University, 1994. https://epublications.marquette.edu/dissertations/AAI9517932.

Ojo, M. A. "The Pentecostal Movement in Nigeria Today." *International Bulletin* 19.3 (1995) 115–16.

Olori, E. O. *Joseph Ayo Babalola: A Rear Prophet*. Ibadan: Gloryland, 1994.

Olukoya, D. K. *Pray Your Way to Breakthroughs*. Lagos: Battle Cry, 2000.

———. *Spiritual Warfare and the Home*. Lagos: MFM, 1996.

Obasanjo, Olusegun. "Interview." *Teju Babyface Show*. Nigeria: WAP TV, April 21, 2018.

Oyor, G. F. *Complete Deliverance and Healing*. Ibadan: GWDIM, 1999.

Sheldrake, P. *Image of Holiness: Explorations in Contemporary Spirituality*. London: Darton Longman & Todd, 1987.

Tang, Alex. "Christian Spirituality: Theology in Action." *Kairos Spiritual Formation Ministries*. Online. https://www.kairos2.com/christian_spirituality.htm.

Victor, Aderibigbe. "Is Nigeria Still the 'Giant of Africa'?" *Guardian*, September 11, 2017. Online. https://guardian.ng/opinion/is-nigeria-still-the-giant-of-africa.

"Why Is Nigeria Called Giant of Africa?" *Quora* (blog), October 2, 2016. Online. https://www.quora.com/Why-is-Nigeria-called-Giant-of-Africa.

www.ingramcontent.com/pod-product-compliance
Lightning Source LLC
Chambersburg PA
CBHW032108220426
43664CB00008B/1177